THE LIMITS OF STATE ACTION

A LIBERTY
CLASSICS
EDITION

Wilhelm von Humboldt

Wilhelm von Humboldt

THE LIMITS OF
STATE ACTION

Edited by J.W. Burrow

Liberty Fund

INDIANAPOLIS

The Limits of State Action © 1969, Cambridge University Press. Reprinted with permission. Comparative Table of Subjects © 1993 by Liberty Fund, Inc. All rights reserved. All inquiries should be addressed to Liberty Fund, Inc., 8335 Allison Pointe Trail, Indianapolis, IN 46250. This book was manufactured in the United States of America.

Frontispiece from Bildarchiv Preussischer Kulturbesitz, Berlin. Drawing by Johann Joseph Schmeller.

Library of Congress Cataloging-in-Publication Data

Humboldt, Wilhelm, Freiherr von, 1767–1835.
    [Ideen zu einem Versuch die Grenzen der Wirksamkeit des Staats zu bestimmen. English]
    The limits of state action / Wilhelm von Humboldt ; edited by J.W. Burrow.
       p. cm.
    ''A Liberty classics edition''—Prelim. p.
    Includes bibliographical references and index.
    ISBN 0-86597-108-0. — ISBN 0-86597-109-9 (pbk.)
    1. State, The.   2. Political science.   I. Burrow, J. W. (John Wyon),
1935–   .   II. Title.
JC501.H8131993
320.1—dc20   92-33512
                                                 CIP

10 9 8 7 6 5 4 3 2 1

Le difficile est de ne promulguer que des lois nécessaires, de rester à jamais fidèle à ce principe vraiment constitutionnel de la société, de se mettre en garde contre la fureur de gouverner, la plus funeste maladie des gouvernements modernes.

Mirabeau l'aîné, Sur l'Éducation publique, p. 69.

The difficult task is to enact only laws that are needed, to remain ever faithful to that truly basic principle of society, to be on guard against the passion for ruling, the most fatal disorder of modern states.

Mirabeau the elder, On Public Education, p. 69.

Contents

CHAPTER I

Object of the inquiry defined—an inquiry seldom prosecuted, though of
the highest importance ▪ Historical view of the limits which States have
practically assigned to their sphere of action ▪ Difference between ancient
and modern States ▪ On the aim of the State organization in general—
Should the solicitude of the State be confined to the preservation of SECUR-
ITY, or should it attempt to provide for the POSITIVE WELFARE of the
nation? ▪ Legislators and authors in favour of the latter opinion—Not-
withstanding their conclusions, this question seems to require a profounder
investigation ▪ This investigation can proceed only from a consideration of
human nature and its highest aims.

CHAPTER II

Man's highest end is the highest and most harmonious development of his
powers in their perfect individuality ▪ Conditions necessary for the attainment of this end: freedom of action and a variety of situations ▪ Closer
application of these positions to the inner life of man ▪ Historical confirmation ▪ Highest principle of the whole inquiry derived from these
considerations.

evils flowing from this condition as regards man's internal development ▪ General principle.

highest and most general grounds, that the State has no access to the real channels of influence on morality, viz. the form of the internal acceptation of religious conceptions ▪ Hence, everything pertaining to religion is wholly beyond the sphere of the State's activity.

CHAPTER XI

On the solicitude of the State for security with respect to such of   94
the citizens' actions as relate directly to others (Civil laws)

mitting them ▪ Limitation of this method to the preventing crimes from being actually committed, which are already resolved on. What means are we to supply for those disapproved of as preventive of crime? ▪ The closest vigilance with regard to crimes committed, and the consequent rareness of impunity ▪ Harmfulness of the right of granting reprieve and mitigation ▪ Arrangements for detecting crime ▪ Necessity for the perfect publicity of all criminal laws ▪ General principles.

effected when the reform proceeds from men's minds and thoughts ▪ General principles of all reform flowing from these positions ▪ Application of these principles to the present inquiry ▪ Principal peculiarity of the system laid down ▪ Dangers to be apprehended in its applications ▪ Necessity for gradual steps in the attempt to realize it ▪ General principle ▪ Connection of this principle with the fundamental principles of the proposed theory ▪ Principle of necessity suggested by this connection ▪ It is superior to that of utility ▪ Conclusion.

Editor's Introduction

ilhelm von Humboldt is widely remembered as the architect of the Prussian educational system and the founder of the University of Berlin. To the student of the history of political ideas, however, he is probably most familiar as the author of a single sentence, taken by John Stuart Mill as the epigraph for his essay *On Liberty:* 'The grand, leading principle, towards which every argument unfolded in these pages directly converges, is the absolute and essential importance of human development in its richest diversity.' Humboldt also, incidentally, a decade later, provided another eminent Victorian, Matthew Arnold, with the epigraph for his *Schools and Universities on the Continent.* The book from which Mill's quotation was drawn was published in 1854, five years before the publication of *On Liberty* and about the time that, as we know, Mill began to consider writing such an essay.[1] It was a translation of Humboldt's *Ideen zu einem Versuch die Grenzen der Wirkamkeit des Staats zu bestimmen*—a title which the English translator, Joseph Coulthard, sacrificing modesty to concision, rendered as *The Sphere and Duties of Government.* Humboldt himself had died in 1835 and the work itself, written when he was a young man in 1791–2, might have been regarded in the 1850s as a museum piece. It had not, however, been published when it was first written, Humboldt anticipating trouble with the Prussian censorship, though sections of it had appeared in Schiller's journal *Neue Thalia* and in the *Berlinische Monatsschrift.*[2]

The revival of interest in it was due chiefly to the subsequent public career and scholarly distinction of its author and to the fact that the post-

[1] J. S. Mill, *Autobiography* (London, 1954), p. 212.
[2] Chapters V, VI, and VIII appeared in the *Berlinische Monatsschrift* in the autumn of 1792. *Neue Thalia* published ch. II, and the first part of ch. III.

humous German edition of Humboldt's works, edited by his brother
Alexander, published the complete, or almost complete, text for the first
time in 1852.[3] It aroused immediate interest, inspiring a French work on
the same lines—Edouard Laboulaye's *L'état et ses limites*—as well as an
English translation of Humboldt's essay. Coulthard's belief that the subject was of 'peculiar interest' for his own time was a reasonable one, for
it was also the theme of such classics of Victorian political thought as
Herbert Spencer's *Social Statics* (1851) and *The Man versus The State*
(1884) as well as Mill's *On Liberty*.

Whether the belated publication of Humboldt's essay actually provided
the springboard for Mill's we cannot be sure, though the dates, and Mill's
frequent references to Humboldt in his text, inevitably suggest a connection.[4] Mill's own account of the matter, apart from the celebrated tribute
to his wife, is somewhat vague, no doubt reflecting fairly accurately the
way in which free-floating ideas, impressions and half-conscious
impulses coalesce in the conception of a book. 'As regards originality, it
[*On Liberty*] has of course no other than that which every thoughtful
mind gives to its own mode of conceiving and expressing truths which
are common property.' Mill goes on to mention Pestalozzi and Goethe
among others, but adds 'the only author who has preceded me . . . of
whom I thought it appropriate to say anything was Humboldt'.[5]

Humboldt had become, of course, by the time his collected works were
published, far more to his contemporaries and successors than simply the
author of a resurrected treatise on the individual and the State. His career
as statesman, philologist, and educationalist, as an assiduous cultivator of
personal relations who was rewarded with the friendship of Goethe and
Schiller, and as the man who taught Mme de Staël German, was an
appropriate image of the deliberate human polymorphism which was his
professed ideal. One only of his many roles was to be the lost leader of
the Prussian liberal constitutionalists. One commentator has suggested

[3] This is a hiatus in ch. III, which subsequent editors have been unable to fill.
[4] J. S. Mill, *On Liberty: With The Subjection of Women and Chapters on Socialism*, ed.
Stefan Collini, Cambridge Texts in the History of Political Thought (Cambridge: Cambridge University Press, 1989), pp. 3, 58, 72, 103, 108; and *Collected Works of John
Stuart Mill*, ed. J. M. Robson, 33 vols. (Toronto: University of Toronto Press, 1963–
91), vol. 18, *Essays on Politics and Society*, pp. 215, 261, 262, 274, 300, 304. [The
editor's original references to the 1968 Everyman's Library edition of *On Liberty* have
been changed to refer to the Cambridge and Toronto editions cited above.]
[5] Mill, *Autobiography*, pp. 216–17.

that had there been a revolution in Germany in 1790 he might have become 'the German Mirabeau'.[6] Friedrich von Genz, a friend of Humboldt's early years—the essay *On the Limits of State Action* began as a letter from Humboldt to Genz—said that he was the cleverest man he had ever met. Mme de Staël, obviously assuming, reasonably enough, that she had met them all, called him simply 'la plus grande capacité de l'Europe'. Arndt said of him that he could lead the great Stein about like a lamb, while Schiller found in him the ideal balance of reason and emotion—a compliment which Humboldt returned.[7] Although it is not surprising that a number of people seem to have been rather afraid of Humboldt.

He was born at Potsdam in 1767, of a Pomeranian noble and official family,[8] and when he wrote the essay which we shall henceforth refer to for convenenience as *The Limits of State Action* at the age of 24 he had just resigned his first minor post in the Prussian administration, having found administration, as he said, '*geistlos*', and resolved to devote himself entirely to the cultivation of his friends, his newly married wife, and himself.[9] In 1802 he made a somewhat tentative return to government service as a Prussian envoy to the Papal court, thus beginning a distinguished scholarly line, for he was followed successively in that post by Niebuhr and Bunsen. In 1808 he returned to Berlin, to become Minister of Public Instruction in Stein's reforming ministry; as masterly, as Seeley said, in the organization of education as Scharnhorst in that of war. Indeed, one might add that if it was really the Prussian schoolmaster who defeated the French in 1870, it was Humboldt who had licensed the schoolmaster.

[6] R. Aris, *History of Political Thought in Germany, 1789–1815* (London, 1936), p. 137.
[7] Ernst Howald, *Wilhelm von Humboldt* (Zurich, 1944), pp. 20–1. J. R. Seeley, *Life of Stein* (3 vols. Cambridge, 1898), III, 153. For Humboldt and Schiller see Howald, p. 84, and D. Regin, *Freedom and Dignity. The Historical and Philosophical Thought of Schiller* (The Hague, 1965), p. 107. Humboldt wrote of Schiller: 'Gedanke und Bild, Idee und Empfindung treten immer in ihm in Wechselwirkung' *Über Schiller und den Gang seiner Geistesentwicklung* (Insel-Bücherei, nr. 38, Leipzig, n.d.), p. 45.
[8] But the Prussian official class was decidedly liberal at this time. Genz considered it tainted with Jacobinism. J. Droz, *L'Allemagne et la Revolution Française* (Paris, 1949), p. 380.
[9] The studies of Humboldt's life on which this biographical account is chiefly based are: Howald, *Wilhelm von Humboldt;* R. Haym, *Wilhelm von Humboldt* (Berlin, 1856); R. Leroux, *Guillaume de Humboldt; la formation de sa pensée jusqu'en 1794* (Paris 1932); Friedrich Schaffenstein, *Wilhelm von Humboldt. Ein Lebensbild* (Frankfurt a.M., 1952).

As a member of Stein's ministry, Humboldt founded the University of Berlin and reorganized the Prussian Gymnasium, stamping its syllabus with his own linguistic and Hellenist leanings and his concern for all-round cultural development. That there was a contradiction between Humboldt's role during this period and the letter, if not the underlying spirit, of some of the doctrines of the *Limits* has often been noted, and explained by the patriotic enthusiasm of the year of Prussia's national awakening. [10] Humboldt subsequently attended the Congress of Vienna as Prussian plenipotentiary and served in several diplomatic posts. In 1818 he became for a brief period Minister of the Interior, leading the opposition to Hardenberg by urging less subservience to Austria and a greater measure of constitutional responsibility. The actual occasion of his final retirement was Prussia's acceptance of the Karlsbad decrees. [11]

Humboldt's devotion to his public career was never entirely whole-hearted, however, and the real timbre of his life is more accurately suggested by his changing intellectual preoccupations and his various published and unpublished writing than by an outline of his official career. Even had he written nothing but personal letters to his friends, he would still have achieved a footnote to German literary history as the correspondent of Goethe and Schiller. In fact, he wrote copiously if spasmodically, and achieved reputations of varying distinction as political theorist, philosopher of history, Hellenist, literary critic, aesthetician, and one of the pioneers of comparative philology. He also, almost inevitably, wrote some rather indifferent poetry. This polymathy of Humboldt is not simply a matter for gratified wonder. It is, as we shall see, crucial to an understanding of his political theory, not only because such polymorphism is a personal expression of his humanist ideal, but because he draws for his basic ideas on a cultural context in which a number of different intellectual activities run along converging or parallel lines.

---

[10] But Humboldt's *volte face* was never absolute; many men have looked forward to the withering away of the State but few ministers have looked forward as Humboldt did to the withering away of their own department. See E. Spranger, *Wilhelm von Humboldt und die Reform des Bildungswesens* (new ed. Tübingen, 1960), p. 104.

    On the question of Humboldt's inconsistency see also Howald, *Wilhelm von Humboldt*, pp. 131–3; Schaffenstein, *Wilhelm von Humboldt. Ein Lebensbild*, pp. 180–3, 225; Seeley, *Life of Stein*, II, 424, 428.

[11] G. S. Ford, *Stein and the Era of Reform in Prussia, 1807–1815* (Princeton, 1922, repr. 1965), pp. 197–205. Also B. Gebhardt, *Wilhelm von Humboldt als Staatsmann* (2 vols. Stuttgart, 1896).

For this reason it would be superficial to approach Humboldt's essay on the limits of the State in what may seem the most obvious way, as an attempt by a young German intellectual to define his attitude, as so many of his compatriots were trying to do, to the revolutionary events in France. Humboldt had, it is true, already written earlier in the same year an essay entitled *Thoughts on Constitutions, suggested by the New French Constitution,* in which he had taken a decidedly Burkean line. There is no evidence, though, that he knew anything of Burke's *Reflections*—later translated by his friend Genz—in 1791. Some of the ideas of Humboldt's earlier essay were incorporated in the *Limits of State Action.* The latter, however, is not very Burkean in tone, except in a few passages, and its central thesis—the attempt rigidly to circumscribe the activities of the State—though it is introduced with a quotation from Mirabeau, is just as applicable to Frederician Prussia or Josephinian Austria as it is to the National Assembly, and in some respects more so.

Humboldt's *Limits of State Action* is by no means solely explicable in terms of current events. It is in fact a singularly rich document, containing a number of different intellectual and cultural seams and moulding them into an intellectual landscape with its own distinctively Humboldtian feel and atmosphere. There was, firstly, Humboldt's ambiguous attitude to the *Aufklärung,* his inheritance of the physiocrat and rationalist doctrines of his boyhood tutors. There were the theories of human perfectibility of Leibniz and Lessing. There was the Kantian assertion of the absolute claims of the moral law, and the Kantian insistence that each individual must be treated as an end and never simply as a means, and that the end of life was essentially an internal matter, an inner freedom of the soul, not simply a condition of external well-being. There was the Rousseauist and *Sturm und Drang* cult of feeling as the source of human vitality. There was the characteristic philhellenism of German neo-classicism, of which Humboldt was a leading figure, which saw in an idealized picture of the ancient Greeks the model of the fully rounded and harmonious human character. There was even a dose of Platonism, which led Humboldt to see the visible world as a kind of cryptogram of the eternal ideas which lie behind it—a doctrine which bobs disconcertingly to the surface of the essay (chapter VIII) though it is not really worked into its theoretical economy.[12]

---

[12] For the fullest account of Humboldt's intellectual development see Leroux, *Guillaume de Humboldt.*

It is necessary to risk some ungainliness and possible bewilderment by dwelling on this heterogeneity, in order to indicate the richness of Humboldt's essay, to emphasize that it was far more than simply a *pièce d'occasion,* and that the fact that it is at least as coherent as most essays in political theorizing represents a considerable synthetic achievement. This may seem at first sight not merely bewildering but implausible. Or it may suggest that Humboldt's essay is simply the product of a well-meaning but over-tolerant eclecticism. It begins to seem less implausible when one remembers that most of these intellectual currents were also present in the work of a German contemporary of Humboldt more familiar to English students of political theory: Hegel. Whatever the objections to Hegel's political theory, and they have been many and violent, he is not generally regarded (though it is a possible line of attack) as a well-meaning eclectic, or simply as as repository of undigested, heterogeneous intellectual impulses. To invoke Hegel in order to dispel suspicions of confusion may seem like raising the devil to exorcise a bump in the night. Yet if it can be allowed that Hegel was able to make something of his intellectual heritage that was undeniably distinctive and coherent, whatever else may be wrong with it, it may seem justified to ask at least for a temporary suspension of disbelief on behalf of Humboldt. In fact one could try to sum up by saying simply that Humboldt, like Hegel, though the results show marked differences, is trying to derive a coherent intellectual position from an inheritance and *milieu* which contain heavy doses both of the Enlightenment and of the Romanticism which is generally set in opposition to it.

In the English intellectual history of the early nineteenth century there was far less of this articulate groping for a synthesis, which is perhaps why English readers are still apt to find the results obscure and unsympathetic. J. S. Mill, who did feel the need, was able, with admittedly a certain amount of simplification, to present his two archetypal figures, Bentham and Coleridge, representing the characteristic intellectual virtues of the eighteenth and nineteenth centuries respectively, as two sides of a dialectic, needing, in fact, to be *aufgehoben* in the Hegelian sense, taken up and synthesized at a higher level. It is such a synthesis that Mill is asking for when, in conclusion, he recommends his readers and by implication himself, to try to fuse the intellectual lessons of Bentham and Coleridge. It is not surprising that he found a congenial spirit in Humboldt, or that he should have taken a sentence written by Humboldt nearly 70 years earlier as the motto for one of his major works.

Humboldt's own emergence from the intellectual world of the German *Aufklärung,* into which he had been initiated by his tutors as Mill had learnt his utilitarianism from his father, was, like Mill's own emancipation, a process partly of emotional crisis and self-discovery, partly of exposure to the literary and philosophical tendencies of the period, and to the influence of friends, especially Georg Forster and Friedrich Jacobi,[13] touched like himself by the late eighteenth-century cult of feeling and the revolt against the drier abstractions of the *Aufklärung* in its most undiluted form. Humboldt found himself, like other youths of cerebral and emotionally unexpansive upbringing and disposition—even in later years acquaintances commented on Humboldt's essential coldness[14]—confronted in his first steps in adult personal relations by the usual elementary and shattering discovery that other people, and particularly women, mattered to him, not merely as an audience for his ideas or as objects of his disinterested benevolence but as influences capable of enriching his life, influencing his ideas and, temporarily at least, destroying his happiness. This sense, which Humboldt never lost, of the fruitful interpenetration of personalities, the sense that others could become, emotionally and intellectually, flesh of his flesh, and he of theirs, prevented his liberalism from ever assuming that characteristic liberal form in which individuals in society confront each other as external objects and obstacles, as rival, independent, and potentially hostile sovereign states. One cannot say of Humboldt's liberalism, as Lionel Trilling remarks of liberalism in general, that 'in the interests of its vision of a general enlargement and freedom and rational direction of human life—it drifts towards a denial of the emotions and the imagination'.[15]

Contemporary events, the French Revolution, Frederick William II's law proclaiming Lutheranism as the State religion, played a part in the formation of Humboldt's fundamental principles, but neither appear to

---

[13] Leroux, *Guillaume de Humboldt,* pp. 205–9, 244 n. 5, 355–7. For studies of Forster, see Droz, *L'Allemagne;* G. P. Gooch, *Germany and the French Revolution* (London, new impr. 1965), ch. XIII; Henry Hatfield, *Aesthetic Paganism in German Literature. Winckelmann to Goethe* (Harvard, 1954).

[14] Howald, *Wilhelm von Humboldt,* p. 13.

[15] Lionel Trilling, *The Liberal Imagination* (Mercury Books, 1964), pp. xiii–xiv.

have been nearly so important as his discovery of girls.[16] In the ensuing struggle to remain open to the new emotional and intellectual possibilities revealed by his discovery of other people, without losing poise and dignity and the sense of his own independent identity, to accept experience and ingest it without being overwhelmed, Humboldt, more fortunate in this respect than Mill, found in his immediate cultural environment in late eighteenth-century Germany a rich assortment of images and concepts and even a myth—the myth of noble Hellas—for interpreting his discovery.

Humboldt's dilemma was essentially, stated in its most abstract terms, that of achieving unity in diversity, of retaining coherence without sacrificing variety, richness, diversity: of giving the various aspects of one's nature their due, and retaining one's sensitivity to experience, even painful experience, while remaining essentially in control of one's cultural metabolism, moulding and shaping its results into a coherent if necessarily unstable whole (see especially chapters II, III, VIII). It is a dilemma which can be formulated in a number of different vocabularies and can be made to sound outlandish or banal depending on how attuned we are to the vocabulary that is chosen. One can express it in a traditional metaphysical vocabulary, as the relation of form to substance or matter, or as the tension between reason and feeling, rules and spontaneity, Classicism and Romanticism, Kantian universal moral imperatives and the vitality and variety of historically nurtured folk-customs and traditions.

These dichotomies are not identical, of course, nor exhaustive. They involve different levels of abstraction and they imply attention to different kinds of illustrative examples, and because the examples are different, the dilemmas themselves will be different. The reason for pointing to their affinities, however, is to suggest that it is not fortuitous that a number of late eighteenth- and early nineteenth-century German authors are equally, or almost equally, aestheticians, moralists, political theorists, and, of course, metaphysicians: Herder, Schiller, Hegel, Schelling, and a number of others, among whom we may include Humboldt. The immediate impulse to such many-sided activity was surely in most cases a sense that a relatively coherent and stable view of the world, that of the *Aufklärung*, was in a number of contexts unacceptably inhibited, uniform

---

[16] 'Il y a là une conception dont l'origine doit être recherchée . . . dans les expériences amoureuses de Humboldt' (Leroux, *Guillaume de Humboldt,* p. 252).

and dominated by concepts too mechanistic and limited in scope to accommodate the full richness of the concrete world and the full range of human potentialities. Such was certainly the inspiration of Goethe's *Naturphilosophie*, to which Humboldt refers (below, p. 13)—perhaps the most notorious example of the doctrinaire many-sidedness of the period.

Because of the nature of these criticisms, the problems of constructing a new conceptual framework would arise in the form of certain fundamental dilemmas. How, in particular, to mediate between what Schiller, in his *Letters on the Aesthetic Education of Mankind* (1794), called *Stofftrieb* and *Formtrieb*, the urge towards the sensuous and concrete and the urge towards rational control and the formulation of rules; how to accommodate a sense of the importance of vitality, concreteness, and diversity without fragmentation and anarchy, without falling into the raw emotionalism and destructive rebelliousness of the *Sturm und Drang*, or, on the other hand, into a total and undiscriminating acceptance, pantheist or historicist, of everything that is the case, from toothache to tyranny, as just part of life's rich tapestry—the latter a tendency already implicit in the Leibnizian optimism of the *Aufklärung*? (For this tendency in Humboldt see below, p. 140.) The journey from one set of metaphors to another is a perilous business.

In political thought, the tendency of German writers during this period to swing violently between these poles is notorious, most notably in the case of Fichte's pendulum-like political career, at different times almost insanely individualist and ruthlessly authoritarian. Characteristic, too, are attempted syntheses which later generations have generally agreed to be merely verbal and spurious: Hegel in particular and the concept of 'positive freedom' in general. This is a political and historical fact whose explanation goes far deeper than the incidents—the execution of Louis XVI or the battle of Jena—which are usually invoked, though no doubt they were the immediate occasion of some of the more dramatic conversions. The tension they sometimes caused to snap was, however, already implicit in the intellectual context of the late eighteenth century. We may point, for example, to the same tension in Rousseau, crudely expressed by the alleged contradiction between the individualism and primitivism of the *Discourses* and *Emile* and the 'totalitarianism' of the *Contrat Social*.

At this point there may be some temptation to simplify: to decide that we are simply confronted by the necessary and perennial tension between 'freedom' and 'order'. There is more to it than this, however, quite apart from the fact that 'order' for Rousseau or Fichte was something very different from what it meant to Hobbes or Frederick the Great. During the period with which we are concerned, discussions of the relation between the individual, society, and the state can generally best be understood in a context which includes metaphysics, morals, psychology, aesthetics, and educational theory (Rousseau, Herder, Schiller, and Humboldt all wrote on education) in which one finds analogues to the political dilemmas, suitably translated into the language of the appropriate genre. Of course, such connections are likely to hold in any period. It is well recognized that there is a useful suggestiveness for the history of political ideas in such phrases as 'Political Romanticism' and 'The revolt against reason'. The latter are far too crude to accommodate Humboldt (or Schiller, or Hegel, for that matter). However, it is true that his manner of recognizing certain tensions in social, political, and personal life was conditioned by the rising intellectual status of such concepts as feeling, spontaneity, variety, and concreteness and that certain characteristically Romantic metaphors are central to his attempts to deal with them.

In the various attempts to welcome and control the newly esteemed Romantic virtues, and to find some resolution of the resulting dilemmas, two metaphors were, in late eighteenth-century Germany—not only there, of course, but there more insistently than elsewhere—found particularly useful. They were derived respectively from the concept of a work of art and the concept of a biological organism. The reasons for their usefulness were basically the same. They both proved immensely suggestive, though both possessed drawbacks. Both are extensively used by Humboldt (chapters II, VIII).

A work of art was, in some respects, an admirable image for a reconciliation of living, multifarious, concrete but earthy substance with elevated, coherent, ethereal form, of unity in diversity—Shaftesbury's conception of a work of art as having an 'inner form' was immensely influential in eighteenth-century Germany—of crude energy or intolerable suffering transmuted, as in Winckelmann's famous description of the Laocoön, into a serene harmony and unity (*stille Grösse und edele Einfalt*). Its disadvantage as a source of metaphors for social relations was that a work of art is something deliberately made.

Solon rather than the *Volksgeist* seems to offer the paradigm of art in politics. True there were ways around this, either by maintaining the thesis that a work of art was not so much the work of the artist's constructive deliberation as of his creative daemon, the sacred wind that blew through him, or by devoting particular attention to works which could plausibly be represented as the spontaneous representation of the folk-spirit: folk-poetry or, as Humboldt's friend F. A. Wolf was to assert, Homer. All the same, the connotations of the work of art as an artifact were sufficiently strong to inhibit its use as a direct analogue for society or the state. The concept of the State as a work of art was precisely what was *not* wanted; it smelt too strongly of Cameralism and benevolent despotism, and of the mechanistic conceptions of the State as an artificially created structure of checks and balances or a bureaucratic hierarchy imposed from above on an inert social mass. 'A properly constituted state must be exactly analogous to a machine, in which all the wheels and gears are precisely adjusted to one another; and the ruler must be the foreman, the mainspring, or the soul—if one may use the expression—which sets everything in motion.'[17] This typical statement by a leading Cameralist thinker, Justi, represents the exact antithesis of Humboldt's belief that the vitality of a nation derives solely from the spontaneous activities and diverse creative energies of the individuals who composed it. Thus, the concept of a work of art tended to enter the political thought of Humboldt, Schiller, and the Romantics not as a direct analogue for the state or society, but indirectly, through its influence on their ethical ideas, notably in Schiller's *Aesthetic Letters* and in Humboldt's conception of personal culture.

Similarly, the concept of an organism was immensely useful in suggesting a combination of inner coherence and self-determination (*Selbstverwaltung*) with a spontaneous vitality fed by the vital juices of material, sensuous existence. An organism has a creative, reciprocal relation to its environment; it is not simply the passive recipient of stimuli (see below, p. 13). But this image also had its disadvantages. Organisms appeared, it was true, to exhibit purposes; they were self-determining, but not *consciously* self-determining. Moreover, if society as a whole were to be regarded as an organism, what would become of the autonomy of the individuals who composed it? One reason, in fact, why Humboldt has to deny so emphatically that the *State* is an organism, and is forced to regard

---

[17] Geraint Parry, 'Enlightened Government and Its Critics in Eighteenth Century Germany', *Historical Journal*, VI (1963), 182.

it simply as a kind of public convenience with strictly limited functions, a mere piece of machinery, is that otherwise, in a political theory so enamoured of the 'organic' virtues, the State, if conceded organic characteristics, would become all in all. The 'organic' political theorist is virtually forced, since he must decide whether the State is like an organism or not, to choose between endowing it with omnicompetence or restricting its functions to a bare minimum.

Hence it is as common to find a cult of the 'organic' virtues among populists, anarchists, and political pluralists of all shades as among State-worshippers. There has, however, been one very notable bridge across which many an organically minded anarchist or semi-anarchist has crossed over into the other camp: the concept of the organic national community, and its political expression, the nation-state. It is therefore not surprising and may seem rather sinister to find that Humboldt as he grew older—there are premonitions of it even in the *Limits* (below, p. 137)—began to make increasing use of this bridge, though his intellectual home, it is fair to say, remained well on the liberal side of it.[18]

The drawbacks to the concepts of the work of art and of the organism as analogues, their implicit denial of spontaneity in the first case and of individual autonomy and self-consciousness in the latter, exacted a certain complexity in their application to the State or society. These particular implications ran directly counter to the exaltation of the free, self-determining, self-conscious moral agent which was an intrinsic part of the ideals of late eighteenth-century German humanism which received its definitive formulation by Kant, and which had deep roots in the *Aufklärung* and in the religious tradition of German Pietism, with its insistence on the inner light. It had also deep social roots in the search for dignity and self-esteem by educated middle-class Germans whose paternalistic governments seemed to treat them like children, while aristocratic exclusiveness and arrogance seemed to deny them their full status as human beings. It is true that some German political theorists did not escape the full implications of the organic analogy and handed their supposedly unhappy, fragmented modern citizens, willy nilly, into the arms of the

[18] For Humboldt's conception of the nation, see Ernst Cassirer, *Freiheit und Form. Studien zur deutschen Geistesgeschichte* (Berlin, 1922), pp. 518–25; F. Meinecke, *Weltbürgertum und Nationalstaat, Werke*, V (Munich, 1962), bk. I, chs. III, VIII; also S. A. Kaehler, *Wilhelm von Humboldt und der Staat* (Munich and Berlin, 1927).

Volk-soul or the bosom of the stream of history in which everything that
happened happened necessarily. But for Humboldt at least, any metaphor
claiming admission to his political thinking had first to make its peace
with the free, self-conscious, self-determining individual.

Humboldt in fact makes considerable use both of aesthetic and organic
metaphors, but there is a third concept which is also relevant to a full
understanding of Humboldt's ethics and political theory, though it is not
made properly explicit in *The Limits of State Action* and for fuller references to it one has to turn to some of his other works, also unpublished
during his lifetime: to his early essay on the laws of human development
(*Über die Gesetze der Entwicklung der menschlichen Kräfte*, 1791), to
his *Plan for a Comparative Anthropology* (*Plan einer vergleichenden
Anthropologie*, 1795), and to his *Reflections on World History* (*Betrachtungen über die Weltgeschichte*, 1814). This is the concept, which Lessing stamped with his name though it was by no means solely his
property, of history as the self-education of mankind. This concept too
contained, or could be invested with, the required ingredients: the presup-
position of an inner, spontaneous vitality, and of an underlying coherence
or pattern working itself out through an immense diversity and gaining
nourishment from it, and of a creative, reciprocal relation to experience,
in which even error and suffering were made meaningful through the concept of education.

Self-education through a creative acceptance of experience is in fact
the master-concept of Humboldt's political theory at both its poles, in his
conception of individual morality and in his tentative hints of a possible
historical progress. His social and political precepts are grounded on the
notion of the supreme importance of *Bildung*, by which he meant the
fullest, richest, and most harmonious development of the potentialities of
the individual, the community, or the human race (*Limits of State Action*,
chapter III).[19] Life lived as it should be, according to Humboldt, consists
of an endless endeavour to reconcile a coherent individuality with the
utmost receptivity to the most diverse experience, an acceptance of an
eternal tension between the need to be uniquely and harmoniously oneself

[19] The chief accounts of Humboldt's theory of *Bildung* are: E. Spranger, *Wilhelm von
Humboldt und die Humanitätsidee* (Berlin, 1909); Leroux, *Guillaume de Humboldt*; and
in English, W. Bruford. 'The Idea of "Bildung" in Wilhelm von Humboldt's Letters',
in *The Era of Goethe, Essays presented to James Boyd* (Oxford, 1959).

and the duty to assimilate as much as possible of life's emotional and intellectual possibilities. As he puts it in *The Limits of State Action*, 'The true end of Man, or that which is prescribed by the eternal and immutable dictates of reason, and not suggested by vague and transient desires, is the highest and most harmonious development of his powers to a complete and consistent whole' (below, p. 10). The Kantian echo of 'eternal and immutable dictates of reason', contrasted with 'vague and transient desires', is clear, and we shall have to return to the implications of this for Humboldt's theory later.

The more distinctive features of Humboldt's ideal are suggested a few lines later, when he stresses the need of human beings for 'variety of situation' if they are to develop their powers to their fullest extent. The duty, which Humboldt stresses, to maintain one's own personality as a 'complete and consistent' whole, moreover, is not merely the counter-weight but the corollary to this insistence on variety. For it is only by retaining and developing one's individuality, one's *Eigentümlichkeit,* that one can contribute to others' 'variety of situation', just as they, in their *Eigentümlichkeiten,* contribute to one's own (below, pp. 12, 27).

This concept of *Bildung* as the achievement of a harmonious individuality nourished by diversity of experience was formulated by Humboldt very early in his life, as can be seen from his letters and his early essays, but it was not achieved without a struggle. As a boy he had admired the Stoics, and throughout his life, even during the most active part of his public career, the impulse to regard life as a play seen from the vantage point of a detached spectator, and to cultivate an inner untouchability, was strong. His cult of accepted experience was in part a deliberate rejection of emotional sterility, an acceptance of the chances of getting hurt. On the other hand, he had obviously an innate, restless, Faustian or collector's streak,[20] independently of the intellectual influences which encouraged it and in terms of which he justified it. His youthful travels were relentless exercises in self-improvement. Even his marriage had to be sanctified as the highest of all opportunities for *Bildung,* a sublime paradox in which two unique individuals became triumphantly one while remaining triumphantly themselves (cf. below, p. 24ff).

[20] Werner Schultz, 'Wilhelm von Humboldt und der Faustische Mensch', *Jahrbuch der Goethe-Gesellschaft,* XVI (1930).

The concept of *Bildung* was not, of course, peculiar to Humboldt either in German literature or social philosophy. The *Bildungsroman* is a literary genre sufficiently distinct to have earned a name.[21] Herder had used the concept of *Bildung* in expounding his own humanist ideal, with an emphasis similar to Humboldt's on the need for diversity. The preoccupation with *Bildung* was in some respects a secular version of German Pietism, itself a variety of Protestantism both strenuous and resolutely spiritual and otherworldly. It also—though this does not apply directly to Humboldt—provided an ideal, practical in its impracticality, to those late eighteenth-century German intellectuals—teachers, pastors, women, newly emancipated Jews—who had been educated beyond the requirements or opportunities of their immediate social circumstances. Humboldt himself, as a young man, belonged to a small *Veredlungsbund,* a high-minded society for mutual improvement of character. Freemasonry, of course, provided another, more institutionalized, outlet of essentially the same kind.

A subtler attraction of the idea of *Bildung* was that it was much better able than the Enlightenment's guiding light of reason to accommodate the newly fashionable virtues of sentiment, sensuousness, enthusiasm, and originality. For *Bildung* could be represented as a quasi-organic and a dialectical process, consisting of an endless acceptance and innumerable provisional reconciliations of the creative tension between the individual and his environment and between the various contending aspects of his own nature. Both organic and aesthetic metaphors could contribute to an understanding of this process. Humboldt himself was convinced that a life successfully dedicated to *Bildung* was itself a work of art. It satisfied the requirements of being both an end in itself, not to be judged by utilitarian or commercial criteria, and of moulding raw experience and natural, spontaneous vitality into a satisfying, harmonious coherence. Moreover, in the school of aesthetics to which Humboldt belonged, the concept of a work of art itself tended to be expounded in organic terms. '[This] concept of poetic creativity—that self-organising process, assimilating disparate materials by an inherent lawfulness into an integral whole—borrows many of its characteristic features from the conceptual model of organic growth'[22] (cf. below, p. 77).

[21] See E. L. Stahl, *Die religiöse und die humanitätsphilosophische Bildungsidee und die Entstehung des deutschen Bildungsromans in 18 Jahrhundert* (Berne, 1934).
[22] M. H. Abrams, *The Mirror and the Lamp. Romantic Theory and the Critical Tradition* (New York, 1958), p. 124, on Coleridge's poetic theory.

The organic metaphor was apt for the exposition of *Bildung*. An organism develops in time, and its form is not imposed on it from without; it is self-determining. It is neither passive in relation to its environment nor disconnected from it; it assimilates what it needs, converting it into its own tissues, imposing form upon heterogeneous brute matter in a miracle of transmutation. Above all, though it is part of nature and cannot exist without its environment, it makes itself, developing as it does out of an inner necessity. Similarly, for Herder, perhaps the greatest of all propagandists of the organic analogy, *Bildung* was, as F. M. Barnard puts it, 'a process of interaction, an "organic" process of "formation", in which men influence each other within a specific social setting'.[23] Exactly the same words can be used of Humboldt.

The concept of *Bildung* also had convenient results when applied, as both Herder and Humboldt applied it, to history considered as the self-education of mankind as a whole. It enabled its exponents to find a respectable and even glorious historical role for the primitive and poetic virtues of earlier civilizations, which the Enlightenment was thought to have undervalued, while still leaving a possible place for the still attractive idea of progress. History, as Humboldt saw it,[24] and as he presented it in his *Thoughts on Constitutions* and later in his *Plan of a Comparative Anthropology* (1795), consisted not of progress in a simple, cumulative sense but of a kind of dialectic, as mankind explored first one range of human potentialities and then another, lurching from one kind of one-sidedness (*Einseitigkeit*—which Humboldt contrasts with *Eigentümlichkeit*) to another (*Limits,* below, p. 141). But there are hints of progress of a kind, because the richer the human experience becomes, by every exploration, every 'one-sided' development, so the *potential* cultural experience of the individual is enriched. The extent to which his potentialities are realized for each individual depends on his opportunities and his capacity for assimilating the cultural experience of mankind, preserved by history, and making of it a coherent and balanced whole. 'In the highest ideal of human nature which the most glowing fantasy can conceive', Humboldt wrote in *Thoughts on Constitutions,* 'each actual

---

[23] F. M. Barnard, *Herder's Social and Political Thought* (London, 1965), p. 93. For the question of Herder's influence on Humboldt, *ibid.* p. 168 n. 50.

[24] R. Leroux, *L'Anthropologie Comparée de Guillaume de Humboldt* (Paris, 1958), pp. 14 ff. and *Guillaume de Humboldt,* pp. 215 ff.

moment is a beautiful flower, but nevertheless only *one*. Only memory can wreathe the garland which binds together past and future'[25] (cf. below, p. 11).

This sounds rather like a tentative and microcosmic version of the Hegelian Absolute Consciousness, in which all contradictions are resolved, just as Hegel's notion of the task of the philosopher as a retrospective one, and his presentation of philosophy as the *history* of philosophy, reminds one of Humboldt's conception of *Bildung*. The most cultivated individual, the most complete philosophy, are the ones which can most successfully assimilate and most fully contain the various cultural and moral commitments—obviously in many cases contradictory—entered into by mankind in the course of history. This is a notion which, more modestly phrased than in Hegel's version of it perhaps, is by no means dead. In a more limited context, T. S. Eliot's discussion of tradition and the individual talent looks like a version of it. Walter Pater's *Gioconda,* most Hegelian of women, was an image of it. It still provides an arguable test of the difference between more and less civilized individuals. It continues to offer a role to academic historians who may no longer believe—to resort to the words of Lord Acton—that 'The science of politics is deposited by the stream of history, like grains of gold in the sands of a river.'

Humboldt's apparent presentation of the cultivated man as a connoisseur in the moral museum of the world's history may strike some as an attenuated and unreal affair compared with the full-blooded if narrowly circumscribed social life of a static society devoid of a sense of history, in which moral imperatives are simply given in education for membership of the tribe, and the question of experimentation does not arise. Others will stress the limited horizons of the latter, their narrow range of choices and their probable incapacity to cope with unprecedented situations without disorientation and loss of self-control or self-respect. This is rather like the dispute whether education should teach one a lot about a little or *vice versa,* and there is no answer. All the same, if Humboldt's ideal is evidently accessible only to a cultivated élite, it is one which does try to

---

[25] 'Ideen über Staatsverfassung', *Gesammelte Schriften*, ed. F. Leitzmann (Berlin, 1903), I, 80–1.

make moral and cultural sense of a situation in which intellectuals are frequently likely to feel themselves. And if Humboldt's remedy smells of pedantry, the most common alternative, a deliberate self-surrender, of a Humean or Hegelian kind, to the customs of the tribe, to making a morality of my station and its duties—assuming I am lucky enough to feel sure what they are—may not be entirely odourless either: some tribes have odd customs, and some stations may properly be closed.

Whether the results of Humboldt's suggested cultural connoisseurship could ever be as poised, natural, and controlled as he implies is another matter. It would be very easy to make it sound ludicrously stilted, artificial, and inconsistent as a way of life. There does indeed seem to have been a certain sense of artifice, if not of artificiality, about his own life,[26] but no one found it ludicrous. We are not, if we are to be fair to Humboldt, to envisage the kind of cold-blooded dilettantism that the act of describing his ideal necessarily evokes. It is in the describing rather than in the living that the cold-bloodedness necessarily arises. Dilettantism is certainly a possible parody of *Bildung,* but another way of seeing it is as a fierce, sustained protest against the limitations of living only one life. It is in a sense unavailing. Humboldt's answer to the inevitability of ultimate defeat is not a Stoic refusal to desire but an acceptance of every opportunity and every possibility of relative success. It is a mistake to think of Humboldt's ideal as a tepid and lofty picking about among the bibelots of life and history. On the contrary, he advocated enthusiastic commitment and acceptance of risks.

He had, unfortunately, little literary gift; he could not give fire and colour to his ideal in words. He could only prescribe it didactically, and didacticism that does not reach the level of literature is apt to sound like priggishness. For us he suffers, of course, from the additional disadvantage of an idiom that is not ours either by language or period. A major part of Humboldt's nineteenth-century reputation, it is sobering to recall, was as a writer of the kind of letter which leaves the recipient a nobler and finer person than it found him or her—not just now a very fashionable mode of self-expression. Humboldt should, one feels, have written a *Bildungsroman*; he did not, though it could be said that he tried to live one.

---

[26] Howald, *Wilhelm von Humboldt,* p. 8.

None of the words we have used so far to characterize Humboldt's attitude—connoisseurship, experimentation, and so on—seem adequate; they suggest too much calm deliberation. Undoubtedly there was a strong vein of narcissism in Humboldt, but the collective sense of his many references to *Bildung* suggests that it is the sheer attractiveness, the emotional pull, of different styles of life that draws him on. The motive of greed is as strong as curiosity or self-esteem, though the three are intermingled. As Humboldt once wrote, 'one must, before one leaves this life, know and absorb as many inner manifestations of humanity as possible. To me an important new book, a new course of study, a new language, seem things that I have torn from the long night of death.'[27] 'More life and fuller, that I want' is not exactly a motto for an experiment, nor is Faust precisely a dilettante. Nor, of course, need we think of the effect upon us of our historical knowledge of different styles of life (another artificial-sounding concept, but it cannot be helped) as anything so crude as a deliberate sampling of the modes of experience characteristic of different historical periods.

It seems doubtful whether Huysmans's Des Esseintes, the hero of *A Rebours,* that historically minded aesthete who tried to do just that, would really have appealed to Humboldt. Humboldt was not simply a sensation seeker. He remained sufficiently a man of the eighteenth century to wish to retain the notion of an ideal humanity. He regarded every extension of one's cultural experience as an enlargement of one's concept of such an ideal. 'From the whole history of mankind', he wrote to Schiller, 'a picture of the human mind and character can be drawn which resembles no single century, and no single nation completely, to which however, all have contributed.'[28] Humboldt's *Plan for a Comparative Anthropology* which he wrote three years after the essay on the limits of state action, and which was also never published during his lifetime, was intended as an attempt to show how this ideal of humanity might be depicted, not *a priori,* with all the limitations of the ethics of a particular

---

[27] 'Ich habe einmal die bestimmte Idee, dass man, ehe man dies Leben verlässt, so viel von innern, menschlichen Erscheinungen . . . kennen und in sich aufnehmen muss als nur immer möglich ist. Ein mir neues wichtiges Buch; eine neue Lehre, eine neue Sprache scheinen mir etwas, das ich der Nacht des Todes entreissen muss' (Letter of 1825, quoted in Howald, *Wilhelm von Humboldt,* pp. 31–2).

[28] Wilhelm von Humboldt, *Briefwechsel mit Schiller* (Stuttgart, 1900), p. 277, quoted in Aris, *History of Political Thought in Germany,* p. 144.

time, but empirically, encompassing the whole richness of human culture, to which history was constantly adding.

In any case, in the notion of *Bildung* informed and enriched by a sense of history and of cultural diversity, Humboldt intended to depict not something we could only do with an embarrassed or perverse self-consciousness, but something we can already hardly help doing, whether we are aware of it or not. Men are to a considerable extent, as Humboldt recognized, conditioned by the traditions they inherit and the collective culture they inhabit. If this were not so, a proposal for a comparative anthropology would be absurd (cf. the remarks in the *Limits,* below, pp. 11, 140–41). But we cannot now help belonging to a culture rich in historical reminiscences. Hence we can and occasionally do use references to historical stereotypes as part of our language of personal descriptions—usually, admittedly, without much historical or psychological finesse: 'Renaissance man', 'puritan', 'Mid-Victorian', '*fin de siècle*' and so on; but that is by the way.[29] In other words, past cultural stereotypes have left living traces, claiming our attention and even allegiance. We can understand and characterize this situation to the extent that we have a sense of the past. If we also welcome it, rather than wishing to extirpate all modes but one in the name of enlightenment, progress, efficiency, common sense or what not, then we have made Humboldt's connection between a sense of the past and its variety and a sense of the opportunities of the present.

If this is true, if a sense of history is an aspect of possible emancipation from the given standards of one's immediate situation, the relation between historiography and discrimination is, or has been, a reciprocal one. For the growing sensitivity, in the late eighteenth and early nineteenth century, to the nuances of distinct historical periods and the possible value of the values they embodied, was intimately connected with the criticism of contemporary society. It is in relation to these criticisms, and to the social situation which gave them plausibility, that one has to see what may otherwise seem to be Humboldt's somewhat picaresque approach to questions of morals and culture. The sense of the relevance of the past and its record, not merely of the crimes and follies of mankind

---

[29] We can also, of course, do the same with fictional characters. 'Literature offers us the raw material for moral judgement and it offers us *far more* material than any one individual life can do'. Graham Hough, *An Essay on Criticism* (London, 1966), p. 28.

but of its experiments in various styles of life and social organization, involved a reappraisal and a criticism of a particular image of contemporary society and of the notion of what constituted modernity. It was, no doubt, vastly oversimplified as a picture of what late eighteenth-century societies and 'enlightened' attitudes were actually like. But it was a caricature which was largely drawn by the victims themselves—the cheerleaders for progress and the publicists of Enlightenment—and as such it could properly be criticized as an aspiration if not as a fact.

The crux of the criticism was that progress was not a simple cumulative process. There was also a debit column, and hence, past states of mankind might suggest not only self-congratulation at having surpassed them but also materials for self-criticism. Of these critiques Rousseau's, invoking, admittedly, a merely hypothetical past, was the most notorious, and most subsequent ones, including Humboldt's critique of the paternalist state, owed something to it, but there were other sources. Meinecke, for example, found one of the chief impulses in the development of *Historismus* as a critique of the idea of progress in *Kleinstaaterei*,[30] the stubborn defence of the local, traditional, and customary elements in the small German kingdoms and principalities against the levelling, rationalizing bureaucracy of the modern state. This was obviously a resistance with which the renegade bureaucrat Humboldt, though the French menace taught him that Germans might need power as well as picturesque diversity, might well sympathize.

But there were other critiques of progress, more directly relevant to Humboldt's humanist ideal, than those of traditionalists looking to their defences. Schiller, for example, was after Rousseau one of the first to make a criticism which has become a platitude, and to link it specifically to a reappraisal of one particular past civilization—that of ancient Greece. As he wrote in the *Aesthetic Letters*:

> The Greeks put us to shame not only by their simplicity, which is alien to our age: they are at the same time our rivals, often indeed our models, in those very excellences with which we are wont to console ourselves for the unnaturalness of our manners. Combining fullness of form with fullness of content, at once philosophic and creative, at the same time tender and energetic, we see them uniting the youthfulness of fantasy with the manliness of reason in a

[30] F. Meinecke, *Zur Geschichte des Historismus, Werke,* IV (Stuttgart, 1959), 218.

splendid humanity, [while] With us, one might almost be tempted to assert, the mental faculties show themselves detached in operation as psychology separates them in idea, and we see not merely individual persons but whole classes of human beings developing only part of their capacities, while the rest of them, like a stunted plant, shew only a feeble vestige of their nature.

The harm is self-induced; the loss of individual totality is the price we pay for our collective achievements:

> It was culture itself that inflicted this wound upon modern humanity. As soon as enlarged experience and more precise speculation made necessary a sharper division of the sciences on the one hand, and on the other, the more intricate machinery of States made necessary a more rigorous dissociation of ranks and occupations; the essential bond of human nature was torn apart, and a ruinous conflict set its harmonious powers at variance. The intuitive and the speculative understanding took up hostile attitudes upon their respective fields, whose boundaries they now began to guard with jealousy and distrust, and by confining our activity to a single sphere we have handed ourselves over to a master who is not infrequently inclined to end up by suppressing the rest of our capacities. While in one place a luxuriant imagination ravages the hard-earned fruits of the intellect, in another the spirit of abstraction stifles the fire at which the heart might have warmed itself and the fancy been enkindled.[31]

There is no diagnosis in Humboldt as articulate and emphatic as this; by comparison his remarks on the subject in the *Limits* (below, pp. 8, 14, 43) are fragmentary. Elsewhere he attributed much of the blame, as also did Schiller in *Die Götter Griechenlands,* to Christianity, to the baleful victory of the pale Galilean.[32] Nevertheless, he fully shares Goethe's and Schiller's adulation of the Greeks as models of a harmonious human totality. He presented them as such in the work he wrote immediately after completing *The Limits of State Action,* his essay *On the Study of Antiquity and especially the Greeks* (1793). Schiller's *Aesthetic Letters* is, as one might expect from the close intellectual kinship and mutual admiration of the two men, closer in spirit to Humboldt than any other work of the period. The complaint of fragmentation, however, as a result of specialization of functions or of undervaluing some elements in human

---

[31] F. Schiller, *Letters on the Aesthetic Education of Mankind,* trans. R. Snell (London, 1954), pp. 37–9.

[32] Bruford, in *The Era of Goethe,* p. 37; Hatfield, *Aesthetic Paganism in German Literature,* pp. 201–2.

personality, was a fairly common one. One finds it, for example, as part of a critique of civilization and of the division of labour, in Adam Ferguson, whose moral philosophy Humboldt had studied as a boy. Even among figures whose cast of mind remained more emphatically that of the Enlightenment, like Turgot, Mme de Staël, and Benjamin Constant,[33] it was accepted that progress and the use of reason were inherently desiccating. What this added up to was the sense of an ambiguous, divided cultural inheritance, not a simple legacy of accumulated knowledge and power. To see Humboldt's pluralistic ideal of culture in this context is to go a long way towards acquitting it of wantonness.

One easy way out of the dilemma, of course, is to adopt one particular idealized past period as a standard, like Winckelmann's Greece or the Schlegels' Middle Ages. Humboldt, in his admiration for the Greeks, came near to doing this in his essay *On the Study of Antiquity*. Essentially, however, his doctrine that every period was a development of one particular human *Einseitigkeit*, his dialectical approach to history, precluded it. Like Schiller in the *Aesthetic Letters* and in his essay *On Naive and Sentimental Poetry*, Humboldt needed a philosophy of history which would allow the Greeks to serve as a model without being the last word, which would marry Helen to Faust and let them breed.

Before considering, however, the extent to which Humboldt succeeded in this, we have to notice another, closely allied, theme in Humboldt's work: his interest in national character and languages. For it was not only past civilizations which seemed to speak with a Babel of voices, each demanding its due. If history could seem a museum of styles and moralities, to the cosmopolitan intellectual, contemporary Europe could seem like a market place for them. Italy and even Germany, in their vastly different ways, seemed to offer valid alternatives to the French accented canons of reason and classical form—those canons whose supposed unchallengability had given such confidence to the historical judgements of a Voltaire. Hence, in the late eighteenth and early nineteenth century the extraordinary prevalence of sweeping generalizations about 'Southern joyousness', 'Latin clarity', 'German spirituality' and so on, and the widespread fascination with national varieties of culture which captivated

---

[33] Benjamin Constant, 'On the Spirit of Conquest', in *Readings from Liberal Writers, English and French*, ed. J. Plamenatz (London, 1965), p. 26.

a number of intellectuals as diverse as Mme de Staël and Stendhal, and, one must add, Humboldt. The interest in these competing siren voices, fiery, passionate Spain, sensuous Italy, wistfully mystical Germany, and the rest, and the belief in possibilities of synthesis, like that long cherished yearning for a fusion of the Greek and German souls as the basis of a new civilization, arose from essentially the same source as that which made philosophies of history such a popular and deadly nineteenth-century game: the sense of an ambiguous inheritance and of contradictory cultural claims and opportunities, needing to be synthesized, transcended, or dialectically comprehended.

It would have been strange if Humboldt, who possessed this sense so strongly, had made no contribution to the similarly absorbing game of national characterization. In fact he did, first in his *Plan of a Comparative Anthropology* and later, in more detail, in his work on comparative philology. The former is a bold attempt to outline the methods by which what Mme de Staël was later to attempt for Germany could be achieved: the delineation of the *Gestalt* of a people and its culture, and an analysis of the contribution such characterizations might make to *Bildung*. Humboldt himself provided merely a programme in this essay. His own contribution to its accomplishment was his work in comparative philology. The *Gestalt* of a people, the mature Humboldt was to agree with Herder, was to be seen most clearly in its language. Without the study of language, he was to write in *Latium and Hellas* (1806), 'every attempt to understand distinctive national character (*Nationaleigentümlichkeit*) would be fruitless, for only in its language is its whole character expressed'.[34] Every language was valuable: 'no language should be condemned or depreciated, not even that of the most savage tribe, for each language is a picture of the original aptitude for language'.[35]

This notion of the unique value of every language as part of the world's richness and variety is an aspect of a similar declaration on behalf of different cultures and historical periods. It was congenial to Germans struggling to raise the status of their native language—though this seems

[34] . . . wäre jeder Versuch über Nationaleigentümlichkeit vergeblich, da nur in der Sprache sich der ganze Charakter ausprägt' (quoted by Howald, *Wilhelm von Humboldt*, p. 115).
[35] Quoted by Otto Jespersen, *Language, Its Nature, Development and Origin* (London, 1922), p. 57.

to have played no significant part in Humboldt's endorsement of it—and to escape from French cultural domination. It also had respectable antecedents in the old Chain of Being theory, with its doctrine of the *plenum*; the variety of the world's organic inhabitants was ordained by God for its own sake, because otherwise the creation would have been less complete and perfect than it is. This doctrine, running counter to the Hebrew utilitarianism which saw the creation simply as something given by God to be used and manipulated for the benefit of man, passed into eighteenth-century German thought through Leibniz's metaphysics.[36] It was influential in shaping the ideas both of Herder and of Goethe's *Naturphilosophie*, with both of which Humboldt has strong affinities. As Goethe put it, each class of creature is an end in itself ('Zweck sein selbst ist jegliches Tier').[37]

This endorsement of every variety simply for being what it is had an obvious application to the existence and the different kinds of appeal of various cultural models. Such universal tolerance, however, left unsolved the problems of the individual, who might feel himself both embarrassed by the riches displayed for him and harassed as a member of a fragmented, discordant or over-specialized culture. Reflection could not be banished, nor could naive totality be re-assumed by an act of will. Precisely the underlying reason for so much interest in and speculation about a multiplicity of cultural norms was that cultural homogeneity, or the belief in it, had been breached by knowledge and by many diverse disruptions of traditional patterns of life. My culture and its intimations might easily seem as imprecise and unsatisfactory a guide as my station and its duties.

Confronted by such a situation there appear to be essentially three possible answers (apart, of course, from the heroic despair of an existentialist assertion that men simply create their values by adopting them). They are not *prima facie* incompatible, and it is a peculiarity of Humboldt to have attempted all three. The first involves an attitude to history as the *sequence* of cultural changes. The sequence can then be regarded as itself meaningful, justified and authoritative. This is the moral core of historicism in the sense to which Sir Karl Popper has given currency. This justi-

---

[36] See Barnard, *Herder's Social and Political Thought,* ch. I; Leroux, *Guillaume de Humboldt,* p. 148.

[37] A. O. Lovejoy, *The Great Chain of Being* (Harvard, 1936), p. 189.

fication can in turn be accepted either because the process is seen as cumulative (the positivist version), or multiple, all the parts being justified as and when they occur, for the sake of the variety they create (Herder) or apocalyptic—a justification in terms of some consummation both inevitable and highly desirable (Marxism, for example). These versions are not absolutely mutually exclusive; they may be combined in various ways, though no theory can emphasize all of them to an equal extent. Thus the positivist theory may contain a dialectical element, while the apocalyptic or the multiple may also include an element of accumulation, as Marx regards technological progress as cumulative. Humboldt, who inclines to the multiple justification, seems to hint at an element of accumulation in the growing richness of cultural alternatives which history keeps churning out (cf. below, p. 14).

The second possible answer does not normally involve any reference to history at all, though in Humboldt's version of it it does. It consists essentially of making a Romantic virtue out of what may well be a social and cultural necessity. Spiritual rootlessness and social dislocation can be christened '*Sehnsucht*', symbolized in various ways as a yearning for the infinite and the unattainable, and converted into the cardinal virtue. This is done in conscious defiance of the limited and relatively precise virtues grounded in a recognized and accepted social situation, which are stigmatized as philistine complacency, rather as though Philip Stanhope had started to write back admonishing letters to Lord Chesterfield. Such a response is normally confined to a literary mode of expression; political and moral philosophers—the latter habitually absorbed in their curious passion for discussing only the most uninteresting virtues—have given it little hospitality. Humboldt, however, shows that Romanticism—it seems fair to use the word—*could* take another political form than the apocalyptic delusions, crude rebelliousness, or abject surrender to the mystique of blood and soil in which we are accustomed to finding it. Humboldt takes up, that is, the Faustian theme of a never satisfied aspiration, an endless spiritual wanderlust, and asks what are its *political* implications. He cannot, however, leave the matter there, for he is not only or even primarily a Romantic. Restlessness and variety are components of *Bildung*; they are not the whole of it. They provide its content but not its form. Like a good German Hellenist, Humboldt also insists on harmony, and like a good Kantian, on obedience to reason and the moral law.

This last requirement brings us to the third possible answer to the sort of moral dislocation we considered earlier: a fervent acceptance of an absolute moral imperative which, however, being concerned with the motives for which an action is done rather than the content of that action, is nevertheless neutral as between the moral claims of different cultural styles, different vocations. Hence one could have all the security and sense of endeavour given by the most rigorous ethical standards, while apparently not being required, in formulating those standards, naively to limit goodness to the norms of any particular period or society. This is the role that Kantian ethics, the definition of a good motive as one which desires to perform good actions for their own sake, plays for Humboldt. This still leaves the content of the actions so performed an open question, however. The most familiar attempts to complete Kant's ethics of motive, his formal characterization of good actions, by supplying a *content* of actions of guaranteed goodness, which can *then* be performed from the right Kantian motives, have taken the form of appeals to the actual, accepted norms of their agent's own society. This is what, with varying degress of completeness, is advocated by Hegel in the *Philosophy of Right* and in England by T. H. Green and F. H. Bradley. For Humboldt, on the other hand, the content is supplied by the individual's experiences and his assimilation of them into an ever greater richness of being, while Kantian ethics plays the part of a limiting condition, ruling out of court *some* experiences: those which would conflict with the Kantian categorical imperative[38] (chapter VIII).

At this point, however, we can no longer escape confronting the questions we have been skirting for some time: does Humboldt actually manage to reconcile his Faustianism and his Hellenism, his ethics of restlessness and his ethics of immutable Kantian imperatives? Does the concept of *Bildung,* in fact, do for Humboldt all that he tries to make it do? The question of content is clear enough: it just *is* the greatest possible variety of opportunity and richness of assimilation. It is the question of the relation of form to content that raises difficulties. What are the limits to the acceptability of experience and how is it to be controlled? What is

---

[38] So act that your action may become a universal law. For Humboldt's Kantianism see Leroux, *Guillaume de Humboldt,* pp. 180 ff.

meant by successful assimilation? What is meant by 'harmony'? Is the requirement to strive for a *harmonious* realization of potentialities the same as the Kantian requirement that acceptable actions must fall within certain moral limits, and be conducted in a certain spirit, which confers inner freedom on the agent, or are these two different requirements, aesthetic in the first case, moral in the second?

Certainly Kantian ethics and Humboldt's humanist ideal of the fully rounded, harmonious personality have something in common. They are both, for example, in contrast to utilitarianism, concerned with persons considered as moral wholes, not simply as the recipients of discrete pleasures or satisfactions. But harmony is an aesthetic, rather than a moral criterion. It is not achieved by submission to any particular ethical imperative, but is *seen* to be achieved, as a certain kind of personal poise and balance, as in the coherence of a work of art—an artistic success for which, despite the efforts of neo-classical, formalist critics, there is no guaranteed formula (below, pp. 78–9). It is significant that Humboldt, like Herder, Schiller and Hegel, objected to Kant's assertion that inclination and duty were necessarily opposed.[39] In the fully harmonious personality there would be no such rift. The belief in such a necessary antithesis was an aspect of the unhappy, fragmented consciousness of modern man, torn between his sensuous and spiritual natures; given an achieved psychic totality, like that of the Greeks, such a belief would be untenable. At this point the aesthetics of personality has the balance of advantage, in Humboldt, over the Kantian conscience. In fact, a religion of culture can hardly be expected to coexist without tension with the claims of an allegedly absolute moral law.

There is, however, one suggestion which, if we could adopt it, would make Humboldt's requirement of harmony into a criterion of a more traditionally ethical—though not Kantian—kind; the suggestion, that is, that it refers ultimately to *quantity*. It is possible, that is to say, to make the requirement to seek the maximum quantity of fulfilled potentialities the *same* as the requirement to preserve a harmonious balance between them. All that would be required, in fact, is a version of an argument familiar from its use in the context of utilitarian ethics. In classical utili-

[39] Leroux, *Guillaume de Humboldt*, p. 277. Cf. Barnard, *Herder's Social and Political Thought*, p. 98 n. 56; Schiller, *Über Anmut und Würde* (1973) Werke, XX (Weimar, 1962), pp. 251 ff.; Walter Kaufman, *Hegel* (London 1966), p. 43.

tarian theory, all satisfactions (pleasures) are deemed to be *per se* good; they become bad, and are to be proscribed, only if they conflict with other, quantitatively greater, pleasures. This follows logically from the original utilitarian maxim that the end is the achievement of the greatest total quantity of pleasure. Similarly, if we take the equivalent maxim of *Bildung* to be the maximization of realized potentialities, we can obtain a similarly quantitative criterion of discrimination: all explorations of experience are good *per se*; they become bad, and to be proscribed, if and only if they preclude still further explorations (e.g., drug-taking, though an extension of experience and so *prima facie* good may in fact be bad because it may, through addiction, lead ultimately to a narrowing rather than a broadening of the subject's experiences). This is not a purely hypothetical suggestion. An argument of this kind was in fact one of the directions English liberal ethics was later to take, once it had shed its utilitarian premises, most notably in the ethics of L. T. Hobhouse, which in many respects begins where Mill's *On Liberty* (and therefore Humboldt also) leaves off. [40]

If Humboldt's theory of *Bildung* was in fact quantitative in this way, then it reached its greatest possible logical coherence, requiring only the initial exhortation to maximize realized potentialities for everything else to follow. But a return to the texts convinces one that this step was never taken by Humboldt himself. 'Harmony' for him, one can feel reasonably sure, was a matter of the aesthetics of personality, perceived by taste or feeling, as one perceived beauty, not by a crypto-Benthamite calculation of the odds. It might coincide with the greatest quantitative realization of potentialities, but it was not logically equivalent to it. No utilitarian but Shaftesbury was surely the ancestor of this conception of Humboldt. [41] Humboldt could not adopt a purely calculating approach because ultimately he is interested, not in discrete experiences any more than in discrete pleasures, but in persons considered as psychic wholes, though constantly changing ones.

[40] L. T. Hobhouse, *Social Development. Its Nature and Conditions* (London, 1924), pp. 37, 74 ff.

[41] It is interesting that in Humboldt's younger days, when he was still nearer to the hedonism of the Enlightenment, he came closer to Hobhouse's formula. In his rules for the members of the *Veredlungsbund* he wrote: 'Sie geniessen jede Freude, die nicht mit dem Verlust höherer Freuden erkauft ist' (quoted by Bruford, *The Era of Goethe,* p. 22).

Humboldt's three guiding lights, therefore, the exhortations to develop oneself by feeding on diverse experiences, to do so harmoniously, and to do so within the limits imposed by the Kantian moral law, remained three logically independent principles. This is not to say that they are necessarily incompatible, but simply that they had to be reconciled, if at all, in deed, in a manner akin to artistic composition. They are not formally deducible from each other. This, of course, raises the question whether Humboldt's own writings succeed in reconciling them. The friction, if any, is obviously most likely to arise between the Kantian and Faustian elements. We have already said that the former limits the permissible extent of the latter. The role the State plays in Humboldt's political theory is precisely that which Kantian moral reason is supposed to play in relation to *Bildung*. It does not initiate; it limits. It exists to enforce in practice the impartial and universal rules which the categorical imperative enjoins in theory: an absolute respect for the equal rights of others. But because its rules *are* universal and hence exert a pressure towards uniformity, they in turn must be strictly limited in the interests of *Bildung*, which is, the active, vital, creative principle. But the tension between the two is always alive, as it was in Humboldt's personal life, in his sense of public duty and his desire to devote himself to self-cultivation as a private person. In his work it appears as occasional outbursts which seem to have little or no settled place in the overall texture of his thinking.

What does Humboldt mean, for example, by his claim that goods are never in conflict (below, p. 27)? This must surely be a Kantian statement: Kantian ethical imperatives do not conflict because they are by definition universifiable. But if Humboldt's statement is applied to the content of *Bildung* it must surely be false: No one man or even one epoch *can* realize all human potentialities, or even all those which are to be approved of. One must choose, and the achieved harmonious personality is, on Humboldt's own showing, surely a *tour de force* rather than an automatic chemical solution. It is true that Humboldt speaks of an 'ideal of humanity', but it is specifically stated to be unrealizable in its entirety at any given time. The existence of a cultural tradition plays a role in *Bildung*, but its relation to Humboldt's individualism is not fully worked out. Matthew Arnold, for example, must have been surprised to read that culture was to be achieved by letting each man do, so far as possible, as he liked. Humboldt and Arnold, of course, confronted different social circumstances: Face to face with benevolent despotism the need for a clerisy must have seemed less urgent than the need for diversity; to Arnold, hating what he saw as the *laissez faire* philistinism of mid-Victorian England, a State-supported clerisy seemed the only answer.

Humboldt did not, however, escape the dilemma altogether: it arose in the heart of his public career, in his attitude to the role of the State in education, and Humboldt's answers were naturally more ambiguous and contradictory than Arnold's emphatic endorsement of it. The inconsistency of Humboldt's attitudes to State education at different times in his career represents more than a capitulation to patriotic enthusiasm: It points to a dilemma in liberal culture itself. How are you to make people aware of the tradition which can both shape their energies into something coherent and by its plurality opens to them new possibilities of freedom unless you in some sense first impose it upon them? Humboldt, even when he became a minister, wanted education kept pluralistic so far as possible, but the dilemma remained. Only an educated people can take full advantage of, or perhaps, under modern conditions, be trusted with, freedom, but any educational system—*pace Emile*—involves taking vital decisions affecting the very character structures of people not yet in a position to choose. The syllabus of the Prussian *Gymnasia* may have been wider than any likely alternative, but it was still a selection from a number of possibilities. One could say, in fact, that because this is perhaps the central liberal dilemma, if Humboldt was going to retreat at any point from the extreme *laissez faire* of *The Limits of State Action,* he was most likely to do so over education, Jena or no Jena. Incidentally, the influence of Humboldt on Mill, if it could be established—through *The Limits of State Action*—and on Arnold—through the latter's admiration for the Prussian educational system—would make a piquant contrast.

Considering again the relation of Kantianism and *Bildung* in Humboldt's essay, what are we to make of the passages (below, pp. 22–3) in which he rhapsodizes over the work of the peasant and the craftsman-artist, and proclaims the absolute value of humble work provided it is freely chosen and the worker finds fulfilment in dedicating himself to his task as an end in itself? There is, of course, nothing unusual in this passage in itself. It may seem all too familiar, looking forward as it does to the Marxist theory of alienation and to William Morris. There is an almost identical passage in Hegel's *Philosophy of History*:

The religion, the morality (*Sittlichkeit*) of a limited sphere of life—that of a shepherd or peasant, e.g.—in its intensive concentration and limitation to a few perfectly simple relations of life—has infinite worth; the same worth as the religion and morality of extensive knowledge, and of an existence rich in the compass of its relations and actions'.[42]

The passage in Humboldt is only peculiar because it is in Humboldt. The reader is bound to compare it with the assertion on p. 63 that 'The idea of virtue, moreover, which has just been presented, is only adapted to a few classes of the political community, of those, namely, whose position enables them to devote their time and means to the process of internal development' (which is pretty obvious) and to conclude that Humboldt is trying to have it all ways. The passage quoted from Hegel takes its legitimate place in an elaborate metaphysics and philosophy of history which specifies the exact place and worth of *Sittlichkeit* in the overall system. Similarly, in a purely Kantian inspired ethics Humboldt's first statement would be entirely at home. It would represent a typical infusion of high Kantian moral idealism into the humdrum ethical situation of my station and its duties, the latter being transfigured into something of supreme moral worth by the purity of the agent's motives. It is less obvious that it is compatible with Humboldt's cultural dandyism. The impression created is of Humboldt laying claim to a piece of high-mindedness to which the rest of his theory does nothing to entitle him, and which therefore appears as mere sentimentality. Essentially the gap between passion and reason, Romantic experimentalism and Kantian inner moral freedom, remained unplugged except by the metaphors of aesthetics.

Nevertheless, Humboldt's Kantianism, like his concept of *Bildung*, gives to his political liberalism a distinctive flavour. One major source of liberal ethical and political theories has been an attempt to avoid disputed moral ground, to cut ethical imperatives, which might be disputed, to a minimum, and to seek the absolutely basic rules without which social life would be impossible, and which may therefore be supposed to be acceptable to all shades of moral opinion. Hence the force of the image of a state of nature. Unless the relentlessness of this search is mitigated, as for example, in Locke's political thought, by a lingering belief that distinc-

---

[42] G. W. F. Hegel, *The Philosophy of History*, trans. J. Sibree (New York, 1956), p. 37.

tively moral as well as prudential rules are discoverable by reason, the result is a would-be value-free theory of politics, founded on a moral *laissez faire* which demands only an acceptance of the basic rules needed to allow each individual to conduct his life and pursue such ends as may appeal to him. Political institutions and fundamental moral rules are not, in this view, nurseries of virtues or trumpet calls to a pure and holy life but traffic lights and highway codes, not prescribing to the traveller where he shall go but providing the framework within which he and others may travel to their separate and individually chosen destinations without colliding.

The concept of the State which such a theory yields is, to switch to Lasalle's metaphor, the nightwatchman State, which is also Humboldt's. Nevertheless, Humboldt's liberalism is not fundamentally of this kind. It rests ultimately not on prudential rules but on a moral exhortation; to accept *Bildung* as the ideal for human beings, with respect for the equal rights of others and acceptance of whatever practical rules and arrangements these principles may entail. Humboldt is chiefly moved, not, like Hobbes, to mediate with a rational prudence between importunate, conflicting egoisms, though he recognizes the necessity, but to exhort against the virtues of well-behaved sheep—a contrast which probably tells us as much about the societies in which the two men lived as about their respective temperaments. The expression of Humboldt's basic principles, as distinct from his exploration of their practical implications, is therefore rhetorical rather than quasi-scientific. It is an invitation to share a view of life, not a draft for a highway code. There is, of course, nothing wrong with this, though it may not appeal to everyone. Professor Plamenatz, for example, has indicated some distaste for what he calls 'the high-minded liberal' as distinct from the ordinary kind (who enjoys his approval) finding the former 'the one with something of the governess about him'.[43] To those unafflicted with governess-phobia, however, this may not seem an overwhelming objection.

Nevertheless, it is essential to insist on the difference of Humboldt's political theory, for all its characteristic and indeed extreme liberal and *laissez faire* proposals, from the kind of liberalism whose ideal is (or was) the smoothly running, strictly segregated traffic of a sophisticated

[43] Plamenatz, in *Readings from Liberal Writers*, p. 26.

motorway system. His ideal of society has in fact more in common with some aspects of socialism. It is an ideal of fellowship in which each individual is both separate yet involved:

> The principle of the true art of social intercourse consists in a ceaseless endeavour to grasp the innermost individuality of another, to avail oneself of it, and penetrated with the deepest respect for it as the individuality of another, to act upon it. Because of this respect one can do this only by, as it were, showing oneself, and offering the other the opportunity of comparison (below p. 27–8).

Humboldt's thought here seems to prefigure the central feature of Schiller's Aesthetic State:

> If in the dynamic state of rights man encounters man as force, and resents his activities, if in the ethical state of duties he opposes him with the majesty of law and fetters his will, in the sphere of cultivated society, in the aesthetic state, he need . . . confront him only as an object of free play. [44]

Humboldt's ideal social world is perhaps a slightly more strenuous affair, though the affinity is clear. It is a contest of personalities for moral and intellectual influence in which it is as blessed to receive as to give—a kind of cultural analogue of Free Trade, in which all are gainers; by being oneself one enriches the world as it presents itself to others, who, in turn, perform the same service for oneself. It is an idealistic picture only in the sense that it abstracts certain features from human contacts; it is at least as realistic as the liberal model of economic competition, or the Hobbesian power struggle, which do the same.

It is impossible neatly to categorize Humboldt's political theory in terms of some generally accepted classification. Pressed for a single epithet one might try 'Rousseauist', but this would be profoundly misleading without an immediate explanation that one means Rousseau the educationalist rather than Rousseau the political theorist. The state of nature, natural rights, the social contract flicker in Humboldt's essay only spasmodically (below, pp. 36, 38, 94, 106, 114). They are never worked up into a full length set-piece in characteristically eighteenth-century fashion. It is the Rousseau of *Emile* to whom Humboldt pays tribute, declaring that someone is needed who will do for politics what Rousseau

---

[44] Schiller, *Letters on the Aesthetic Education of Mankind*, p. 137.

had done for education, disdaining concern with rules, precepts and techniques, and considering politics from the point of view of the spontaneous, natural development of men's inner characters (below, p. 67). The *Contrat Social* is not mentioned, and the notion of a General Will seems explicitly repudiated, though not by name (below, p. 36).

In view of this lack of concern with rules and model institutions, with what a later apostle of culture, Matthew Arnold, was to call 'machinery', it is perhaps not surprising that, just as Humboldt makes relatively little direct use of the usual hypothetical state of nature/natural rights/social contract bag of tricks, neither does he deal in the manner of Montesquieu with the best form of government and with the defence of liberty by mechanical checks and balances built into the constitution. He is not, he says, immediately concerned with who should exercise power but simply with the limits within which power ought to be exercised (p. 3). He does, however, touch on the distinction between the State and what he calls the national union (*Nationverein*), based on free association, in the conclusion to chapter III (also below, pp. 91, 137). In his preference for the voluntary association for performing general social tasks Humboldt is not only harking back to the long established distinction between the State and civil society but is also anticipating much nineteenth-century political theory of a populist, anarchist, and syndicalist kind. The common intellectual roots of all these doctrines appear to be Herder's concept of the organic community and the Rousseauist/Kantian notion that moral self-determination is the essence of human dignity, and that to condition men's behaviour by external sanctions to ends which they do not consciously accept for their own sake is to deprive them of that dignity. As Humboldt says, 'Whatever does not spring from a man's free choice, or is only the result of instruction and guidance, does not enter into his very being, but still remains alien to his true nature' (below, p. 23). This contrast between outward behaviour and inner character is inherent, of course, in Rousseauist educational doctrines. For Humboldt it supplies the basis for his critique of benevolent paternalism in government.

Humboldt's attack, as it develops, makes three essential criticisms. Firstly, by treating its subjects as children the paternalist State, however benign, denies them the central feature of their humanity, the freedom to choose and the opportunity spontaneously to develop their potentialities by learning, as Emile had to do, from the consequences of their own actions (p. 20). Secondly, it diminishes the quality of the experiences from which they learn because by imposing its own uniformity of character on its citizens it deprives them of the fruitful clash and contact of well-nurtured individualities; it flattens, as it were, the social landscape (below, p. 18). Thirdly, by acting only on men's outward behaviour, and by doing for them much that they should learn to do for themselves, it weakens initiative and independence and hence, in the long run, society itself: 'the man whom [the State] has accustomed to lean on an external power for support is thus given up in critical emergencies to a far more hopeless fate' (below, p. 21).

The first two criticisms look rather like a transposition into cultural terms of *laissez faire* arguments in economics; Humboldt was familiar with these, though they were almost certainly not his immediate inspiration here. The third is the argument, not unfamiliar to us, that the Welfare State weakens the moral fibre of the nation. Humboldt, whether we warm to him on this account or not, must have been one of the first to enunciate it. Previous defenders of liberty had generally assumed that the State would interfere with the subject's liberties to do him obvious harm rather than obliquely to sap his energies by doing him good. Humboldt's remark, quoted above, does have considerable force applied to the Frederician Prussian State, for commentators both then and now have agreed that such a collapse was precisely what occurred after Jena.[45] The guiding purpose of the Stein reforms in which Humboldt participated was to encourage a more active kind of citizenship.

Humboldt in his essay, however, does not fully develop his positive concept of the free association of citizens. He is most directly concerned simply to provide the criteria by which the permissible limits of the State's activity may be determined. He distinguished three functions of government in the name of which the State may claim to interfere and to coerce its subjects: first, to defend its existence; second, to provide for social welfare; third, to protect citizens from infringements of their liberties by others. The first he confines within very narrow limits. The sec-

---

[45] Gordon Craig, *Politics of the Prussian Army 1640–1945* (London, 1955), pp. 17–21, 36. Cf. Mme de Staël: 'Toute semblait devoir être de la politique dans Frédéric; ainsi donc, ce qu'il faisait du bien rendait l'état du pays meilleur, mais ne perfectionnait pas la moralité de la nation' (*De l'Allemagne,* Librarie Garnier, 2 vols. Paris, n.d., I, 82–3).

ond Humboldt virtually rules out altogether. We are left with the third. Humboldt considers at length what it may entail in practical terms. His principle, familiar to us from Mill and de Tocqueville, is that the only justification for governmental interference is to prevent harm to others. A man's own good, as Mill says, is not a sufficient warrant.

Of course, this view of the State's functions may not differ in practice from a natural rights theory of the traditional Lockean kind. It is interesting, therefore, that Humboldt does not make more use of the state of nature/natural rights formula. This may have been due to the fact that its fictional and arbitrary character was becoming too obvious—as it was to Bentham—as more and more ideological weight was being placed upon it. The Declaration of the Rights of Man may not have seemed an encouraging precedent. But probably the chief reason Humboldt does not make it bear the chief weight of his argument—the same reason, essentially, for which he criticized the new French constitution—was that it tended to be defended by a kind of static theory of fixed and definite human needs, in the satisfaction of which men must be free from governmental interference. A right *sounds* like a possession to be enjoyed, rather than a territory which one explores, and it was with the latter that Humboldt was concerned.

Of course, you can quite easily give the natural rights theory a progressive twist, making it open-ended in this way. You can say, in other words, that the area of privacy defined by a natural right is that area which is necessary for the fullest development of the human personality compatible with equal opportunities for everyone else. You can, that is, translate Mill's criterion of 'self-regarding actions' into natural rights language. Humboldt does, in fact, speak of rights. But if you are not concerned, as Humboldt was not at this point, with the *source* of governmental authority but only with its proper limits, there is no particular need to speak of rights as *natural*.

Historically, of course, natural rights theories had been closely associated, not only with the static view that there was a specifiable human nature with a content of fixed and specific needs, but with questions of the source of political authority. The doctrine that men retained some of their natural rights in political society tended to be defended by arguments about what rights men, possessing such a nature, would, if choosing freely in a state of nature, have refused to give up when establishing a government in order to enjoy the benefits of political association. Humboldt was not chiefly concerned with what men, considered as bundles of specific needs, would choose at any given time, because for him the human personality was an organism with infinite potentialities for change and development, whose future was essentially unforeseeable. It is true that, considering human beings in this way, Humboldt's criteria for the limits of state interference are needs: the need of the human organism to develop spontaneously, which entailed choosing freely, and of a variegated environment to stimulate and nourish its growth. But Humboldt bases his case on the prerequisites of a *process,* which he regards as desirable, not primarily on what men, conscious of their needs and interests, would or would not choose to claim at any given time.[46]

In this respect Humboldt makes a significant break with seventeenth- and eighteenth-century liberalism, or at least with the conceptual scheme in terms of which it was expressed. He anticipates the way intellectual liberalism was to develop in the nineteenth century. Nineteenth-century political theories of various kinds took as their guiding principle not consent, actual or tacit, which attributes a paramount authority to the choices of the present or of some hypothetical past generation, but the concept of human progress. This, of course, could result in moves to extreme *laissez faire* or extreme *dirigiste* positions, according to whether it was held that the mechanism of progress was unfettered competition of some kind, or whether you believed that the forceps of the state should be borrowed to bring to birth the new society. But Humboldt's conception of progress was a different and much less circumscribed one than that of most of the nineteenth-century theorists who tried to found libertarian politics on a theory of human progress. For Herbert Spencer, for example, progress was a succession of clearly marked stages and its mechanism was free competition and the survival of the best adapted—the industrious, thrifty, and prudent. For Humboldt progress, if one can call it that, was simply an endless exploration of further and further possibilities, in principle unpredictable. The human spirit blew where it listed, and though cultural competition and cross-fertilization were indispensable to it there was no infallible mechanism.

---

[46] See, e.g., Humboldt, *Betrachtungen über die Weltgeschichte,* in *Gesammelte Schriften,* ed. Leitzmann, III, 351 ff. and Cassirer, *Freiheit und Form,* p. 515.

Again, to consider another variety of liberal progressivism, T. H. Buckle and J. S. Mill hold that through the unfettered competition of ideas and ways of living men gain knowledge of truths, with the aid of which they can then improve the conduct of their lives. This is a concept which is quite alien to Humboldt's exploratory Faustianism, and reminds us that English liberalism was subjected to heavy doses of English and even French positivism. For though education was the key concept of Humboldt's political theory, education for him meant essentially the modification of our sensibility through culture and experience. 'Inexactness or incompleteness in our scientific knowledge' is explicitly stated by him to be one of the lesser evils of restrictions on free inquiry (below, p. 66). On the other hand, any diminution of the richness and variety of the external world was to be deplored, for it was the source of future experiences. Humboldt held strongly that true knowledge was something experienced: 'I now understand fully how one can know nothing of mankind, of life and of the world that one has not brought to birth deep in one's own being, or rather, that one has not proved upon oneself. Humanity and Nature cannot be grasped intellectually, as it were; one can only get somewhere near them actively.'[47]

This essentially Romantic view of knowledge greatly intensified, of course, the tendency we have already considered to think of history and its 'lessons' dialectically (see below, p. 141), and to look for a synthetic philosophy of history in whose overall pattern all contradictions shall be seen to be resolved. For if one thinks of learning from history as trying to identify with and, as it were, live through the diverse characters of different periods and civilizations, the problem of retaining balance and a sense of one's own intellectual identity, of almost literally keeping one's head, becomes a far more complex and difficult business than it is for those who regard learning from history as gaining a knowledge of causes and effects, or learning about the follies of our ancestors and resolving to do better.

---

[47] 'Ich begreife erst jetzt ganz, wie man von Menschen, dem Leben und der Welt nichts wissen kann, was man nicht tief aus seinem eigenen Dasein schöpft oder vielmehr an sich selber wahr macht. Menschheit und Natur lassen sich nicht begreifen, wie man es nennt; man kann sich ihnen nur lebendig . . . nähern' (quoted by Howald, *Wilhelm von Humboldt*, p. 34.) Cf. Leroux, *Guillaume de Humboldt*, p. 395.

What, in conclusion, can one usefully say about Humboldt's political theory? This rather depends on what one thinks one can usefully say about any past political theory. And that is not perhaps so self-evident as it is sometimes taken to be. It hardly seems necessary to go laboriously through his list of prohibitions and permissions, marking them with ticks and crosses according to whether they appeal to us now or not. Not that the questions he raises about the extent of State interference are not important, but there are less onerous ways of discussing them than by an exegesis of the work of a dead Prussian Minister of Education. Equally it does not seem particularly tempting to follow the example of those who can get angry with Fichte and Hegel for allegedly helping to cause Hitler by shedding a pious tear over Humboldt for failing to prevent him. Or—a devilish piece of sophistication this—to blame him for being too impractical in his idealism, and hence letting the devil in by default. There is no absolute necessity, simply because we are discussing German history, to turn into disgruntled Whigs, interpreting intellectual history in terms of the Disastrous Revolution. In such a context it might well be tempting to use Humboldt to adorn the tale, a sort of Bonnie Prince Charlie of German liberalism. The price, however—to accept that it helps us to understand what a late eighteenth- or early nineteenth-century author is saying, or the intellectual and social *milieu* in which he says it, if we are constantly looking over his shoulder to see the shadow of Bismarck's cloven hoof or Hitler's forked tail—is a heavy one.

Humboldt is sufficiently interesting both historically and theoretically without the need to make this assumption. He combines a number of diverse intellectual strands and achieves with them a certain balance and coherence—which is not the same thing as absolute consistency—which one finds nowhere else. His is a distinctive voice, though the languages he speaks are common to a number of his contemporaries. He enlarges one's sense of what a liberal political theory may be: not by his extreme *laissez faire* doctrine—liberalism can boast plenty of doctrinaires of that kind—but because it is very hard to think of another liberal writer who allows into his political theory so strong a sense of a particular kind of tension and paradox. It is something with which virtually everyone is familiar, yet in political theory it is often radically oversimplified: namely, the complexity of our attitudes to and need of other people. Humboldt's liberalism emphatically does not rest on a 'conception of the individual as essentially the proprietor of his own person and capacities, owing nothing to society for them', in which 'the individual was seen neither as a moral whole, nor as part of a larger social whole, but as an owner of himself'.[48] This is a picture of what Schiller called the *Notstaat*, the state of needs: 'Either he [man] hurls himself at objects and wants to snatch them to him in desire; or else the objects force their way obstructively into him, and he thrusts them from him in abhorrence . . . He never perceives others in himself, only himself in others.'[49]

Humboldt's liberalism is not a rationalization of such a state. He has an Aristotelian sense of the ways in which human beings enrich each other's lives in society, together with a quite un-Aristotelian sense that one can neither predict nor set limits to human moral and cultural experimentation. Humboldt's exaltation of the greatest possible comprehensiveness of assimilated experience at times reads like a kind of informal adumbration of the status given to the greatest possible comprehensiveness of consciousness in Idealist political philosophy. One is inclined to regard the Romantic notion of self-enrichment through a communion of souls as one of the cultural sources of the Idealist notion of Absolute Consciousness, together with its more strictly philosophical sources in Hegelian ontology and the theory of universals. Consider in this context, for example, Humboldt's remarkable reference to 'a single complete whole in which all individualities are resolved' (below, p. 58). This, however, remains uncharacteristic though significant.

More typically, Humboldt's combination of Kantian ethics and Idealist epistemology with political liberalism inevitably reminds one of T. H. Green. Essentially, however, the two theorists could scarcely have been culturally and temperamentally further apart. For Green, a moralist in every fibre, and a philistine, 'self-improvement' consisted simply in a more and more vigorous application of the ethics of pure duty. Humboldt's cultural experimentalism lay wholly outside his range. Humboldt recognizes that men are necessary to each other, that they are constantly

---

[48] C. B. Macpherson, *The Political Theory of Possessive Individualism* (London, 1962), p. 3. Cf. Humboldt: 'Bei dieser Materie der Gewerbefreiheit, und einigen andern Lieblingstheorien der neuesten Zeit scheint man auf die Menschen bloss als isolirte, erwerbende, hervorbringende und geniessende Wesen zu sehen, nicht aber auf sittliche Elemente der grössern und kleinern Gemeinheiten im Staat, und des Staats selbst.' ('Zur ständischen Verfassung in Preussen', *Gesammelte Schriften,* ed. Leitzmann, XII, 421.)

[49] Schiller, *Letters on the Aesthetic Education of Mankind,* p. 114.

modifying each other by example, and enriching their sense of the possible styles of living. He also recognizes their hostility and need for protection against each other and against the rigid imposition of some particular communal way of living and thinking. Liberals, by definition, recognize the latter but have tended to treat this recognition as if it were an exhaustive description. Hence the caricatures of liberalism, dear to both traditionalists and Marxists, as a theory or body of theories in which individuals confront each other simply as independent and potentially hostile powers, exchanging goods and making treaties called contracts. None of these historians' and philosophers' maps and caricatures of the liberal mind altogether fits Humboldt. This in itself is a sufficient reason for attending to him.

J. W. BURROW
University of Sussex

EDITOR'S NOTE

I have based my translation on Joseph Coulthard's version of 1854. The translation by J. C. Coulthard has been completely revised for this edition, which has been checked against the text of A. Leitzmann's edition (vol. I of *Humboldts Gesammelte Schriften,* Berlin, 1903). Footnotes taken from Leitzmann's edition are keyed in to the text by numerical indicators and followed by [L]. The editor's notes are keyed in by numerical indicators; those by Humboldt himself are keyed in by symbols.

Humboldt's style in his later years became notorious for its obscurity. The present work, though sometimes ungainly and occasionally digressive, is seldom really obscure. It has to be remembered, however, that the work as a whole was never revised for publication by the author. In extensively revising the translation I have attempted simply to ensure that the English is at no point more obscure than the original.

I am very grateful to my friends Franz Kuna and Quentin Skinner for reading and criticizing the Introduction. My thanks are also due to Mrs. Carol Lee, who typed a difficult manuscript impeccably.

Note on translation of particular terms. The word *Recht* has been translated variously as 'right' or 'justice' as English usage seemed to require—'justice' when the reference is to principles, 'right' where actual legal or natural rights are meant. Humboldt's term *Kräfte* has also been translated either as 'powers' or 'energies', according to English idiom. It should be noted that the word translated as 'morality' is in every case *Sittlichkeit,* not the Hegelian *Moralität.*

NOTE ON THE PRESENT EDITION

For this edition of *The Limits of State Action*, Liberty Fund has used the edition published in 1969 by Cambridge University Press. In both the Editor's Introduction and the text, we have silently corrected typographical errors and changed occasional punctuation to reflect more modern usage. The bibliographies have been expanded, and Professor Stuart D. Warner has prepared a collation to aid the reader interested in comparing selected themes in this volume with John Stuart Mill's *On Liberty.*

OTHER WORKS BY
WILHELM VON HUMBOLDT

Cowan, Marianne, trans. *Humanist Without a Portfolio: An Anthology of the Writings of Wilhelm von Humboldt*. Detroit, 1963.

Humboldt, Wilhelm von. *Humboldts Gesammelte Schriften* [Collected Works]. 17 vols. Berlin, 1903–36.

Humboldt, Wilhelm von. *On Language: The Diversity of Human Language-Structure and Its Influence on the Mental Development of Mankind*. Translated by Peter Heath. Cambridge, 1988.

Humboldt, Wilhelm von. "On the Task of the Historian." In *German Essays on History*, edited by Rolf Sältzer and translated by Joanna Sheldon. New York, 1991.

Works by Humboldt other than the present text which have particular bearing on his political thought are:

Ideen über Staatsverfassung, durch die neue französische Konstitution veranlasst (1791)

Über die Gesetze der Entwicklung der menschlichen Kräfte (1791)

Über das Studium des Altertums und des griechischen inbesondere (1793)

Plan einer vergleichenden Anthropologie (1795)

Das achtzehnte Jahrhundert (1796–97)

Betrachtungen über die Weltgeschichte (1814)

Denkschrift über Preussens ständische Verfassung (1819)

None of these works were published in Humboldt's lifetime.

SELECT BIBLIOGRAPHY

The following are the most important works on Humboldt and the aspects of his thought dealt with in this volume.

Biographical and General

BAUER, JULIETTE. *Life of Wilhelm von Humboldt*. London, 1852.

HAYM, R. *Wilhelm von Humboldt*. Berlin, 1856.

HOWALD, E. *Wilhelm von Humboldt*. Zürich, 1944.

ISHAM, HOWARD. "Wilhelm von Humboldt." *The Encyclopedia of Philosophy*, vol. IV. New York, 1967.

LEROUX, R. *Guillaume de Humboldt; la formation de sa pensée jusqu' en 1794*. Paris, 1952.

SCHAFFENSTEIN, F. *Wilhelm von Humboldt. Ein Lebensbild.* Frankfurt a. M., 1952.
SWEET, PAUL R. *Wilhelm von Humboldt: A Biography.* 2 vols. Columbus, 1978–80.

Humboldt as a Statesman

GEBHARDT, BRUNO. *Wilhelm von Humboldt als Staatsmann.* 2 vols. Stuttgart, 1896–99.
MEINECKE, FRIEDRICH. "Wilhelm Humboldt und der deutsche Staat." In *Staat und Persönlichkeit.* Berlin, 1933.
SCOTT, D.F.S. *Wilhelm von Humboldt and the Idea of a University,* Inaugural Lecture. University of Durham, 1960.
SPRANGER, E. *Wilhelm von Humboldt und die Reform des Bildungswesens.* New ed., Tübingen, 1960.

Humboldt's Political Thought

ARIS, R. *The History of Political Thought in Germany, 1789–1815.* London, 1936.
BATTISTI, SIEGFRIED. *Freiheit und Bindung: Wilhelm von Humboldts "Ideen zu einem Versuch, die Grenzen der Wirksamkeit des Staats zu bestimmen" und das Subsidiaritätsprinzip.* Berlin, 1987.
BEISER, FREDERICK C. *Enlightenment, Revolution, & Romanticism: The Genesis of Modern German Political Thought 1790–1800.* Cambridge, Mass., 1992.
BERGLAR, PETER. *Wilhelm von Humboldt.* Hamburg, 1970.
CHALLEMEL-LACOUR, M. *La Philosophie Individualiste: Etude Sur Guillaume de Humboldt.* Paris, 1864.
CHAPMAN, JOHN. "The Sphere and Duties of Government" [Review of *The Sphere and Duties of Government,* Translated from the German of Baron Wilhelm von Humboldt, By Joseph Coulthard, Jun. (London: John Chapman, 1854).] *The Westminster Review,* New Series 6 (1854): 473–506.
CRANSTON, MAURICE. "Wilhelm von Humboldt." *Inquiry* 12 (1979).
GOOCH, G. P. *Germany and the French Revolution.* London, new impr. 1965.
KAEHLER, S. A. *Wilhelm von Humboldt und der Staat.* Munich and Berlin, 1927.
KRIEGER, L. *The German Idea of Freedom.* Chicago, 1957.
LABOULAYE, EDOUARD. "L'Etat et ses Limites." In *L'Etat et ses Limites, Suivi d'Essais Politiques,* pp. 1–102, Paris, 1863.
LEROUX, ROBERT. "Guillaume de Humboldt et J. Stuart Mill," *Etudes Germaniques* 6 (1951): 262–274, and 7 (1952): 81–87.
MEINECKE, FRIEDRICH. *Cosmopolitanism and the National State.* Translated by Robert Kimber. Princeton, 1970.
MEINECKE, F. *Weltbürgertum und Nationalstaat, Werke.* Vol. V, Bk. 1. Munich, 1962.
MUHLACK, ULRICH. *Das zeitgenössische Frankreich in der Politik Humboldts,* Historische Studien no. 400. Lubeck, 1967.

RAICO, RALPH. "Wilhelm von Humboldt." *New Individualist Review* 1 (1961): 18–27. Reprinted in *New Individualist Review*. Indianapolis, 1981.

REISS, H. S. "Introduction" to *Political Thought of the German Romantics*. Translated and selected by H.S. Reiss. Oxford, 1955.

REISS, H. S. "Justus Möser und Wilhelm von Humboldt. Konservative und liberale politische Ideen in Deutschlund des 18. Jahrhunderts." *Politische Vierteljahresschrift* 8(1) (1967).

ROSENBLUM, NANCY L. *Another Liberalism: Romanticism and the Reconstruction of Liberal Thought*. Cambridge, 1987.

SWEET, PAUL R. 'Young Wilhelm von Humboldt's Writings (1789–93) Reconsidered." *Journal of the History of Ideas* 34 (1973): 469–482.

VOGEL, URSULA. "Liberty Is Beautiful: Von Humboldt's Gift to Liberalism." *History of Political Theory* 3 (1982): 77–101.

Studies of *Bildung*, Education, and Language

ADLER, G. J. *Wilhelm von Humboldt's Linguistical Studies*. New York, 1866.

BRUFORD, W. "The Idea of 'Bildung' in Wilhelm von Humboldt's Letters." In *The Era of Goethe. Essays presented to James Boyd*. Oxford, 1959.

BRUFORD, W. *The German Tradition of Self-Cultivation: "Bildung" from Humboldt to Thomas Mann*. Cambridge, 1975.

CASSIRER, ERNST. *The Philosophy of Symbolic Forms*, vol. I. Translated by Ralph Manheim. New Haven, 1953.

SORKIN, DAVID. "Wilhelm von Humboldt: The Theory and Practice of Self-Formation (*Bildung*), 1791–1810." *Journal of the History of Ideas* 44 (1983): 55–73.

SPRANGER, E. *Wilhelm von Humboldt und die Humanitätsidee*. Berlin, 1909.

VOEGELIN, ERIC. "The German University and the Order of German Society: A Reconsideration of the Nazi Era." In *The Collected Works of Eric Voegelin*, Vol. 12, *Published Essays 1966–1985*. (Baton Rouge, 1990).

VONDUNG, KLAUS. "Unity Through Bildung: A German Dream of Perfection." *Independent Journal of Philosophy* 5/6 (1988): 47–55.

Humboldt's Hellenism

HATFIELD, HENRY. *Aesthetic Paganism in German Literature: Winckelmann to Goethe*. Harvard, 1954.

STADLER, P. B. *Wilhelm von Humboldts Bild der Antike*. Zurich and Stuttgart, 1959.

THE LIMITS OF STATE ACTION

CHAPTER I

Introduction

o discover to what end State institutions should be directed, and what limits should be set to their activity, is the design of the following pages. The importance of this question is self-evident, and if we compare the most noteworthy political constitutions with each other, and with the opinions of the most eminent philosophers and politicians, we shall, with reason, be surprised to find it so insufficiently discussed and vaguely answered.

Those who have either themselves remodelled the framework of State constitutions, or proposed schemes of political reform, seem mostly to have concerned themselves with specifying the respective shares which the nation or any of its parts should have in the administration and with assigning the proper function of each in the plan of government, so that none shall infringe the rights of the others. But in every attempt to frame or reorganize a political constitution, there are two main objects, it seems to me, to be distinctly kept in view, neither of which can be overlooked or made subordinate without serious injury to the general purposes; these are—first, to determine, for the nation in question, who shall govern, who shall be governed, and to arrange the actual working of the administration; and secondly, to prescribe the exact sphere to which the government, once constructed, should extend or confine its operations. The latter object, which more immediately affects the private life of the citizen, and more especially determines the limits of his free, spontaneous activity, is, strictly speaking, the true ultimate purpose; the former is only a necessary means for arriving at this end. And yet, however, it is to the attainment of the first of these ends that man directs his most earnest attention; and this exclusive pursuit of one definite purpose is the way human activity usually manifests itself. It is in the prosecution of some single object, and in striving to reach it by the combined application of his moral and physical energies, that the true happiness of man, in his full vigour and development, consists. Possession, it is true, crowns exertion with rest; but it is only in the illusions of fancy that it has power to charm us. If we consider the position of man in the universe—if we remember the constant tendency of his energies towards some definite activity, and recognize the influence of surrounding nature, which is constantly provoking him to exertion, we find that rest and possession exist only in imagination. Only the partial or one-sided man finds repose in the cessation of one line of action; and in the man whose powers are wholly undeveloped, one single object alone elicits a few manifestations of energy. The dissatisfaction we notice accompanying possession, especially in the case of the finer sensibilities, does not at all apply to that ideal of human perfection which is conceivable by imagination; but it is true, in the fullest sense, of the wholly uncultured man, and proportionately true of every intermediate gradation between this utter want of culture and that ideal standard mentioned above.[1] It seems, then, to follow that the conqueror enjoys his victory more than the actual occupation of the territory he has won, and that the dangerous commotion of reform itself is dearer to the reformer than the calm enjoyment of its fruits. So it is that the exercise of dominion is more immediately agreeable to human nature than freedom; or, at least, that the care to secure freedom is more satisfying than the actual enjoyment of it. Freedom is but the possibility of a various and indefinite activity, while government, or the exercise of dominion, is a single, yet real activity. The longing for freedom, therefore, is at first only too frequently suggested by the deep-felt consciousness of its absence.

It remains undeniable, however, that the inquiry into the proper aims and limits of State agency must be of the highest importance—perhaps greater importance than any other political question. That such an investigation alone concerns the ultimate object of all political science has been already pointed out; but it is a truth that also allows extensive practical application. Real political revolutions or new governmental organizations are never without many concurrent and fortuitous circumstances, and

---

[1] Humboldt's line of argument may seem confused here. The meaning becomes clearer if one bears in mind that fine sensibility and low cultivation are not necessarily presented as antitheses.

always produce various unfortunate consequences; whereas a sovereign—whether it be democratic, aristocratic, or monarchical—can extend or restrict its sphere of action quietly and unnoticed, and, in general, attains its ends more surely as it avoids startling innovations. The best conducted human activities are those which most faithfully resemble the operations of the natural world. The seed, for example, which drops into the awaiting soil, unseen and unheeded, brings a richer and more blessed growth than the violent eruption of a volcano, which, however necessary, is always destructive; also there is no other system of reform so well adapted to our own times, which justifiably boast of their superiority in culture and enlightenment.

It may easily be foreseen, therefore, that the important inquiry into the proper limits of State agency must lead to a consideration of greater freedom for human energies, and a richer diversity of circumstances and situations. Now the possibility of any higher degree of freedom presupposes a proportionate advance in cultivation—a decreasing need to act in large, compacted masses—a richer variety of resources in the individual agents. If, then, the present age really possesses this increased culture and this power and diversity of resources, the freedom which it rightly demands should unquestionably be allowed it. And so its methods of reform would be suitable to a progressive civilization such as we suppose it to be. Generally speaking, it is the drawn sword of the nation which checks the physical power of its rulers; but in our case, culture and enlightenment sway their thoughts and subdue their will, so that the actual concessions of reform seem due to them rather than to the nation. If to see a people breaking their fetters, in the full consciousness of their rights as men and citizens, is a beautiful and ennobling spectacle, it must be still more fine and uplifting to see a prince himself loosing the bonds and granting freedom to his people—not as an act of grace, but as the fulfilment of his first and most indispensable duty; for it is finer to see an object achieved through a reverent regard for law, than conceded to the demands of absolute necessity; and the more so, when we consider that the freedom which a nation strives to attain by overthrowing existing institutions is only like hope compared with enjoyment, or preparation compared with completion, by comparison with that which a State, once constituted, can grant.

If we cast a glance at the history of political organizations, we shall find it difficult to decide, in the cast of any one of them, the exact limits within which its activity was restricted, because we discover in none the systematic working out of any deliberate plan, grounded on certain basic principles. We shall observe that the freedom of the citizen has always been limited from two points of view; that is, either from the necessity to organize and secure the constitution, or from expediency, to provide for the moral and physical condition of the nation. These considerations have prevailed alternately, as the constitution, in itself powerful, has required additional support, or as the views of the legislators have been more or less widened. Often indeed both of these causes may be found operating together. In the ancient States, almost all the institutions relating to the private life of the citizens were of a strictly political character. Having little authority in itself, the constitution mainly depended for its duration on the will of the nation, and hence it was necessary to bear in mind means by which due harmony might be preserved between the character of established institutions and the national will. The same policy is still observable in small republican States; and in the light of these circumstances alone, it would be correct to say that the freedom of private life always increases in exact proportion as public freedom declines, whereas security always keeps pace with the latter. It is true the ancient legislators very often, and the ancient philosophers invariably, directed their attention to the inner life of the individual; and, in their eyes, the moral worth of human nature seemed to deserve the highest regard: we have an illustration in Plato's *Republic,* of which Rousseau has very truly observed that it has more the character of an educational than a political treatise.[2] Now if we consider the most modern States in this respect we shall find the aim of acting for the individual citizen, and of providing for his welfare, to be clear and unmistakable from the number of laws and institutions directed to this end, and which often give a very distinct form to private life. The superior internal consistency of our constitutions—their greater independence of national character and feeling—the deeper influence of mere thinkers, who are naturally disposed to wider views—the multitude of inventions which teach us how better to cultivate the common objects of national activity; and lastly, and above all, certain ideas of religion which represent the governing power as responsible, to a certain extent, for the moral and future welfare of the citizens, have all contrib-

[2] In *Emile,* bk. I.

uted to introduce this change and develop this positive care. But if we look into the origin of particular institutions and police laws, we find that they frequently originate in the real or pretended necessity of imposing taxes on the subject, and in this we return to the example of the ancient States, inasmuch as such institutions grow out of the same desire to maintain the constitution which we noticed in them. As to those limitations of freedom, however, which do not so much affect the State as the individuals who compose it, we are led to notice a vast difference between ancient and modern governments. The ancients devoted their attention more exclusively to the harmonious development of the individual man, as man; the moderns are chiefly solicitous about his comfort, his prosperity, his productiveness. The former looked to virtue; the latter seek for happiness. And hence it follows that the restrictions imposed on freedom in the ancient States were, in some important respects, more oppressive and dangerous than those which characterize our times. For they directly attacked that inner life of the soul, in which the individuality of human beings essentially consists; and hence all the ancient nations betray a character of uniformity [*Einseitigkeit*], which is not so much due to their want of higher refinement and more limited intercommunication, as to the systematic communal education of their youth (almost universal among them), and the deliberately established communal life of the citizens. But, from another point of view, these ancient institutions preserved and heightened the vigorous activity of the individual man. The very desire, which they had always before them, to train up temperate and energetic citizens gave a higher impulse to their whole spirit and character. With us, it is true, man is individually less restricted; but the influence of surrounding circumstances is only the more limiting, though it does seem possible to begin to struggle against these external hindrances, with our own internal resources. And yet the peculiar nature of the limitations imposed on freedom in our States; the fact that they regard rather what man possesses than what he really is, and that with respect to the latter they do not, like the ancients, cultivate, even to uniformity, the physical, intellectual, and moral faculties; and lastly and especially, the prevalence of certain determining ideas, more binding than laws, suppress those energies which are the source of every active virtue, and the indispensable condition of any higher and more diversified culture. With the ancients, moreover, their greater energy served to compensate for their uniformity; but with the moderns uniformity is aggravated by the evil of diminished energy. This difference between the States of antiquity and those of our own times is in general thoroughly evident. Whilst in these later centuries the rapid strides of progress, the number and dissemination of artistic inventions, and the greatness of our works especially attract our attention, antiquity captivates us above all by that inherent greatness which is comprised in the life of the individual, and perishes with him—the bloom of fancy, the depth of spirit, the strength of will, the perfect oneness of the entire being, which alone confer true worth on human nature. Their strong consciousness of this essential worth of human nature, of its powers and their consistent development, was to them the impulse to every activity; with us these too often seem merely abstractions, in which the sense of the individual is lost, or at least in which his inner life is not so much regarded as his ease, his material comfort, his happiness. The ancients sought for happiness in virtue; the moderns have too long been endeavouring to develop the latter from the former;* and even he† who could conceive and portray morality in its purest form, thinks himself bound to supply happiness to his ideal of human nature through the medium of a highly artificial machinery, and this rather as a reward from without, than as a good obtained by man's own exertions. I need not

---

* This difference is never so strikingly evident as when we make the comparison between the ancient and modern philosophers. As an example, I quote some remarks of Tiedemann[3] on one of the finest passages in Plato's *Republic:* 'Quanquam autem per se sit justitia grata nobis: tamen si exercitium ejus nullam omnino afferret utilitatem, si justo ea omnia essent patienda, quae fratres commemorant; injustitia justitiae foret praeferenda; quae enim ad felicitatem maxime faciunt nostram, sunt absque dubio aliis praeponenda. Jam corporis cruciatus, omnium rerum inopia, fames, infamia, quaeque alia evenire justo fratres dixerunt, animi illam e justitia manantem voluptatem dubio procul longe superant, essetque adeo injustitia justitiae antehabenda et in virtutum numero collocanda' (Tiedemann in *argumentis dialogorum Platonis*, Ad. 1, 2, *de Republica*). 'Now although justice is pleasing to us in its own nature, still if the practice of it did not confer any advantage whatever, if the just man had to endure all that the brothers relate, injustice would be preferable to justice; for the things which especially contribute to our happiness, are unquestionably to be preferred to others. Now bodily torture, utter indigence, hunger, infamy, and whatever else the brothers observed to befall the just man, far outweigh, doubtless, that spiritual pleasure which flows from justice; and so injustice would have to be preferred to justice, and ranked in the number of virtues.'

³ Tiedemann, *Dialogorum Platonis argumenta exposita et illustrata* (Zwiebrücken, 1786).

† Kant, on the Summum Bonum in his *Elements of Moral Metaphysics* (Riga, 1785), and in the *Critique of Practical Reason*.

say more of this striking difference, but will draw these hints to a conclusion with an illustrative passage from Aristotle's *Ethics*: 'For that which peculiarly belongs to each by nature, is best and most pleasant to every one; and consequently, to man, the life according to intellect [is most pleasant], if intellect especially constitutes Man. This life therefore is the most happy.'*

It has been from time to time disputed by publicists, whether the State should provide for the security only, or for the whole physical and moral well-being of the nation. Concern for the freedom of private life has in general led to the former propositions, while the idea that the State can give something more than mere security, and that the injurious limitation of liberty, although a possible, is not an essential, consequence of such a policy, has counselled the latter. And this belief has undoubtedly prevailed, not only in political theory, but in actual practice. This is shown in most of the systems of political jurisprudence, in the more recent philosophical codes, and in the history of constitutions generally. Agriculture, handicrafts, industry of all kinds, business, arts and learning itself, all receive life and direction from the State. The introduction of these principles has given a new form to the study of politics (as is shown for instance by so many recent financial and legislative theories)[4] and has produced many new departments of administration, such as boards of trade, finance, and national economy. But however generally these principles may be accepted, they still appear to me to require a more radical investigation; and this investigation . . .[5]

* Aristotle, *Nichomachean Ethics*, bk. X, ch. 7.
[4] Humboldt is here probably referring to the eighteenth-century German school of political theory known as Cameralism.
[5] At this point there is a gap in the manuscript.

CHAPTER II[1]

Of the individual man, and the highest ends of his existence

he true end of Man, or that which is prescribed by the eternal and immutable dictates of reason, and not suggested by vague and transient desires, is the highest and most harmonious development of his powers to a complete and consistent whole. Freedom is the first and indispensable condition which the possibility of such a development presupposes; but there is besides another essential—intimately connected with freedom, it is true—a variety of situations.[2] Even the most free and self-reliant of men is hindered in his development, when set in a monotonous situation. But as it is evident, on the one hand, that such a diversity is a constant result of freedom, and on the other hand, that there is a species of oppression which, without imposing restrictions on man himself, gives a peculiar impress of its own to surrounding circumstances; these two conditions, of freedom and variety of situation, may be regarded, in a certain sense, as one and the same. Still, it may contribute to clarity to point out the distinction between them.

Every human being, then, can act with only one dominant faculty at a time; or rather, our whole nature disposes us at any given time to some single form of spontaneous activity. It would therefore seem to follow from this that man is inevitably destined to a partial cultivation, since he only enfeebles his energies by directing them to a multiplicity of objects.

[1] This chapter and the first half of the next first appeared in Schiller's *Neue Thalia* (1792), II, 131–69.

[2] This passage was singled out for quotation by Mill. J. S. Mill, *On Liberty*, Cambridge ed., p. 58; Toronto ed., p. 261.

But man has it in his power to avoid this one-sidedness, by attempting to unite the distinct and generally separately exercised faculties of his nature, by bringing into spontaneous cooperation, at each period of his life, the dying sparks of one activity, and those which the future will kindle, and endeavouring to increase and diversify the powers with which he works, by harmoniously combining them, instead of looking for a mere variety of objects for their separate exercise. What is achieved, in the case of the individual, by the union of the past and future with the present is produced in society by the mutual cooperation of its different members; for, in all the stages of his life, each individual can achieve only one of those perfections, which represent the possible features of human character. It is through a social union, therefore, based on the internal wants and capacities of its members, that each is enabled to participate in the rich collective resources of all the others. The experience of all, even the rudest, nations furnishes us an example of a union formative of individual character, in the union of the sexes. And, although in this case the difference as well as the longing for union appears more marked and striking, it is still no less active in other kinds of association where there is actually no difference of sex; it is only more difficult to discover in these, and may perhaps be more powerful for that very reason. If we were to follow out this idea, it might perhaps lead us to a clearer insight into those relations so much in vogue among the ancients, and more especially the Greeks, among whom we find them engaged in even by the legislators themselves: I mean those so frequently, but unworthily, given the name of ordinary love, and sometimes, but always erroneously, that of mere friendship. The effectiveness of all such relations as instruments of cultivation entirely depends on the extent to which the members can succeed in combining their personal independence with the intimacy of the association;[3] for whilst, without this intimacy, one individual cannot sufficiently possess, as it were, the nature of the others, independence is no less essential, in order that each, in being possessed, may be transformed in his own unique way. On the one hand, individual energy is essential to both parties and, on the other hand, a difference between

---

[3] Humboldt may well here be thinking of the small society for mutual self-improvement, the *Veredlungsbund*, which he formed with the Berlin bluestocking Henriette Herz. Humboldt had eventually found the lack of emotional privacy, insisted upon by the rules of the society, irksome.

them, neither so great as to prevent one from comprehending the other, nor so small as to exclude admiration for what the other possesses, and the desire to assimilate it into one's own character.

This individual vigour, then, and manifold diversity combine themselves in originality; and hence, that on which the whole greatness of mankind ultimately depends—towards which every human being must ceaselessly direct his efforts, and of which especially those who wish to influence their fellow-men must never lose sight: individuality of energy and self-development. Just as this individuality springs naturally from freedom of action, and the greatest diversity in the agents, it tends in turn directly to produce them. Even inanimate nature, which, proceeding according to unchangeable laws, advances by regular steps, appears more individual to the man who has been developed in his individuality. He transports himself, as it were, into nature itself; and it is in the highest sense true that each man perceives the beauty and abundance of the outer world, in the same degree as he is conscious of them in his own soul. How much closer must this correspondence become between effect and cause—this reaction between internal feeling and outward perception—when man is not only passively open to external sensations and impressions, but is himself also an agent?

If we attempt to test these principles by a closer application of them to the nature of the individual man, we find that everything in the latter reduces itself to the two elements of form and substance. The purest form beneath the most delicate veil, we call idea; the crudest substance, with the most imperfect form, we call sensuous perception. Form springs from the combinations of substance. The richer and more various the substance that is combined, the more sublime is the resulting form. A child of the gods is the offspring only of immortal parents; and as the blossom ripens into fruit, and from the seed of the fruit the new stalk shoots with newly clustering buds, so does the form become in turn the substance of a still more exquisite form. The intensity of power, moreover, increases in proportion to the greater variety and delicacy of the substance, since the internal cohesion increases with them. The substance seems as if blended in the form, and the form merged in the substance. Or, to speak without metaphor, the richer a man's feelings become in ideas, and his ideas in feelings, the more transcendent his nobility, for upon this constant intermingling of form and substance, or of diversity with the individual unity, depends the perfect fusion of the two natures which co-exist in man, and upon this, his greatness. But the intensity of the fusion depends upon the energy of the generating forces. The highest point of human existence is this flowering.* In the vegetable world, the simple and less graceful form seems to prefigure the more perfect bloom and symmetry of the flower which it precedes, and into which it gradually expands. Everything hastens towards the moment of blossoming. What first springs from the seed is not nearly so attractive. The full thick trunk, the broad leaves rapidly detaching themselves from each other, seem to require some fuller development; as the eye glances up the ascending stem, it marks the grades of this development; more tender leaves seem longing to unite themselves, and draw closer and closer together, until the central calyx of the flower seems to satisfy this desire.†5 But destiny has not blessed the tribe of plants in this respect. The flower fades and dies, and the germ of the fruit reproduces the stem, as rude and unfinished as the former, to ascend slowly through the same stages of development as before. But when, in man, the blossom fades away, it is only to give place to another still more beautiful; and the charm of the most beautiful is only hidden from our view in the endlessly receding vistas of an inscrutable eternity. Now, whatever man receives externally is only like the seed. It is his own active energy alone that can turn the most promising seed into a full and precious blessing for himself. It is beneficial only to the extent that it is full of vital power and essentially individual. The highest ideal, therefore, of the co-existence of human beings seems to me to consist in a union in which each strives to develop himself from his own inmost nature, and for his own sake. The requirements of our physical and moral being would, doubtless, bring men together into communities; and as the conflicts of warfare are more honourable than the fights of the arena, and the struggles of exasperated citizens more glorious than the hired efforts of

---

* 'Blüthe, Reife', *Neues deutsches Museum*, June 1791.4

    4 This anonymous article put forward the idea that maturity (*Reife*) which follows flowering (*Blüthe*) represents the highest perfection in nature. Flowering has more charm but less perfection.

† Goethe, *Über die Metamorphose der Pflanzen.*

5 This passage is strongly marked by the teleological character of German transcendental biology. See G. S. Carter, *A Hundred Years of Evolution* (1958); R. Friedenthal, *Goethe, His Life and Times* (1965), ch. 27; and W. Haas, 'Of Living Things', *German Life and Letters* (1956–7).

mercenaries, so the exertions of such spontaneous agents succeed in exciting the highest energies.

And is it not exactly this which so inexpressibly captivates us in contemplating the age of Greece and Rome, and which in general captivates any age in contemplating a remoter one?[6] Is it not that these men had harder struggles with fate to endure, and harder struggles with their fellow-men? that greater and more original energy and individuality constantly encountered each other, and created wonderful new forms of life? Every later epoch—and how rapidly must this decline now proceed!—is necessarily inferior in variety to that which it succeeded: in variety of nature—the vast forests have been cleared, the morasses dried up and so on; in variety of human life, by ever-increasing intercommunication and agglomeration.* This is one of the chief reasons why the idea of the new, the uncommon, the marvellous, is so much more rare, so that affright or astonishment are almost a disgrace, while the discovery of fresh and, till now, unknown expedients, and also all sudden, unpremeditated and urgent decisions are far less necessary. For, partly, the pressure of outward circumstances is less, while man is provided with more means for opposing them; partly, this resistance is no longer possible with the simple forces which nature gives to all alike for immediate use. Again, it is partly that a higher and more extended knowledge renders expedients less necessary, and the very increase of learning blunts the energy necessary to it. It is, on the other hand, undeniable that, whereas physical variety has declined, it has been succeeded by an infinitely richer and more satisfying intellectual and moral variety, and that our superior refinement can recognize more delicate distinctions and gradations, and our cultivated and sensitive character, if not so strongly developed, as that of the ancients, can transfer them into the practical conduct of life—distinctions and gradations which might have escaped the notice of the sages of antiquity, or at least would have been discernible by them alone. To the human race as a whole, the same has happened as to the individual: the ruder features have faded away, the finer only have remained. And in

---

[6] The tension in Humboldt's ideas between the notion of cultural progress and his Hellenism and Rousseauist primitivism is very marked in the tone of this and the preceding paragraph.

* Rousseau has also noticed this in his *Emile*.[7]

[7] *Emile*, bk. V.

view of this sacrifice of energy from generation to generation, we might regard it as a blessed dispensation if the whole species were as one man; or the living force of one age could be transmitted to the succeeding one, along with its books and inventions. But this is far from being the case. It is true that our refinement possesses a peculiar force of its own, perhaps even surpassing the former in strength, according to the measure of its refinement; but the question is whether the earlier development, through the more robust and vigorous stages, must not always be the prior transition. Still, it is certain that the sensuous element in our nature, as it is the first germ, is also the most vivid expression of the spiritual.

Whilst this is not the place, however, to enter on a discussion of this point, we are justified in concluding, from the other considerations we have urged, that we must at least preserve, with the most eager concern, all the energy and individuality we may yet possess, and cherish anything that can in any way promote them.

I therefore deduce, as the natural inference from what has been argued, *that reason cannot desire for man any other condition than that in which each individual not only enjoys the most absolute freedom of developing himself by his own energies, in his perfect individuality, but in which external nature itself is left unfashioned by any human agency, but only receives the impress given to it by each individual by himself and of his own free will, according to the measure of his wants and instincts, and restricted only by the limits of his powers and his rights.*

From this principle it seems to me that reason must never retract anything except what is absolutely necessary. It must therefore be the basis of every political system, and must especially constitute the starting-point of the inquiry which at present claims our attention.

CHAPTER III

On the solicitude of the State for the positive welfare of the citizen

K eeping in view the conclusions arrived at in the last chapter, we might embody in a general formula our idea of State agency when restricted to its proper limits, and define its objects as all that a government could accomplish for the common weal, without departing from the principle just established; while, from this position, we could proceed to derive the still stricter limitation, that any State interference in private affairs, where there is no immediate reference to violence done to individual rights, should be absolutely condemned. It will be necessary, however, to examine in succession the different departments of a State's usual or possible activity, before we can circumscribe its sphere more positively, and arrive at a full solution of the question proposed.

A State, then, has one of two ends in view; it designs either to promote happiness, or simply to prevent evil; and in the latter case, the evil which arises from natural causes, or that which springs from man himself. If it restricts its concerns to the second of these objects, it aims merely at security; and I would here oppose this term security to every other possible end of State agency, and comprise these last under the general heading of Positive Welfare. Further, the various means adopted by a State affect in very different degrees the extension of its activity. It may endeavor, for instance, to secure its ends directly, either by coercion or by the inducements of example and exhortation; or it may combine all these sources of influence in the attempt to shape the citizen's outward life, and forestall actions contrary to its intention; or, lastly, it may try to exercise a sway over his thoughts and feelings, so as to bring his inclinations, even, into conformity with its wishes. It is particular actions only that come under political supervision in the first of these cases; in the second, the general conduct of life; and, in the last instance, it is the very character of the citizen, his views, and modes of thought, which are brought under the influence of State control. The actual working of this restrictive agency, moreover, is clearly least in the first of these cases, more so in the second, and greatest in the third; either because, in this, it touches the sources from which the greater number of actions arise, or because the very possibility of such an influence presupposes a greater multiplicity of institutions. But however seemingly different the departments of political action to which they respectively belong, we shall scarcely find any one institution which is not more or less intimately connected with several of these. We may take, for example, the close interdependence that exists between the promotion of welfare and the maintenance of security; furthermore, when any influence affecting particular actions only creates a habit through force of repetition, it comes ultimately to modify the character itself. Hence, in view of this interdependence of political institutions, it is very difficult to find a suitable way of classifying the different aspects of the subject with which we are concerned. But, in any case, it will be best to examine at the outset whether the State should extend its concern to the positive welfare of the nation, or content itself with provisions for its security; and, confining our view of institutions to what is strictly essential either in their objects or consequences, to discuss next, as regards both of these aims, the means that the State may properly make use of in accomplishing them.

I am speaking here, then, of the entire efforts of the State to raise the positive welfare of the nation; of all solicitude for the population of the country, and the subsistence of its inhabitants, whether shown directly in such institutions as poor laws, or indirectly, in the encouragement of agriculture, industry, and commerce; of all regulations relative to finance and currency, imports and exports, etc. (in so far as these have positive welfare in view); finally, of all measures employed to remedy or prevent natural devastations, and, in short, of every political institution designed to preserve or augment the physical welfare of the nation. For moral welfare is not generally regarded so much for its own sake, as with reference to its bearing on security, and I shall therefore come to it later.

Now all such institutions, I maintain, have harmful consequences, and are irreconcilable with a true system of polity; a system conceived in the light of the highest aspirations yet in no way incompatible with human nature.

1. A spirit of governing predominates in every institution of this kind; and however wise and salutary such a spirit may be, it invariably produces national uniformity, and a constrained and unnatural manner of acting. Instead of men grouping themselves into communities in order to discipline and develop their powers, even though, to secure these benefits, they may have to forgo a part of their exclusive possessions and enjoyments, they actually sacrifice their powers to their possessions. The very variety arising from the union of numbers of individuals is the highest good which social life can confer, and this variety is undoubtedly lost in proportion to the degree of State interference. Under such a system, we have not so much the individual members of a nation living united in the bonds of a civil compact; but isolated subjects living in a relation to the State, or rather to the spirit which prevails in its government—a relation in which the undue preponderance of the State already tends to fetter the free play of individual energies. Like causes produce like effects; and hence, in proportion as State interference increases, the agents to which it is applied come to resemble each other, as do all the results of their activity. And this is the very design which States have in view. They desire comfort, ease, tranquillity; and these are most readily secured to the extent that there is no clash of individualities. But what man does and must have in view is something quite different—it is variety and activity. Only these develop the many-sided and vigorous character; and, there can be no one, surely, so far degraded as to prefer, for himself personally, comfort and enjoyment to greatness; and he who draws conclusions for such a preference in the case of others may justly be suspected of misunderstanding human nature, and of wishing to make men into machines.

2. Further, a second harmful consequence ascribable to such a policy is that these positive institutions tend to weaken the vitality of the nation. For as the substance is annihilated by the form which is externally imposed upon it, so it gains greater richness and beauty from what is internally produced by its own spontaneous action; and in the case under consideration it is the form which annihilates the substance—what is itself non-existent suppressing and destroying what really exists. The chief characteristic of human nature is organization. Whatever is to flourish in it must first have germinated there. Every manifestation of energy

presupposes the existence of enthusiasm; and few things nourish enthusiasm so well as the notion of present or future possession. Now man never regards what he possesses as so much his own, as what he does;[1] and the labourer who tends a garden is perhaps in a truer sense its owner, than the listless voluptuary who enjoys its fruits. It may be that such reasoning appears too general to admit of any practical application. Perhaps it seems even as though the extension of so many branches of science, which we owe chiefly to political institutions (for the State alone can mount experiments on a large scale), contributed to raise the power of intellect, and thereby our culture and character in general. But the intellectual faculties themselves are not necessarily ennobled by every addition to our knowledge; and even if it were granted that these means actually achieved such a result, this does not so much apply to the entire nation, as to that particular portion of it which is connected with the government. The cultivation of the understanding, as of any man's other faculties, is generally achieved by his own activity, his own ingenuity, or his own methods of using the discoveries of others. Now, State measures always imply more or less compulsion; and even where this is not directly the case, they accustom men to look for instruction, guidance, and assistance from without, rather than to rely upon their own expedients. The only method of instruction, perhaps, of which the State can avail itself consists in its declaring the best course to be pursued as though it were the result of its investigations. But whether it coerces the citizen by some compulsory arrangement, directly by law or indirectly in some way, or by its authority by rewards, and other encouragements attractive to him, or, lastly, merely by arguments, it will always deviate very far from the best system of instruction. For this unquestionably consists in proposing, as it were, all possible solutions of the problem in question, so that the citizen may select, according to his own judgement, the course which seems to him the most appropriate; or, still better, so as to enable him to discover the solution for himself, from a careful consideration of all the objections. In the case of adult citizens, the State can only adopt this negative system of instruction by extending freedom, which allows all obstacles to arise, while it develops the skill, and multiplies the opportunities neces-

---

[1] The compression of Humboldt's argument at this point leads to the appearance of a contradiction. The argument is that things acted upon are more truly 'possessed' than possessions, and hence evoke more enthusiasm.

sary to meet them. By adhering to a really national system of education, however, it can operate positively on the early training and culture of the young. We shall later embark on a close examination of the objection which might be advanced here in favour of these institutions; namely, that in the execution of such enterprises as those to which we refer, it is more important that the thing be done, than that the person who performs it should be thoroughly instructed in his task; more important that the land be well tilled, than that the husbandman be the most skilful agriculturist.

But to continue: the evil results of a too extensive solicitude on the part of the State are still more strikingly shown in the suppression of all active energy, and the necessary deterioration of the moral character. This scarcely needs further argument. The man who is often led easily becomes disposed willingly to sacrifice what remains of his capacity for spontaneous action. He fancies himself released from an anxiety which he sees transferred to other hands, and seems to himself to do enough when he looks to their leadership and follows it. Thus, his notions of merit and guilt become unsettled. The idea of the first no longer inspires him; and the painful consciousness of the last assails him less frequently and forcibly, since he can more easily ascribe his shortcomings to his peculiar position, and leave them to the responsibility of those who have made it what it is. If we add to this, that he may not, possibly, regard the designs of the State as perfectly pure in their objects or execution—that he may suspect that his own advantage only, but along with it some other additional purpose is intended, then, not only the force and energy, but also the purity of his moral nature suffers. He now conceives himself not only completely free from any duty which the State has not expressly imposed upon him, but exonerated at the same time from every personal effort to improve his own condition; and even fears such effort, as if it were likely to open out new opportunities, of which the State might take advantage. And as for the laws actually enjoined, he tries as much as possible to escape their operation, considering every such evasion as a positive gain. If we reflect that, among a large part of the nation, its laws and political institutions have the effect of limiting the sphere of morality, it is a melancholy spectacle to see the most sacred duties, and mere trivial and arbitrary enactments, often proclaimed from the same authoritative source, and to see the infraction of both met with the same measure of punishment. Further, the pernicious influence of such a positive policy is no less evident in the behaviour of the citizens to each other. As each individual abandons himself to the solicitous aid of the State, so, and still more, he abandons to it the fate of his fellow-citizens. This weakens sympathy and renders mutual assistance inactive; or, at least, the reciprocal interchange of services and benefits will be most likely to flourish at its liveliest, where the feeling is most acute that such assistance is the only thing to rely upon; and experience teaches us that oppressed classes of the community which are, as it were, overlooked by the government, are always bound together by the closest ties. But wherever the citizen becomes indifferent to his fellows, so will the husband be to his wife, and the father of a family towards the members of his household.

If men were left wholly to themselves in their various undertakings, and were cut off from all external resources, other than those which their own efforts obtained, they would still, whether through their own fault or not, fall frequently into difficulties and misfortune. But the happiness for which man is plainly destined is no other than that which his own energies procure for him; and the very nature of such a self-reliant position sharpens his intellect and develops his character. Are there no instances of such evils where State agency fetters individual spontaneity by too detailed interference? There are many, doubtless; and the man whom it has accustomed to lean on an external power for support is thus given up in critical emergencies to a far more hopeless fate. For, just as the very act of struggling against misfortune, and encountering it with vigorous efforts, lightens the calamity, so delusive expectations aggravate its severity tenfold. In short, taking the most favourable view, States like those to which we refer too often resemble the physician, who only retards the death of his patient by nourishing his disease. Before there were physicians, man knew only health and death.

3. Everything towards which man directs his attention, whether it is limited to the direct or indirect satisfaction of his merely physical wants, or to the achievement of external objects in general, is closely related with his internal sensations. Sometimes, moreover, alongside this external purpose and related to it there is some inner impulse and often, even, this is the sole spring of his activity, the former being only, necessarily or incidentally, connected with it. The more unity a man possesses, the more freely does his choice of these external matters spring from his inner

being, and the more frequent and intimate is the cooperation of these two sources of motive, even when he has not freely selected these external objects. An interesting man, therefore, is interesting in all situations and all activities, though he only attains the most matured and graceful consummation of his activity when his way of life is harmoniously in keeping with his character.

In view of this consideration, it seems as if all peasants and craftsmen might be elevated into artists; that is, men who love their labour for its own sake, improve it by their own plastic genius and inventive skill, and thereby cultivate their intellect, ennoble their character, and exalt and refine their pleasures. And so humanity would be ennobled by the very things which now, though beautiful in themselves, so often serve to degrade it. The more a man accustoms himself to live reflectively and sensitively, and the more refined and vigorous his moral and intellectual powers become, the more he longs to choose only such external objects as furnish more scope and material for his internal development; or, at least, to overcome the adverse conditions into which fate may cast him, and transform them. It is impossible to estimate a man's advance towards the great and the beautiful, when he ceaselessly strives for this supreme object, the development of his inner life; so that it may remain the chief source, the ultimate goal of all his labours, and all that is corporeal and external may seem merely its instrument and veil.

How striking, to take an illustration, is the historical picture of the character fostered in a people by the undisturbed cultivation of the soil. The labour they devote to the land, and the harvest with which it repays their industry, bind them with sweet fetters to their fields and firesides. Their participation in beneficent toil, and the common enjoyment of its fruits, entwine each family with bonds of love, from which even the ox, the partner of their work, is not wholly excluded. The seed which must be sown, the fruit which must be gathered annually, occasionally with disappointed hopes, make them patient, trusting and frugal. The fact of their receiving everything immediately from the hand of nature, the ever-deepening consciousness that, although the hand of man must first scatter the seed, it is not from human agency that growth and increase come, the constant dependence on favourable and unfavourable weather, awaken presentiments, sometimes fearful, sometimes joyful, of the existence of higher beings—in the rapid alternations of fear and hope—and dispose

them to prayer and thanksgiving. The visible image of the simplest sublimity, the most perfect order, and the gentlest beneficence mould their
lives into forms of simple grandeur and tenderness, and dispose their
hearts to a cheerful submission to custom and law. Always accustomed to
produce, never to destroy, agriculture is essentially peaceful, and, while
far from wrongdoing and revenge, is yet capable of the most dauntless
courage when roused to resist the injustice of unprovoked attack and the
destroyers of its peace.

But, still, freedom is undoubtedly the indispensable condition, without
which even the pursuits most congenial to individual human nature can
never succeed in producing such salutary influences. Whatever does not
spring from a man's free choice, or is only the result of instruction and
guidance, does not enter into his very being, but still remains alien to his
true nature; he does not perform it with truly human energies, but merely
with mechanical exactness.[2] The ancients, and more especially the
Greeks, were accustomed to regard every occupation as harmful and
degrading which was immediately connected with the exercise of physical strength, or the pursuit of external advantages, and not exclusively
confined to the development of the inner man. Hence, many of their philosophers who were most eminent for their philanthropy approved of
slavery; thereby adopting a barbarous and unjust expedient, and agreeing
to sacrifice one part of mankind in order to secure the highest power and
beauty to the other. But reason and experience combine to expose the
error which lies at the root of such a fallacy. There is no pursuit whatever
that may not be ennobling and give to human nature some worthy and
determinate form. The manner of its performance is the only thing to be
considered; and we may here lay down the general rule, that a man's
pursuits react beneficially on his culture, so long as these, and the energies allied with them, succeed in filling and satisfying the wants of his
soul; while their influence is not only less salutary, but even pernicious,
when he directs his attention more to the results to which they lead, and
regards the occupation itself merely as a means. For anything which
charms us by its own intrinsic worth awakens love and esteem, while
what is only looked on as a means to ulterior advantage merely appeals to

---

[2] Cf. J. S. Mill: 'One whose desires and impulses are not his own, has no character, no
more than a steam-engine has a character' (*On Liberty*, Cambridge ed., pp. 60–1;
Toronto ed., p. 264).

self-interest; and the motives of love and esteem tend as directly to ennoble human nature, as those of interest to degrade it. Now, in exercising
such a positive care as we are considering, the State can only consider
results, and establish rules whose observance will most directly conduce
to their achievement.

Never does this limited point of view lead to such pernicious results as
in those cases where moral or intellectual ends are the object of human
endeavor; or, at least, where some end is regarded for itself, and apart
from the consequences which are only necessarily or incidentally implied
in it. This becomes evident, for instance, in all scientific researches and
religious opinions, in all kinds of human association, and in that union in
particular which is the most natural, and the most vitally important both
for the individual and for the State, namely, matrimony.

Matrimony, or as it may perhaps be best defined, the union of persons
of the two sexes, based on the difference of sex, may be regarded in as
many different aspects as the attitudes taken to that difference, and as the
inclinations of the heart, and the objects which they present to the reason,
assume different forms; and in such a union every man will show his
whole moral character, and especially the force and peculiarity of his sensibilities. Whether a man is more disposed to the pursuit of external
objects, or to the exercise of the inner faculties of his being; whether reason or feeling is the more active principle in his nature; whether he is led
to embrace things eagerly, and quickly abandon them, or involves himself
slowly but continues faithfully; whether he is capable of deeper intimacy,
or only loosely attaches himself; whether he preserves, in the closest
union, a greater or less self-sufficiency; and an infinite number of other
considerations modify, in various ways, his relations in married life.
Whatever form they assume, however, the effects upon his life and happiness are unmistakable; and upon the success or failure of the attempt to
find or create a reality in harmony with his inner feelings, depends the
higher consummation or alternatively the vegetation of his being. This
influence manifests itself most forcibly in those men, so peculiarly interesting in their character and actions, who form their perceptions with the
greatest ease and delicacy, and retain them most deeply and lastingly.
Generally speaking, the female sex may be more justly reckoned in this
class than the male; and it is for this reason that the female character is
most intimately dependent on the character of the family relations in a

nation. Wholly exempt as she is from most outward occupations, and absorbed almost entirely only by those which leave the soul untouched—stronger in what she can be than in what she can do—more full of expression in her serenity, than in her expressed perceptions—more richly endowed with all the means of immediate, indefinable expression, a more delicate frame, a more moving eye, a more winning voice—destined rather, in her relations with others, to expect and receive, than to initiate—naturally weaker in herself, and yet, not on that account, but through loving admiration of strength and greatness in another, clinging more closely—ceaselessly striving in her union to experience and grasp what the other experiences, to form the other in her own being, and reproduce it moulded into new forms of creation—inspired at the same time with the courage which loving care and the consciousness of strength infuse into the soul—not defiant but enduring—woman is, strictly speaking, nearer to the ideal human nature than man; and whilst it is true that she more rarely reaches it, it may only be that it is more difficult to ascend by the steep, immediate path than by the winding one. Now, how much such a being—so sensitive, yet so complete in herself, who therefore responds to everything with her whole being—must be disturbed by external disharmony, is incalculable. Hence the infinite social consequences of the culture of the female character. If it were not somewhat fanciful to suppose that every human excellence is presented, as it were, in one kind of being, we might believe that the whole treasure of morality and order is enshrined in the female character. As the poet profoundly says,

Nach Freiheit strebt der Mann, das Weib nach Sitte. [3]

While the former strives to remove the external barriers which hinder his development, woman's careful hand draws the salutary inner limits within which alone the fullness of strength can be refined to proper ends; and she defines the limits with more delicate precision, in that she grasps more deeply the inner nature of humanity, and sees more clearly through the intricate confusion of human relations, for all her senses are alert, and she avoids the sophistications which so often obscure truth.

If it were necessary, history would afford sufficient confirmation of this argument, and show the close connection that exists between national

---

[3] 'Man strives for freedom, woman for order' (Goethe, *Torquato Tasso,* II, 1).

morality and respect for the female sex. It is clear from these considerations that the results of marriage are as various as the characters of the
persons concerned, and that, as it is a union so closely related to the very
nature of the respective individuals, it must have the most harmful consequences when the State attempts to regulate it by law, or through the
force of its institutions to make it rest on anything but simple inclination.
When we remember, moreover, that the State can only contemplate the
final results in such regulations—as, for instance, population, education
of children, etc.—we shall be still more ready to admit the justice of this
conclusion. It may reasonably be argued that a care for such objects conducts to the same results as the highest care for the most beautiful development of the inner man. For, after careful observation, it has been found
that the uninterrupted union of one man with one woman is most conducive to population; and it is likewise undeniable that no other union
springs from true, natural, harmonious love. And, further, it may be
observed that such love leads to the same results as those very relations
which law and custom tend to establish, such as the procreation of children, family training, community of living, participation in the common
goods, the management of external affairs by the husband, and the care of
domestic arrangements by the wife. But the radical error of such a policy
appears to be that the law commands, whereas such a relation cannot
mould itself according to external arrangements, but depends wholly on
inclination; and wherever coercion or guidance come into collision with
inclination, they divert it still further from the proper path. Wherefore it
appears to me that the State should not only loosen the bonds in this
instance, but, if I may apply the principles stated above (now that I am
not speaking of matrimony in general, but of one of the many injurious
consequences arising from restrictive State institutions, which are in this
instance especially noticeable), that it should entirely withdraw its active
care from the institution of matrimony, and both generally and in its particular variations should rather leave it wholly to the free choice of the
individuals, and the various contracts they may enter into. I should not
be deterred from the adoption of this principle by the fear that all family relations might be disturbed, or their formation in general hindered;
for although such a fear might be justified in particular circumstances
and places, it could not be fairly entertained in an inquiry into the
nature of men and States in general. For experience frequently shows

us that just where law has imposed no fetters, morality most surely binds; the idea of external coercion is entirely foreign to an institution which, like matrimony, rests only on inclination and an inward sense of duty; and the results of such coercive institutions are not at all what is intended.

4. *The solicitude of a State for the positive welfare of its citizens must further be harmful, in that it has to operate upon a promiscuous mass of individualities, and therefore does harm to these by measures which cannot meet individual cases.*

5. *It hinders the development of Individuality . . .*[4]

In the moral life of man, and generally in his practical conduct in so far as they are guided by the same rules, which may, however, be limited to the basic principles of justice, he still endeavors to keep before his eyes the highest conception of the most individual development of himself and others. He strictly subordinates all other considerations of interest to this pure and spiritual law that he has recognized. But all the aspects of human nature which a man may cultivate exist together in a wonderful interdependence, and while their coherence is more striking (if not really closer) in the intellectual than in the physical sphere, it is infinitely more remarkable in that of morality. It follows that men are not to unite themselves in order to forgo any portion of their individuality, but only to lessen the exclusiveness of their isolation; it is not the object of such a union to transform one being into another, but to open communication between them. Each is to compare what he is himself with what he receives by contact with others, and, to use the latter to modify but not to suppress his own nature. For as truth is never found conflicting with truth in the domain of intellect, so too in the region of morality there is no opposition between things really worthy of human nature. Close and varied unions of individual characters are therefore necessary, in order to destroy what cannot co-exist in proximity, and does not, therefore, essentially conduce to greatness and beauty, while they cherish and foster the qualities which can coexist harmoniously, and make them fruitful in new and finer ways. Hence the principle of the true art of social intercourse consists in a ceaseless endeavour to grasp the innermost individuality of another, to avail oneself of it, and, with the deepest respect for it as the

---

[4] There is a hiatus in the manuscript at this point.

individuality of another, to act upon it.[5] Because of this respect one can
do this only by, as it were, showing oneself, and offering the other the
opportunity of comparison. This art has been hitherto singularly
neglected. Such neglect may excuse itself by claiming that social intercourse should be a refreshing recreation, and not a toilsome duty, and
that, unfortunately, in many people it is scarcely possible to discover an
interesting individual aspect. Still, everyone must have too much respect
for himself to look for recreations which leave his highest faculties inactive, and too much reverence for human nature, to pronounce any of his
companions completely useless or insensitive. He, at least, who makes it
his business to exercise an influence over his fellow-men must not ignore
the possibility; and hence, inasmuch as the State, in its positive care for
the external and physical well-being of the citizen (which are closely connected with his inner being), cannot avoid creating hindrances to the
development of individuality, we find another reason why it should not
be permitted to exercise such interference except in the case of the most
absolute necessity.

These, then, may be the chief harmful consequences which flow from a
positive solicitude of the State for the welfare of the citizen; and although
they may be especially involved in certain of its particular manifestations,
they appear to me to be generally inseparable from the adoption of such a
policy. It was my intention hitherto to confine myself to considering the
State's care for physical welfare, and I have so far proceeded strictly from
this point of view alone, carefully setting aside everything that referred
exclusively to moral well-being. But I took occasion at the outset to mention that the subject does not admit of any strict division; and this may
serve as my excuse, if much that naturally arises from the previous development of the argument applies to the care for positive welfare in general.
I have hitherto made the assumption, however, that the State institutions
referred to are already established, and I have therefore still to speak of
certain difficulties which present themselves in the actual framing of such
institutions.

6. Nothing, certainly, would be more necessary here than to weigh the
advantages intended by such institutions against the disadvantages which

[5] Cf. J. S. Mill: 'In proportion to the development of his individuality, each person
becomes more valuable to himself and is therefore capable of being more valuable to
others' (*On Liberty,* Cambridge ed., p. 63; Toronto ed., p. 266).

always arise, and especially the limitations of freedom involved. But it is always very difficult to weigh consequences in this manner and perhaps impossible to do so completely. For every restrictive institution comes into collision with the free and natural development of energy, and gives rise to an infinite multiplicity of new circumstances; and even if we suppose the smoothest course of events, and set aside all serious and unlooked-for accidents, the number of consequences which follow from it is unforeseeable. Any one who has an opportunity of occupying himself with the higher departments of State administration must certainly feel conscious from experience how few political measures have really an immediate and absolute necessity, and how many, on the contrary, have only a relative and indirect importance, and simply follow from previous measures. Now, in this way a vast increase of measures is rendered necessary, which become diverted from the original end. Not only does such a State require larger sources of revenue, but it needs in addition an increase of artificial regulations for the maintenance of mere political security: the separate parts work less well together—the supervision of the government requires far more vigilance and activity. Hence comes the need, unhappily too often neglected, to make the difficult calculation whether the available resources of the State are adequate to provide the means for what has been undertaken; and should this calculation reveal a real disproportion, it only suggests the necessity of fresh artificial arrangements, which, in the end, overstrain the power of the State—an evil from which (though not from this cause only) many of our modern States are suffering.[6]

We must not overlook here one particular harmful consequence, since it so closely affects human development; and this is that the administration of political affairs itself becomes in time so full of complications that it requires an incredible number of persons to devote their time to its supervision, in order that it may not fall into utter confusion. Now, by far the greater portion of these have to deal with the mere symbols and formulas of things; and thus, not only are men of first-rate capacity withdrawn from anything which gives scope for thinking, and useful hands are diverted from real work, but their intellectual powers themselves suf-

---

[6] This passage and the one which follows no doubt owe something to Humboldt's own experience of government service, which, at the time of writing, he had just left in disgust.

fer from this partly empty, partly narrow employment. New careers, moreover, are introduced by the needs of State business, and these render the servants of the State more dependent on the governing classes of the community, in whose pay they are, than on the nation in general. Familiar as they have become to us by experience, we need not describe the numerous evils which flow from such a dependence—what looking to the State for help, what a lack of self-reliance, what false vanity, what apathy even, and poverty. The same evils from which these harmful consequences arise are immediately produced by them in turn. When once thus accustomed to the transaction of State affairs, men more and more lose sight of the essential object, and concentrate on the mere form; they thereupon attempt new improvements, perhaps good in intention, but without sufficient adaptation to the required end; and the harmful effect of these necessitates new forms, new complications, and often new restrictions, and thereby creates new departments, which require for their efficient supervision a vast increase of functionaries. Hence it arises that in most states from decade to decade the number of the public officials and the extent of registration increase, while the liberty of the subject proportionately declines. In such an administration, moreover, it follows of course that everything depends on the most vigilant supervision and careful management, since there are such increased opportunities of falling short in both; and hence one tries to ensure, up to a point correctly, that everything passes through as many hands as possible in order to avoid the risk of errors and embezzlement.

But according to this method of transacting affairs, business becomes in time merely mechanical, while the men who are engaged in it relapse into machines, and all genuine worth and honesty decline in proportion as trust and confidence are withdrawn. Finally, as the occupations of which I am speaking must be vested with high importance, the idea of what is momentous or trivial, of what is dignified or contemptible, of what are essential and what are subordinate aims, becomes reversed. The necessity for business of this kind compensates, on the other hand, by many obviously beneficial results, for its evils, so I will not here dwell longer on this part of the subject, but will proceed at once to the ultimate consideration—to which all the foregoing is simply a necessary preparation: the general distortion of outlook which is produced by the positive interference of the State.

7. In the kind of policy we are supposing, then, men are neglected for things, and creative powers for results. A political community, organized and governed according to this system, resembles an agglomerated mass of living but lifeless instruments of action and enjoyment, rather than a multitude of active and enjoying energies. In disregarding the spontaneity of active beings, such States seem to confine their view to the attainment of happiness and enjoyment alone. But although the calculation would be correct in so far as the test of happiness and enjoyment is the sensations of the person enjoying them, it would still underestimate the dignity of human nature. For why otherwise should this very system, which aims at tranquillity, willingly resign the highest human enjoyment, as if fearing disturbance. Joy is greatest in those moments in which man is aware that his individuality and creative energy are at their highest pitch. It is doubtless true that at such times also he is nearest the depth of his greatest misery; for the moment of intensity can only be succeeded by a similar intensity, and fate decides whether it shall be joy or despair. But if the feeling of the highest that human nature can attain deserves the name of happiness, even pain and suffering assume another character. The soul becomes the true seat of happiness or misery, and it does not fluctuate with the tide of circumstance which carries it along. The system we have condemned only leads us to a fruitless struggle to escape pain. But he who truly knows the nature of enjoyment can endure pain, which in spite of everything harries those who flee it; thus he learns to rejoice unceasingly in the steady march of destiny; and the prospect of greatness first and last entices him. Thus he comes to feel what is so rare (except to the enthusiast) that even the moment of what he feels to be his own destruction, may be a moment of the highest ecstasy.[7]

Perhaps I may be charged with having exaggerated the evils enumerated here; but, allowing that there may be important differences in their operation, according to the degree and method of State interference, I must repeat, with this reservation, that it was my task to follow out the working of that interference in its fullest consequences. In general, I would hope that all considerations of a general nature contained in these pages would be considered entirely apart from the details of actual prac-

---

[7] It is not altogether surprising to find that Humboldt in later life, like Schelling and Wagner, took an interest in oriental mysticism. He became an enthusiast for the Bhagavad Gita.

tice. In practice we do not often find any case fully and purely developed, we do not see the true working of single elements separately. And we must not forget that once harmful influences are set in motion, the evil increases with rapidly accelerating strides. Just as a greater force united to a greater produces results doubly multiplied, so do two minor ones quickly degenerate into infinitesimal results. How can one follow the rapidity of these steps? Should we concede, however, that these consequences might be less than we have supposed, we might claim that our own theory might be far more beneficial in the truly inestimable blessings that must flow from the application of its principles, if that application should ever be wholly possible. For the ever-active, restless energy inherent in the very nature of things struggles against every pernicious institution, and actively promotes everything beneficial; so that it is in the highest sense true, that the most active evil influence can never equal the good which is everywhere and at all times being spontaneously produced.

I could here present as an agreeable contrast a picture of a people in the enjoyment of absolute, unfettered freedom, and of the richest diversity of individual and external relations; I could show how, even in such a state, finer and higher and more wonderful forms of diversity and originality must still appear, than even any in Antiquity, which still so unspeakably fascinates us despite the harsher features which inevitably characterize the individuality of a ruder civilization; I could depict a state in which energy would keep pace with refinement and richness of character, and in which, from the endlessly ramified interconnection between all nations and quarters of the globe, the basic elements of human nature themselves would seem more numerous; I could then proceed to show what new forces would ripen, when every being was developing itself spontaneously; when even surrounded, as it would be, by the most beautiful forms, it assimilated them into its own inner being with that unhampered spontaneity which is fostered by freedom. I could point out with what delicacy and refinement the inner life of man would unfold its strength and beauty; how it would become the ultimate object of his activity, and how everything physical and external would be transfused into the inner moral and intellectual being, and the bond which connects man and nature would gain lasting strength, when nothing intervened to disturb the reaction of all human pursuits upon the mind and character; how no single agent would be sacrificed to the interest of another; but while each held fast the measure of energy bestowed on him, he would for that very reason be inspired with a still more beautiful eagerness to direct it to the benefit of the others; how, when every one was developing in his individuality, more varied and finer modifications of the beautiful human character would spring up, and one-sidedness would become more rare, since it is generally the result of feebleness and insufficiency; and how each man, when nothing else would avail to make others assimilate themselves to him, would be obliged to modify his own nature by the continuing necessity of union with others; how, in such a people, no single energy or hand would be lost to the task of ennobling and enhancing human existence; and lastly, how through this focal concentration of energies, the views of all would be directed to this ultimate end alone, and would be turned aside from every other object that was false or less worthy of humanity. I might then conclude, by showing how the beneficial consequences of such a constitution, diffused throughout the people of any nation whatever, would even remove an incalculable amount of that human misery which is never wholly eradicable, of the destructive devastations of nature, of the ravages of human animosity, and of the excesses of a too sensual indulgence. But I content myself with having given a general outline of the contrasting picture; it is enough for me to throw out a few suggestive ideas, for riper judgements to test.

If I come now to the ultimate result of the whole argument, the first principle of this part of the present inquiry must be that *the State is to abstain from all solicitude for the positive welfare of the citizens, and not to proceed a step further than is necessary for their mutual security and protection against foreign enemies; for with no other object should it impose restrictions on freedom.*

I should now turn to the means through which such a solicitude manifests itself in action, but, as the principles I wish to establish wholly disapprove of the thing itself, it is needless to dwell on these. I will content myself with the general observation that the means by which freedom is limited with a view to welfare are very various in their character: laws, exhortations, bounties, which are direct in their operation; and immunities, monopolies, etc. and the power acquired by the sovereign as chief landowner, which are indirect; and that all of them, whether direct or indirect, or however they may differ in kind or degree, are accompanied by pernicious consequences. Should it be objected to these assertions that it appears somewhat strange to deny to the State a privilege which is allowed to every individual, namely to propose rewards, to extend loans, to be a landowner, there would be nothing to say against this if it were possible for the State to consist of a double personality in practice, as it does in theory.[8] In such a case it would be the same as if a private individual had secured to himself a vast amount of influence. But when we reflect (still keeping theory distinct from practice) that the influence of a private person is liable to diminution and decay, from competition, dissipation of fortune, even death; and that clearly none of these contingencies can be applied to the State; we are still left with the principle that the latter is not to meddle in anything which does not refer exclusively to security, a principle whose force is enhanced in that it has not been supported by arguments derived from the nature of coercion alone. A private person, moreover, acts from other motives than the State. If an individual citizen offers bounties which I will agree to suppose are as efficient inducements as those of the State (although this is never perhaps the case), he does so for some interest of his own. Now, from his continual intercourse with his fellow-citizens, and the equality of his condition with theirs, his interest must be closely connected with their advantage or disadvantage, and hence with the circumstances of their respective positions. The end moreover which he wishes to attain is already to some extent anticipated in the present, and therefore produces beneficial results. But the grounds on which the State acts are ideas and principles, which often lead astray the most accurate calculations; and if the reasons arise from considering the State in its private capacity, it may be observed that this is only too often hazardous for the welfare and security of the citizen and further, that the situation of the citizen is never on a level of equality with that of the State. Even if we do consider the State as a private person, it is then no longer the State as such which acts; and the very nature of such reasoning forbids its application in this context.

The point of view from which these last considerations arise, and from which indeed our whole argument proceeds, has no other concern than simply man's energies, as such, and his internal development. Such reasoning could justly be called one-sided if it wholly disregarded the conditions which must exist for those energies to operate at all.

---

[8] Humboldt is referring to the distinction between public and private law.

And while mentioning this, we must not overlook the question that
naturally arises here, which is whether these things which we would
withdraw from the competence of the State could ever flourish without
it, by themselves. We might here consider in turn the different kinds of
handicraft, agriculture, industry, commerce, and all those separate
activities which I have hitherto considered together, and bring in the
aid of technical knowledge to show the advantages and disadvantages
of freedom and *laissez faire* [*Selbstüberlassung*]. Lack of such technical knowledge prevents my entering on such a discussion. I also
believe it to be no longer essential to the main question. Still, such an
investigation well and, what is especially important, historically conducted would be very useful in making these ideas more persuasive,
and judging at the same time the possibility of their being put in practice, however materially modified, for the existing order of things in
any political community would scarcely allow of their unmodified
application. I shall content myself here with a few general reflections.
Every occupation, of whatever nature, is more efficiently performed if
pursued for its own sake alone, rather than for the results to which it
leads. So deeply grounded is this in human nature that what has at first
been chosen for its utility in general becomes ultimately attractive in
itself. Now this arises simply because action is dearer to human nature
than mere possession, but action only in so far as it is spontaneous. It
is precisely the most vigorous and energetic who would prefer inactiv-
ity to compulsory labour. Further, the idea of property grows only in
company with the idea of freedom, and it is to the sense of property
that we owe the most vigorous activity. Every achievement of a great
end requires unity of purpose. This needs no proof. Consider the measures for the prevention of great calamities, famines, floods, etc. But
this unity might as easily proceed from national as from merely governmental arrangements. It is only necessary to extend to the nation
and its different parts the freedom of association. Between a national
and a governmental institution there is always a vast and important difference. The former has only an indirect, the latter a direct influence;
and hence with the former there is always greater freedom of contracting, dissolving and altering associations. It is highly probable that
all political unions were originally nothing more than such national
associations. And here experience shows us the fatal consequences of

combining, with provisions for security, measures to attain other ultimate ends. Whoever is responsible for security must possess absolute
power. But this power he extends to the pursuit of other projects; the
power of an institution increases the further it gets from its source, and
the original contract is forgotten. A political institution, however, only
has force in so far as it adheres faithfully to this original compact and
its authority. This reason alone might seem sufficient; but, granting
even that the fundamental compact was rigidly observed, and that the
State union was, in the strictest sense, a national association, still the
will of the individuals could only be ascertained through a system of
representation; and it is impossible for the representative of a plurality
to be a true organ of all the opinions of those represented. Now the
point to which the whole argument conducts us is the necessity of
securing the consent of every individual. But this very necessity renders the decision by a majority of voices impossible; and yet no other
could be thought of in the case of a State which extended its activity to
include matters affecting the positive welfare of the citizen. Nothing
would be left to the unconsenting but to withdraw from the community
in order to escape its jurisdiction, and prevent the further application of
a majority suffrage to their individual cases. And yet this is almost
impossible when we reflect that to withdraw from the social body
means the same as withdrawing from the State. Furthermore, it is better to enter into separate unions in specific associations, than to contract them generally for unspecified future contingencies; finally, it is
very difficult to establish associations of free men within a nation.
Now if this seems to make more difficult the attainment of ultimate
purposes, it is still certain that every larger association is in general
less beneficial; and it should not be forgotten that whatever is established with difficulty gains greater endurance from the consolidation of
long-tested powers. The more a man acts on his own, the more he
develops himself. In large associations he is too prone to become
merely an instrument. These associations, moreover, are often guilty of
taking the shadow for the substance, which always hinders self-development. The dead hieroglyphic does not inspire like living nature. For
an example, I need only take the case of poor laws. Does anything tend
so effectually to deaden and destroy all true sympathy—all hopeful yet
modest entreaty—all trust in man by man? Does not everyone despise

the beggar, who finds it more convenient to be cared for in an alms-house than, after struggling with want, to find, not a mere hand fling-ing him a pittance, but a sympathizing heart? I admit, in conclusion, that without the great masses, as it were, with which the human race has been working in these last centuries, human progress might not have advanced with such rapid strides; but speed is not everything. The fruit would have been longer in maturing, but still it would really have ripened; and would it not have been more precious? Granting this, it is needless to dwell longer on this objection. But two others remain to be tested: Whether even the maintenance of security would be possible, with those limitations of the State's activity we have here prescribed? and secondly, whether to provide the means which the State must dis-pose of to carry on its activities does not entail a more manifold encroachment upon private relations between citizens by the State machine.

CHAPTER IV

Of the solicitude of the State for the negative welfare of the citizen ▪ For his security

T
o counteract the evil which arises from the tendency man has to transgress his proper limits,*[1] and the discord produced by such unjust encroachment on the rights of others, is the essential object of the creation of the State. If it were the same in these cases, as with the physical ills of nature, or with the working of that moral evil which disturbs the natural order of things through excessive enjoyment or privation, or through other actions inconsistent with that order—then such unions would no longer be necessary. The physical evil would be encountered by the unaided efforts of human courage, skill, and foresight; the moral, by the wisdom which is matured in experience; and with either, in any case, the removal of the evil would end the struggle. Therefore, any ultimate, absolute authority, such as uniquely distinguishes the concept of the State, would be wholly unneeded. But, as it is, human disputes are utterly different, and make absolutely necessary at all times the existence of some such supreme power. For in these dissensions one conflict springs immediately from another. Wrong begets revenge; and revenge is a new wrong. And hence it becomes necessary to look for some species of revenge which does not admit of any further revenge—that is the punishment inflicted by the State—or for a settlement of the contro-

---

* What I am here obliged to convey by a circumlocution, the Greeks expressed in the single word, πλεονεξία, for which, however, I do not find an exact equivalent in any other language. We could say, perhaps, in German: 'Begierde nach mehr' (a desire for more); yet still this would not include the notion of unrightfulness which is conveyed in the Greek expression—at least, if not in the literal meaning of the word, in the constant use of it in their writings. The word 'Uebervortheilung' (taking more than one's share), although still not so full in significance, may approach somewhat nearer to the idea.

1 Cf. J. S. Mill, *On Liberty*, Cambridge ed., pp. 78–9; Toronto ed., pp. 278–9.

versy which the parties are obliged to accept, namely, a judicial decision. There is nothing, moreover, which necessitates such stringent coercion and such unconditional obedience as man's rivalry with his fellow-men, whether we are thinking of the expulsion of foreign enemies, or the preservation of security within the State. Now, without security, it is impossible for man either to develop his powers or to enjoy the fruits of so doing; for, without security, there is no freedom. But this is a condition which man is wholly unable to realize by his own individual efforts; the reasons we have touched on rather than fully developed show this to be true, and it is confirmed by experience; our States, closely knit together as they are by so many treaties and alliances and by mutual fear, which so often prevents the actual outbreaks of violence, are far more favourably placed than we can think of man in the state of nature as being, yet nevertheless they do not possess that freedom which under the most ordinary constitution the meanest subject enjoys. Whilst, therefore, I have hitherto found reasons for denying the competence of the State in many important matters, because the nation can do them equally well and without incurring the evils which flow from State interference, I must for similar reasons direct it to security, as the only thing* which the individual cannot obtain for himself and by his own unaided efforts. I would therefore lay down as the first positive principle—a principle to be more carefully defined and limited in what follows—that the maintenance of security, both against the attacks of foreign enemies and internal dissensions, constitutes the true and proper concern of the State.

Hitherto I have attempted only to define this true end of the State in a negative way, by showing that the State should not extend the limits of its concern any further than this.

This assertion is confirmed by history, in that the kings in all earlier nations were in reality nothing more than leaders in war, and judges in times of peace. I say, kings. For (if I may be allowed the digression), in those very periods in which men most cherish the feeling of freedom—possessing, as they do, little property, and only knowing and prizing personal force, and finding the highest enjoyment in its unrestricted exercise—in those very periods, however strange it may seem, history shows us nothing but kings and monarchies. We observe this in all the Asiatic

---

* 'La sûreté et la liberté personnelle sont les seules choses qu'un être isolé ne puisse s'assurer par lui-même' (Mirabeau, *Sur l'Education publique*, p. 119.)

political unions, in those of the earliest ages of Greece, of Italy, and of those tribes who loved freedom most devotedly of all—the German.* If we reflect on the reasons for this, we are struck with the truth, that the choice of a monarchy is a proof that those who select it enjoy the highest freedom. The idea of a chief ruler arises only, as was said earlier, from the deep-felt necessity for some military leader and umpire of disputes. Now one general or umpire is unquestionably the best solution. Concern that the person selected may ultimately become a master is unknown to the man who is truly free; he does not even dream of such a possibility; he does not believe anyone would have the power to subvert his liberty, nor that any free man would wish to be a master; indeed, the desire for domination, the insensibility to the beauty of freedom, show that a man is in love with slavery, merely not wishing to be a slave himself, and so it is that as the science of morals originated in crime and theology in heresy, so politics sprang into existence with servitude. However, our monarchs certainly do not have the honey-sweet tongues of the kings in Homer and Hesiod.†

---

* 'Reges (nam in terris nomen imperii id primum fuit)', etc. (Sallust, *Catilina*, c. 2) (Kings—for that was the first title of earthly authority, etc.). Κατ' αρχας άπασα πολις Ἑλλας εβασιλευετο (Dion Halicarn., *Antiquit. Rom.*, lib. 5) (all the Grecian States were at first governed by kings, etc.).

†
Ὄντινα τιμήσουσι Διὸς κοῦραι μεγάλοιο,
Γεινόμενόν τ ἐσίδωσι διοτρφέων βασιλήων,
Τῶ μὲν ἐπὶ γλώσση γλυκερὴν χείουσιν ἐερσην,
Τοῦ δ' ἔπε' ἐκ οτόματος ῥεῖ μείλιχα.

Τούνεκα γὰρ βασιλῆες ἐχέφρονες, οὖνεκα λαοῖς
βλαπτόμενοις ἀγορῆφι μετάτροπα ἔργα τελεῦσι
Ῥηϊδίως, μαλακοῖσι παραιφάμενοι ἐπέεσσιν.

(Hesiod, *Theog.*, 81 ff., 88 ff.)

When the watching daughters of Zeus attend with their grace
the honoured birth of a prince of god-nurtured race,
down on his tongue they let a honeydew fall
and his lips pour eloquence out . . .

Therefore so blest a ruler is counted wise;
when the people assembled are erring, his words have force
with gentle ease to persuade the better course.

Jack Lindsay

From *The Oxford Book of Greek Verse in Translation*, edited by T. F. Higham and C. M. Bowra (O.U.P. 1938).

CHAPTER V[1]

On the solicitude of the State for security against foreign enemies

f it were not useful in explaining our principal idea to apply it successively to individual cases, it would not be essential to the present inquiry to make any reference to the subject of security against foreign enemies. But this digression is the less regrettable, so long as I confine my attention to the influence of war on national character, taking the point of view that I have chosen as the guiding principle of the whole inquiry.

Now, regarded in this light, war seems to be one of the most salutary phenomena for the culture of human nature; and it is not without regret that I see it disappearing more and more from the scene. It is the fearful extremity through which all that active courage—all that endurance and fortitude—are steeled and tested, which afterwards achieve such varied results in the ordinary conduct of life, and which alone give it that strength and diversity, without which facility is weakness, and unity is inanity.

It may, perhaps, be argued that there are other means of achieving this—that there are many kinds of activity full of physical danger, and, if I may be allowed the expression, moral dangers also, which beset the firm, unfaltering statesman in the council room, and the free-spirited thinker in his solitary cell. But I cannot divest myself of the belief that as everything spiritual is only a finer development of the physical, so it is in this case. The past still lives, as the stem, as it were, from which these active virtues could continue to spring. But the memory of the past is

---

[1] This chapter and the next were first published in the *Berlinische Monatsschrift* (October and December, 1792).

constantly receding into oblivion; while the number of those in the nation who are influenced by it is always diminishing, its influence even on them tends also gradually to decline. Other pursuits, such as voyaging, mining, and so on, though equally dangerous, lack, to a greater or lesser extent, that inherent idea of greatness and glory so inseparably associated with warlike achievement. This idea is not fanciful, based as it is on the concept of overwhelming power.

As for the elements, we do not try so much to oppose and subdue them, as to escape their effects or endure them—

> Mit Göttern
> Soll sich nicht messen
> Irgend ein Mensch.*2

Deliverance is not victory; what fate beneficently offers, which human courage and ingenuity merely use, is not the result or proof of superior power. In war, moreover, everyone thinks that right is on his side, and that there are wrongs to be avenged; and while man, in a state of nature, thinks it a higher object to redeem his honour than to accumulate the means of subsistence, it is a feeling which even the most civilized cannot disclaim.

No one will suppose that the death of a fallen warrior is more beautiful in my eyes than the death of the fearless Pliny, or, to name men perhaps too little honoured, the death of Robert and Pilâtre de Rozier.3 But such instances are rare; and who knows whether they would ever, even, occur without the memory of those former examples. Moreover I have not deliberately selected the most favourable examples of war. Take the Spartans at Thermopylae: what an influence such an illustrious example of heroism in its sons is likely to exercise on a nation. I know that such courage and self-sacrifice can and does show itself in any situation in life; but can we blame an impressionable man if he is most struck by its most vivid example, and can one deny that such an example has the greatest influence? With all that I have heard of evils more terrible than death, I

---

* Goethe, *Grenzen der Menschheit.*
2 'No man may measure himself against the gods.'
3 Pilâtre de Rozier was an unsuccessful balloonist, who died attempting to cross the English Channel in 1785. 'Robert' is Humboldt's mistaken version of the name of his companion, Romain [L].

never yet knew any but an enthusiast who despised death while still enjoying life to the full. Least of all would we look for such a spirit in antiquity, where things were still esteemed more than names and the present more highly prized than the future. My view of the warrior, then, does not apply to such as were trained up and devoted to warlike pursuits, as in Plato's *Republic*,[4] but to men who take life and death, like other things, for what they really are, and who, having the highest things in view, can dare to risk them. All those situations in which contrasting extremes are most closely and variously intermingled are the most interesting and improving; but of what is this so true as war—where inclination and duty, and the duty of the man and that of the citizen, seem incessantly in conflict, and where, nevertheless, all these conflicts find their fullest solution, as soon as justified self-defence has put weapons into our hands?

To regard war in this light, in which alone it can be considered as either beneficial or necessary, seems to indicate, in my opinion, the nature of the policy to be observed by the State with respect to it. In order to promote the spirit which it engenders, and to diffuse it throughout the whole body of the nation, freedom must be guaranteed. Now this already argues against the maintenance of standing armies. Moreover, these and other modern methods of warfare in general are very far from ideal for promoting human culture. If the warrior in general becomes degraded to a machine as soon as he surrenders his freedom, this degradation must be still more complete and deplorable in our methods of conducting war, in which so much less than formerly depends upon the valour, strength, and skill of the individual. How fatal must the uniformity consequent on such a sacrifice become, when, in time of peace, a considerable portion of the nation is condemned to this machine-like existence—not for a few years only, but often for life—merely to provide against a possible war? Perhaps it is nowhere more obvious than here that with the progressive development of the theory of human enterprises, their usefulness to the men immediately concerned declines. Undoubtedly the art of war has made incredible strides in modern times, but it is equally unquestionable that the nobler characteristics of the warrior have proportionately disappeared, and that it is only in antiquity that we find them in their highest

---

[4] Plato, *Republic*, bk. III.

beauty; or, at least, if this seems exaggerated, that the warlike spirit appears now to bring little but harmful consequences for the nations which entertain it, while in the ancient world we see it so commonly productive of beneficial results. Our standing armies carry war, so to speak, into the very bosom of peace. Now, a warlike spirit is only honourable in conjunction with the highest peaceful virtues, and military discipline, only when allied with the highest feeling of freedom; if these are severed—and how this separation is promoted by the existence of marshalled armies in the midst of peace—the former rapidly degenerates into wild and lawless ferocity, and the latter into slavery.

Still, although I would condemn the maintenance of standing armies, it may be well to observe that I only introduce the subject in this place, in so far as it is required by the point of view I am concerned with. I am far from overlooking their great and undoubted usefulness, which counterbalances the headlong tendency to ruin, to which their faults would otherwise impel them, like everything else on earth. They are a part of the whole, which has been produced not by any plans of vain human reason, but by the sure hand of destiny. To show us by the side of our ancestors, fully and fairly depicted in all the complex uniqueness of our modern life, one would have to show how all its characteristics interact with each other and how they share the praise and blame for all the good or bad that distinguishes it.

I must moreover have been very unfortunate in the exposition of my views, if I am supposed to infer that the State should, from time to time, seek pretexts for war. It may give freedom to its people, and a neighbouring nation may enjoy a like degree of freedom. Men, in every age, are men; and do not lose their original passions. War will arise of itself; and if, under these circumstances, it should not so arise, it is then at least certain that peace has not been gained by compulsion, nor produced artificially by paralysis; and then the peace of nations will be a greater blessing, as the peaceful ploughman is a more pleasing picture than the bloodstained warrior. And if we believe in a progressive civilization of the whole human race, it is indeed certain that the later ages will become gradually more peaceful; but in such a development peace will spring from the internal capacities of men themselves, and men—free men— will have become peaceful. Now—a single year of European history proves it—we enjoy the fruits of peace, but not a spirit of peacefulness.

Human energies, which are always striving towards a ceaseless activity, either unite when they encounter each other, or clash in conflict. The form which this conflict may assume—whether war, or competition, or other nuances which may arise—depends chiefly on the measure of their refinement.

If I may now draw an inference from these arguments helpful to my ultimate purpose, I would lay down the principle—*that the State should in no way attempt to encourage war, but neither should it forcibly interfere to prevent it, when required by necessity; that it should allow perfect freedom to the diffusion of warlike impulses through the spirit and character of the nation, while it especially refrains from all positive institutions calculated to prepare the nation for war; or, where these last are absolutely necessary—as, for instance, in the training of the citizens to the use of arms—that it should give them a direction likely to induce, not only the skill, daring, and subordination of the mere soldier, but animate those under its discipline with the spirit of true warriors, or rather of noble-minded citizens, ready at all times to fight in the defence of their country.*

CHAPTER VI

On the solicitude of the State for the mutual security of the citizens ▪ *Means for attaining this end* ▪ *Institutions for reforming the mind and character of the citizen* ▪ *National education*

I now have to turn to a more profound and explicit investigation into the concern of the State for the mutual security of the citizens. For it does not seem enough merely to commit the care for security to the political power as a general and unconditional duty, but we also need to define the specific limits of its activity in this respect; or, at least, should this general definition be difficult or wholly impossible, to show the reasons for this, and discover the characteristics by which these limits may, in given cases, be recognized.

Even a very limited experience is sufficient to convince us that this interference may be either very limited or very extensive. It can confine itself to correcting actual disorders or it may take precautions for preventing their occurrence, or even adopt the policy of moulding the mind and character of the citizen after the fashion most suitable to its preconceived scheme of social order. Even this extension admits of different degrees. The violation of personal rights, for example, or of the immediate rights of the State, may be investigated and punished, or—by regarding the citizen as accountable to the State for the use of his abilities, and therefore as one who robs it, as it were, of its property when he does anything to weaken or destroy them—a watchful eye may be kept on even those actions which affect none but the agent himself. I shall therefore take all these kinds of interference together and speak in general of all those institutions which have in view the promotion of public security. As I have said, the nature of the subject precludes any strict demarcation, and all those institutions which relate to the moral welfare of the citizen will naturally need to be considered here, for if they do not, in all cases, aim at security and order exclusively, these are in general the main objects of such institutions. I shall therefore adhere to the system I have hitherto adopted. I have so far begun by considering the greatest possible extension of State interference, and then tried step by step to discover where it can be diminished, until at length the concern for security is all that remains. I must now adopt the same method in the case of regulations for security; I will therefore begin by considering their greatest extent, in order to arrive, by successive limitations, at fundamental principles. Should this be regarded as somewhat lengthy and tedious, I am ready to admit that a dogmatic exposition would require exactly the opposite method. But, by confining oneself strictly to an inquiry like the present one, one can at least be sure of having omitted nothing of real importance, and of developing the principles in their natural and consecutive order.

It has, of late, been usual to insist on the expediency and propriety of preventing illegal actions, and of calling in the aid of moral means to accomplish this; but I will not disguise that, when I hear such exhortations, I am glad to think such encroachments on freedom are becoming more rare among us, and in almost all modern constitutions daily less possible.

It is not uncommon to appeal to the history of Greece and Rome in support of such a policy; but a clearer insight into the nature of their constitutions would at once show how inconclusive such comparisons are. Those States were essentially republics; such institutions of this kind as we find in them were pillars of the free constitution, and were regarded by the citizens with an enthusiasm which made their harmful restrictions on private freedom less deeply felt, and their active character less pernicious. They enjoyed, moreover, a much wider range of freedom than ourselves, and anything that was sacrificed was sacrificed only to another form of activity: participation in the affairs of government. Now, in our States, which are in general monarchical, all this is utterly different; and whatever moral means the ancients might employ, such as national education, religion, moral laws, would with us be less fruitful, and productive of far greater harm. We ought not to forget, moreover, in our admiration for antiquity, that what we are so apt to consider the results of wisdom in the ancient legislators was mostly nothing more than the effect of popular custom, which, only when decaying, required the authority and support of legal sanction. The remarkable correspondence that exists between the laws of Lycurgus and the manners and habits of most uncultivated nations has already been clearly and forcibly illustrated by Ferguson;[1] and as the nation grows in culture and refinement, we only discern the faint shadow of such early popular institutions. Lastly, I would observe that men have now reached a pitch of civilization beyond which it seems they cannot ascend except through the development of individuals; and hence all institutions which act in any way to obstruct or thwart this development, and press men together into uniform masses, are now far more harmful than in earlier ages of the world.

It seems to follow, even from these few and general reflections, that national education—or that which is organized or enforced by the State—is at least in many respects very questionable. The grand, leading principle, towards which every argument hitherto unfolded in these pages directly converges, is the absolute and essential importance of human development in its richest diversity;[2] but national education, since at least it presupposes the selection and appointment of some particular instructor, must always promote a definite form of development, however careful to avoid such an error. And hence it is attended with all those disadvantages which, as we have already seen, flow from such a positive policy; and I need only add that every restriction becomes more directly fatal when it operates on the moral part of our nature—that if there is one thing more than another which absolutely requires free activity on the part of the individual, it is precisely education, whose object it is to develop the individual. It cannot be denied that the most beneficial results occur when the citizen becomes spontaneously active in the State itself, in the manner determined by his peculiar lot and circumstances, and when by the conflict, so to speak, between the position pointed out to him by the State, and that which he has spontaneously chosen, he is in part himself

---

[1] Adam Ferguson, *An Essay on the History of Civil Society* (1766) 'Of Rude Nations prior to the Establishment of Property'.

[2] This is the passage quoted by J. S. Mill as the epigraph to *On Liberty* (Cambridge ed., p. 3; Toronto ed., p. 215).

changed, and the State constitution also experiences some modification; and although such influences are not of course immediately evident, they are still distinctly traceable in the history of all States, in the modifications of their national character. Now this interaction always diminishes to the extent that the citizen is trained from childhood to become a citizen. Certainly, it is beneficial when the roles of man and citizen coincide as far as possible; but this only occurs when the role of citizen presupposes so few special qualities that the man may be himself without any sacrifice; which is the goal I have exclusively in mind in this inquiry.

However, the fruitful relationship between man and citizen would wholly cease if the man were sacrificed to the citizen. For although the consequences of disharmony would be avoided, still the very object would be sacrificed which the association of human beings in a community was designed to secure. From which I conclude that the freest development of human nature, directed as little as possible to citizenship, should always be regarded as of paramount importance. He who has been thus freely developed should then attach himself to the State; and the State should test itself by his measure. Only through such a struggle could I confidently hope for a real improvement of the national constitution, and banish all fear of the harmful influence of civil institutions on human nature. For even although these were very imperfect, we could imagine how the force of human energies, struggling against the fetters, and asserting, in spite of them, its own greatness, would ultimately prevail. Still, such a result could only be expected when those energies had been allowed to unfold themselves in all their natural freedom. For what extraordinary efforts must be required to maintain and expand energies cramped by such fetters since earliest youth. Now all systems of national education, governed as they are by the spirit of regulation, impose on nature a special civic form.

When such a form is clearly defined, and beautiful, although one-sided, as we find it to be in the States of antiquity and even now perhaps in many republics, not only do things work more smoothly, but the thing itself is less deplorable. But in our monarchical constitutions, happily enough for human development, such a definite form as that which we describe does not exist. It is clearly among their advantages, however numerous may be the accompanying evils, that since the State is regarded merely as a means, not so much energy is sacrificed to it as in republics.

So long as the citizen obeys the laws, and maintains himself and those dependent on him in comfort, without doing anything calculated to prejudice the interests of the State, the latter does not trouble itself about the particular manner of his existence. Here therefore national education— which, as such, still keeps in view, however imperceptibly, the culture of the citizen in his capacity of subject, and not, as is the case in private education, the development of the individual man—would not be directed to the encouragement of any particular virtue or disposition; it would, on the contrary, be designed to produce a balance, since nothing tends so much to produce and maintain tranquillity, which is precisely the object most eagerly desired by such States. But such an artificial equilibrium, as I have already observed elsewhere, leads to sterility or lack of energy; while, on the other hand, the pursuit of particular objects which is characteristic of private education produces an equilibrium more surely without sacrifice of energy, through a variety of relationships.

But even though we were to deny to national education all positive contribution to culture of any kind, if we were to make it its duty simply to encourage the spontaneous development of men's faculties, this would still prove impracticable, since whatever has unity of organization invariably produces a corresponding uniformity of results,[3] and thus, even when based on such principles, the utility of national education is still inconceivable. If it is only intended to prevent the possibility of children remaining uninstructed, it is much more convenient and less harmful to appoint guardians where parents are remiss, or to subsidize them when they are indigent. Furthermore, national education fails in accomplishing its object, namely, the reformation of morals according to the model which the State considers most suitable. However great the influence of education may be, and however it may extend to the whole course of a man's actions, still, the circumstances which surround him throughout his whole life are far more important. And hence, if all these do not harmonize with its influences, education alone cannot achieve its objects.

In fine, if education is only to develop a man's faculties, without regard to giving human nature any special civic character, there is no need for the State's interference. Among men who are really free, every

---

[3] Cf. J. S. Mill: 'A general State education is a mere contrivance for moulding people to be exactly like one another' (*On Liberty*, Cambridge ed., p. 106; Toronto ed., p. 302).

form of industry becomes more rapidly improved—all the arts flourish more gracefully—all the sciences extend their range. In such a community, too, family ties become closer; parents are more eagerly devoted to the care of their children, and, in a state of greater well-being, are better able to carry out their wishes with regard to them. Among such men emulation naturally arises; and tutors educate themselves better when their fortunes depend upon their own efforts than when their chances of promotion rest on what they are led to expect from the State. There would, therefore, be no want of careful family training, nor of those private educational establishments which are so useful and indispensable.*

But if national education is to impose some definite form on human nature, one can be perfectly certain that it actually does nothing towards preventing transgressions of law, or establishing and maintaining security. For virtue and vice do not depend on being any particular kind of person, nor are necessarily connected with any particular aspect of character; much more depends on the harmony or discordancy of all the different features of a man's character—on the proportion that exists between his energies and the sum of his inclinations, etc. Every distinct development of character is capable of its peculiar excess, and to this it constantly tends to degenerate. If then an entire nation has committed itself to some particular kind of development, it comes in time to lose all power of resisting the prevailing bias to this one peculiarity, and along with it all power of regaining its equilibrium. Perhaps it is in this that we discover the reason for such frequent changes in the constitution of ancient States. Every fresh constitution exercised an undue influence on the national character, and this, once developed, degenerated in turn and necessitated a new one.

Lastly, even if we admit that national education may succeed in the accomplishment of all its purposes, it does too much. For in order to maintain the security it envisages, the reformation of the national morals is not at all necessary. But as my reasons for taking this position refer to the whole concern with morality on the part of the State, I reserve them for a later part of this inquiry, and turn meanwhile to consider some par-

---

* 'Dans une société bien ordonnée, au contraire, tout invite les hommes à cultiver leurs moyens naturels: sans qu'on s'en mêle, l'éducation sera bonne; ella sera même d'autant meilleure, qu'on aura plus laissé à l'industrie des maîtres et à l'émulation des élèves' (Mirabeau, *Sur l'Education publique*, p. 11).

ticular measures which are often suggested by this concern. I need only conclude from what has been argued here that national education seems to me to lie wholly beyond the limits within which the State's activity should properly be confined.*

---

* 'Ainsi c'est peut-être un problème de savoir, si les législateurs Français doivent s'occuper de l'éducation publique autrement que pour en protéger les progrès, et si la constitution la plus favorable au développement du moi humain, et les lois les plus propres à mettre chacun à sa place, ne sont pas la seule éducation que le peuple doive attendre d'eux' (Mirabeau, *Sur l'Education publique*, p. 11). 'D'après cela, les principes rigoureux sembleraient exiger que l'Assemblée Nationale ne s'occupât de l'éducation que pour l'enlever à des pouvoirs ou à des corps qui peuvent en dépraver l'influence' (*ibid*. p. 12).

CHAPTER VII

Religion[1]

Besides the education of the young, there is another important means of exercising an influence on the morals and character of a nation, through which the State endeavours to educate, as it were, the full-grown man, accompanies him throughout the whole course and conduct of his life—his ways of thinking and acting—and aims at giving them some specific and preconceived direction, or forestalling probable deviations from the path it prescribes—this is religion.

History shows us that all States have used this source of influence, but with very different designs, and in very different degrees. In the ancient nations it was completely interwoven with the political constitution, it was, in fact, a guiding principle and essential pillar of the State; and hence all that I have said of other ancient institutions applies no less aptly to religion. When the Christian religion, instead of the earlier local deities of nations, taught men to believe in a universal God of humanity, thereby throwing down one of the most dangerous barriers which separated the different tribes of the great human family from each other; and when it thus succeeded in laying the foundation for all true human virtue, human development, and human cooperation, without which enlightenment and even science and learning would have long, and perhaps always, remained the rare property of a few, it also directly worked to loosen the strong bond that formerly existed between religion and the political constitution. But when, afterwards, the incursion of the barbarian tribes had

---

[1] This chapter almost exactly repeats Humboldt's earlier essay *Über Religion* (1789) though it is even more hostile to State interference. The question it discusses had been made a public issue by a recent law of Frederick William II in 1788 declaring Lutheranism the State religion and threatening penalties for those who did not conform.

banished enlightenment—when a misconception of that very religion inspired a blind and intolerant rage for proselytism; and when, at the same time, the political form of States underwent such changes that citizens were transformed into subjects, and these not so much the subjects of the State as of the person in whom the government was vested—the concern for religion, its preservation and extension, was left to the conscientiousness of princes, who believed it confided to their hands by God himself. In our times this prejudice has, comparatively speaking, ceased to prevail; but the promotion of religion by laws and State institutions has been no less urgently recommended by considerations of internal security, and of morality, its strongest bulwark. These, then, I regard as the principal distinctive epochs in the history of religion as a political element, although I am not prepared to deny that all these reasons, and especially the last, have been cooperating throughout, while at each period, doubtless, one of them prevailed.

In the endeavour to act upon morality through the medium of religious ideas, it is especially necessary to distinguish between the propagation of a particular form of religion, and the diffusion of a spirit of religiousness in general. The former is undoubtedly more oppressive in its character, and more harmful in its consequences; but, without it, the latter is hardly possible. For when once the State believes morality and religiousness to be inseparably associated, and considers that it can and may avail itself of this method of influence, it is scarcely possible not to take one religion in preference to any others under its protection, according to its conformity to true, or generally accepted, ideas of morality. Even where it aims at wholly avoiding this partiality, and assumes the position of protector or defender of all religious parties, it can only judge by outward expressions, and must therefore indirectly favour the beliefs of such parties, suppressing other possible beliefs of individuals; and in any case, it shows its concern for one opinion at least, in that it strives to render the influence of belief in a God the prevailing one. It will be evident, moreover, that, owing to the vagueness and ambiguity of all expressions, which enable them to convey so many different ideas by the same general word, the State itself would be obliged to supply some definite interpretation of the term religiousness, before it could apply it in any way as a clear rule of conduct. So that I would absolutely deny the possibility of any State interference in religious affairs which should not be more or less responsible for encouraging certain distinct opinions, and was not therefore open to arguments against it on that account. Neither can I grant the possibility of any such interference, without the accompaniment of some guiding and controlling influence—some restraint on the freedom of the individual. For, however widely certain kinds of influence may differ from coercion—such as exhortation, or the mere creation of opportunities—there still exists, even in the last of these (as we have already tried to demonstrate more fully in the case of several similar institutions), a certain preponderance of the State's views, which is calculated to repress and diminish freedom.

I have thought it necessary to make these preliminary observations in order to anticipate an objection that might, perhaps, be advanced as I proceed, which is that in the views I hold of the consequences of a patronage of religion, my attention was confined to the encouragement of certain particular forms, to the exclusion of the possibility of a care for religion in general; and I hoped moreover in this way to avoid needlessly fragmenting my inquiry by a too minute review of the possible individual cases.

All religion rests upon a need of the soul. I am speaking here, obviously, of religion in its relation to morality and happiness. I am not considering religion in so far as reason perceives, or fancies it perceives, any religious truth; for the perception of truth is independent of all influence from the will or desire; nor in so far as revelation tends to strengthen any particular belief; since even historical belief should be exempt from all such influences. We hope, we dread, because we desire. Wherever there is no vestige of spiritual culture, this need is purely sensuous. Fear and hope with regard to the phenomena of external nature, which are transformed by imagination into personal agencies, constitute the whole sum of religion. But when culture dawns on the spirit, this is no longer sufficient and satisfying. The soul then yearns towards a revelation of perfection, of which a spark faintly glimmers in itself, but of which it has an intuition existing in a far higher degree outside itself. This first intuition gradually merges into wonder; and conceiving of himself as in some relation to this higher existence, man's wonder ripens into love, from which there springs a longing to assimilate himself to this outward manifestation of perfection. This development of the religious idea is even true of nations in the lowest grade of civilization; for it is in this way that, even among the rudest tribes, the chiefs of the people are brought to believe themselves lineally descended from the gods, and destined, after death, to return to them. Only the actual conception of the divine nature varies according to the different ideas of perfection which prevail in particular ages and nations. The gods of the remoter ages of Greece and Rome, and those worshipped by our own earliest forefathers, were simply ideals of bodily strength and prowess. As the idea of sensuous beauty arose and gradually became refined, the sensuous personification of beauty was exalted to the throne of deity; and hence arose what we might call the religion of art. When men ascended from the sensuous to the purely spiritual, from the beautiful to the good and true, the sum of all moral and intellectual perfection[2] became the object of their adoration, and religion became the province of philosophy. It might perhaps be possible to estimate the comparative worth of different religions according to this ascending scale, if it were true that religion derived its distinguishing characteristics from nations and sects, and not from the nature of single individuals. But, as it is, religion is wholly subjective, and depends solely on each individual's unique conception of it.

When the idea formed of divinity is the fruit of true spiritual culture, its reaction on the inner perfection of the individual is at once beneficial and beautiful. All things assume a new form and meaning in our eyes when regarded as the creations of a providential design, and not the work of senseless chance. The ideas of wisdom, order, and purpose—ideas so necessary to the conduct of our own actions, and even to the culture of the intellect—strike deeper root into our souls when we discover them everywhere around us. The finite becomes, as it were, infinite; the perishable, enduring; the fleeting, stable; the complex, simple—when we contemplate one great regulating cause on the summit of things, and regard what is spiritual as endlessly enduring. Our search after truth, our striving after perfection, gain greater certainty and consistency when we can believe in the existence of a being who is at once the source of all truth, and the sum of all perfection. The soul becomes less sensible of the chances and changes of fortune, when it learns how to connect hope and confidence with such calamities. The feeling of receiving everything we possess from the hand of love tends equally to exalt our moral excellence

---

[2] *Vollkommenheit* (perfection) may also be translated as 'completeness.'

and enhance our happiness. Through a sense of gratitude for enjoyment—through trust in a hoped-for joy—the soul is drawn out of itself; it no longer constantly broods in jealous isolation over its own sensations, its own plans, hopes, and fears. Should it lose the exalting feeling of owing everything to itself, it still enjoys the rapture of living in the love of another, a feeling in which its own perfection is united with the perfection of the other. It becomes disposed to be to others what others are to it; it does not wish to see in them the same insensibility that it has itself renounced. I have only touched here on the most outstanding features of the subject; to enter into it more fully, after the masterly exposition of Garve,[3] would be both useless and presumptuous.

But although the influence of religious ideas unmistakably harmonizes and cooperates with the process of moral perfection, it is no less certain that such ideas are in no way inseparably associated with that process.[4] The simple idea of moral perfection is great, and inspiring, and exalted enough to require no other veil or form; and every religion is based on personification to a greater or less degree, represents itself in some shape of appeal to the senses, in some kind of anthropomorphism. The idea of perfection will still hover in front of a man, even if he is not accustomed to think in terms of the sum of all moral excellence in one absolute ideal, and to conceive of himself as in a relation with an ideal being: it will be to him the incentive to activity, and the stuff of all his happiness. Firmly assured by experience of the possibility of raising his soul to a higher degree of moral perfection, he will strive with valiant ardour to reach the goal he has set before him. The thought of his possible annihilation will no longer alarm him, when his delusive imagination no longer sees nothingness in his own non-existence. His unalterable dependence on external fate no longer daunts him: comparatively indifferent to external joys and privations, he regards only what is purely moral and intellectual; and no freak of destiny can disturb the calm, inner life of his soul. His spirit feels itself raised above the flux of things through its perfect self-sufficiency, through the richness of its own ideas and the consciousness of its inner

---

[3] Christian Garve, *Philosophische Anmerkungen und Abhandlungen zu Ciceros 'Büchem von den Pflichten, II'* (Breslau, 1783), 23 [L]. Christian Garve was the first German translator of Adam Ferguson. He was an Idealist metaphysician and apologist for Enlightened Despotism.

[4] This was the fundamental contention of Humboldt's essay, *Über Religion*.

strength. And then when he looks back to his past, and retraces his progress, step by step; when he sees how he made use of circumstances, now
in this way, now in that; how he gradually arrived at what he now is;
when he sees cause and effect, ends and means united in himself, and,
full of the noblest pride of which finite beings are capable, exclaims,

> Hast du nicht alles selbst vollendet,
> Heilig, glühend Herz?[5]

then all thoughts of his lonely life—of helplessness, of failing support
and consolation, disappear. These are thoughts which, as we believe, are
mostly found in those in whose minds the idea of a personal, superintending, rational cause of the chain of finite being is lacking. This self-consciousness, moreover, this living solely in and through himself, need not
render the moral man hard and insensitive to others, or shut out from his
heart every loving sympathy and benevolent impulse. This very idea of
perfection, the goal of all his actions, is really not a mere cold abstraction
of the reason, but a warm impulse of the heart, which draws his own
being towards that of others. For in them too there exists a similar capacity for greater perfection, and this he may be able to elicit or improve
upon. He is not yet filled with the highest idea of morality, so long as he
can be content to regard himself or others as isolated—so long as in his
mind all spiritual being does not flow together into a single complete
whole in which all individualities are resolved. Perhaps his union with
other beings like himself is still more intimate, and his sympathy with
their fortunes warmer, in proportion as their fates and his own seem to
him to be dependent only on themselves.

If it is objected to this picture, and it is a fair objection, that to realize it
would be beyond the normal capacity of the human mind and character,
one must remember that this is equally the case for religious feelings to
become the basis in a man's character, of a truly beautiful life, equally
free from coldness on the one hand and enthusiasm on the other. The
force of this objection could only be admitted, moreover, if I had particularly demanded the cultivation of that harmony which I have just
endeavoured to portray. But, as it is, my only object was to show that

---

[5] 'Hast thou not accomplished everything thyself, holy, ardent heart' (Goethe,
Prometheus, II, 63).

human morality, even the highest and most consistent, is not at all dependent on religion, or in general necessarily connected with it, and incidentally to contribute a few additional reasons for rejecting the faintest shadow of intolerance, and for promoting the respect which we should always entertain for the individual thoughts and feelings of our fellow-men. If it were necessary still further to justify this view of morality, it would be easy to draw a contrasting picture of the pernicious influences as well as the good to which the most religious feelings are susceptible. But it is painful to dwell on such unpleasant themes, and history already supplies enough examples. It may provide more evidence in favour of the principles we advocate to cast a hasty glance at the nature of morality itself, and at the close relation of religious systems, as well as of religious feeling, to human sensibility.

Now, neither what morality prescribes as a duty, nor what enforces its dictates and recommends them to the will, is dependent on religious ideas. I will not dwell on the consideration that such a dependence would even impair the purity of the moral will.[6] In reasoning derived from experience, and to be applied to it, this position might not be thought sufficiently valid. But the qualities of an action which make it a duty arise partly from the nature of the human soul, and partly from their particular application to human relations; and, although it is certain that these qualities are especially recommended by religious feeling, this is neither the sole medium of impressing them on the heart, nor by any means applicable to every kind of character. On the contrary, religion depends wholly for its efficacy on the individual disposition, and is, in the strictest sense, subjective.[7] The man whose character is cold and essentially reflective— for whom knowledge is never sensuous—for whom it is enough to see clearly the connection between facts and behaviour for him to bend his will accordingly, needs no religious motive to induce him to virtuous action, and, as far as such a character can be, to be virtuous. But it is wholly otherwise where the sensibility is particularly strong, and every thought rapidly merges into feeling. And yet even here the nuances are endless. For example, where the soul feels a strong impulse to pass out of

---

[6] Humboldt seems here to be referring to the Kantian doctrine that only completely disinterested actions are moral actions as such.

[7] Cf. J. S. Mill: 'different persons also require different conditions for their spiritual development' (*On Liberty,* Cambridge ed., p. 68; Toronto ed., p 270).

itself, and establish a union with others, religious ideas will be an efficient stimulus. But, on the other hand, there are characters in which there
is such an intimate relation between all feelings and ideas, which have
such depths of understanding and emotion that they acquire a strength and
self-reliance which neither feels the need for nor permits that surrender of
the whole self to another, that trust in an external power, in which religious influences show themselves. Even the circumstances which draw
men back to religious ideas are different for different characters. With
one man, every powerful emotion, joyful or sorrowful, suffices; with
another, only the outflow of gratitude for pleasure. Perhaps such characters as the last are far from being the least estimable. On the one hand,
they are strong enough not to look for external help in trial and misfortune, while they have, on the other hand, too keen a sense of the feeling
of being loved, not to associate with the idea of enjoyment the concept of
a loving benefactor. The longing for religious ideas, moreover, often has
a still nobler, purer, and, so to speak, a more intellectual source. Whatever man beholds in the world around him, he perceives only through the
medium of the senses; the pure essence of things is nowhere immediately
revealed to him; even what inspires him with the most ardent love, and
takes the strongest hold on his whole nature, is shrouded in the thickest
veil. There are some whose whole life is an active striving to penetrate
this veil, whose whole pleasure consists of a presentiment of truth in the
enigma which is wrapped in the symbol, whose hope is uninterruptedly to
contemplate it in other periods of their existence. Now it is when, in
wonderful and beautiful harmony, the mind is thus restlessly searching,
and the heart longing for this immediate contemplation of the creative
being, when the aridity of concepts is inadequate to the profound power
of thought, the shadowy images of the imagination and the senses, to the
living warmth of feeling—it is then that belief immediately follows the
particular bent of reason, to enlarge every concept beyond all barriers, as
far as the ideal itself. Then it adheres to the idea of a Being which com-
prehends all other beings, and, purely and without any medium, exists,
contemplates, and creates. But, on the other hand, in some minds a cau-
tious discretion confines belief within the realm of experience: often,
indeed, the emotions are satisfied with this ideal, usually regarded as
peculiar to reason, but they find a more pleasurable fascination in the
attempt to weave man's sensuous and spiritual natures closer together;

and, confining themselves to this world, to give a richer significance to the symbol, and to truth a more intelligible and suggestive symbolism. Hence man is often compensated for the loss of the drunken exaltation of hopeful anticipation, by a constant consciousness of the success of his attempts not to allow his attention to wander away into infinity. The less bold way is the more certain; the conception of reason to which he closely clings is clearer, though less rich; the intimations of the senses, although less faithful to the truth, are closer to experience, and therefore more useful to him. On the whole, there is nothing which the mind so gladly and wholeheartedly admires as a wise order preserved among a countless number of different and even antagonistic individuals. Yet this admiration is far more characteristic of some minds than others; and these more readily embrace a belief according to which one being created and regulates the universe, and maintains it by a wise surveillance. To others, individuality seems more sacred; they are more attracted by this idea than by that of a universal order; and to such minds an opposite system is more usually and more naturally suggested; one in which the individual essence, developing itself out of its own resources, and modified by reciprocal influences, itself creates that perfect harmony in which alone the human heart and mind can find rest. I am far from supposing that I have exhausted in these inadequate descriptions a subject which is so copious as to defy classification. My only object has been to show, by a few illustrative examples, that not only all true religious feeling, but every true system of religion, proceeds, in the highest sense, from the inner structure of human sensibility.

Now, it is doubtless true that the conceptions of design, order, providence, and perfection, or all that is purely intellectual in religious ideas, is wholly independent of peculiar sensibilities or the necessary differences of character. But while we allow this, we need to add that we are not now regarding these ideas in the abstract, but rather in their influence on men, who are not purely intellectual to the same extent; and to observe further that such ideas are not by any means the exclusive property of religion. The idea of perfection is at first derived from our impressions of animate nature, and, thence transferred to the inanimate, it approaches, step by step, to the notion of an absolute, unlimited totality. But animate and inanimate nature have the same lessons for all, and might it not be possible to advance through all the preceding steps, and still to pause before the last? Now, if all religiousness depends so absolutely on the various phases and modifications of character, and more particularly of feeling, the influence it exercises on morality cannot be based on the form and content of accepted propositions, but on the particular manner of their acceptance—on conviction and belief. This conclusion may now, I hope, be taken as established, for I shall make further use of it later. The only objection, perhaps, to which my treatment of this entire question may fairly be open is that I have confined my observations to men who are favoured both by nature and by circumstances, and are for that reason so rare, and interest us so much. But I hope to show that I am far from overlooking the masses of which society is mainly composed; it strikes me as ignoble to begin from any but the highest point of view whenever human nature is the subject of inquiry.

If, after these general considerations on religion, and the nature of its influence in human life, I now return to the question whether the State should employ it as a means for reforming the morals of its citizens, it will be granted that the methods adopted by the legislator for the promotion of moral culture are always appropriate, and efficient, according to the extent that they foster the internal development of abilities and inclinations. For all moral culture springs solely and immediately from the inner life of the soul, and can only be stimulated in human nature, and never produced by external and artificial contrivances. Now, it is unquestionable that religion, which is wholly based on ideas, sensations, and internal convictions, affords precisely such a means of influencing a man's nature from within. We develop the artist by accustoming his eye to the masterpieces of art; we nourish his imagination by a study of the beautiful models of antiquity; and in the same way, moral development is achieved through the contemplation of moral perfection, in the school of social intercourse, in history suitably presented, and lastly in the contemplation of its highest, most ideal perfection in the image of Divinity. And yet, as I have already shown, this last glimpse of moral perfection is scarcely appropriate for every eye, or rather, to abandon metaphor, this manner of conception is only adapted to certain varieties of character. But even if this method of self-development were universally possible, it would only be efficient when grounded on the perfect cooperation of all ideas and sensations, or when unfolded from the inner life of the soul, rather than imposed on it from without. Hence the only means which the legislator can use must be by removing obstacles that prevent the citizen from becoming aware of religious ideas,[8] and by promoting a spirit of free inquiry. If, going further, he seeks directly to promote a religious spirit;[9] if he protects certain definite religious ideas; or if, lastly, he dares to require a belief according to authority instead of a true and sincere conviction, he will hinder the spirit's aspiration and the development of the powers of the soul; and, although he may work on the citizen's imagination through his feelings and succeed in bringing his actions into conformity with the law, he can never produce true virtue. For this is independent of all particular forms of religious belief, and incompatible with any that is required by, and believed on, authority.

If, however, the influence of certain religious principles tends to encourage only law-abiding actions, is this not enough to entitle the State to spread them, even at the sacrifice of general freedom of thought? The State's object is surely fully accomplished when its laws are strictly observed; and the legislator seems to have done his duty when he has succeeded in framing wise laws, and seen how to secure their observance by the citizen. The idea of virtue, moreover, which has just been presented, is only adapted to a few classes of the political community, of those, namely, whose position enables them to devote their time and means to the process of internal development. The State has to care for the majority, and these are incapable of that higher degree of morality.

It would be a sufficient answer to this objection to reiterate the principle established in the former part of this essay—that the State is not in itself an end, but is only a means towards human development; and hence, that it is not enough for the legislator to succeed in maintaining his authority, so long as the means through which that authority operates are not at the same time good, or, at least, innocuous. But apart from this fundamental principle, it is erroneous to suppose that only the citizen's actions and their legal propriety are important for the State. A State is such a complex and intricate machine that its laws, which must always be few in number, and simple and general in their nature, cannot possibly prove fully adequate here. The greater part is always left to the voluntary

[8] In Humboldt's earlier essay *Über Religion*, the text at this point reads: 'by *causing* the citizen to become aware of religious ideas'. Humboldt, *Gesammelte Schriften* (ed. F. Leitzmann; Berlin, 1903), I, 70. Italics mine.
[9] This phrase is omitted in *Über Religion, loc. cit.*

and cooperative efforts of the citizens. To demonstrate this, it is only necessary to contrast the prosperity of a cultivated and enlightened people with the deficiencies of the ruder and less civilized. It is for this reason that all who have occupied themselves with political affairs have invariably been animated with the desire to render the well-being of the State the direct, personal interest of the citizen. They have tried to turn the State into a machine, which would be kept working by the inner force of its springs, and not require the continual application of new external impulses. Indeed, if modern States can claim any marked superiority over those of antiquity, it is chiefly in the fact that they have more fully and clearly realized this principle. That they have done so, the very circumstance of their employing religion as a means of culture is itself a proof. But still, even religion, in so far as it is designed to produce good actions alone, by the faithful observance of certain positive principles, or to exercise a positive influence on morals in general—even religion is an extraneous agency, and works only from without. Hence it should always remain the ultimate object of the legislator—an object which a true knowledge of human nature will convince him is attainable only by granting the highest degree of freedom—to raise the culture of the citizen to such a point that he may find every incentive to cooperation in the State's designs, in the consciousness of the advantages which the political institution offers his own individual interests. Such an understanding, however, implies enlightenment and a high degree of mental culture, which can never spread where the spirit of free inquiry is fettered by laws.

Meanwhile, the propriety of such interference is only acknowledged, because of the conviction that outward peace and morality cannot be secured without fixed, generally accepted religious principles, or, at least, without the State's supervision of the citizen's religion, and that without these it would be impossible to preserve the authority of the law. However, the influence exercised by religious dogmas received in this fashion, and indeed by any manifestation of a religious spirit called forth by political institutions, needs a stricter and closer examination. Now, as regards the acceptance of religious truth by the less cultivated masses of the people, most reliance is to be placed in the idea of future rewards and punishments. But these do nothing to lessen the propensity to immoral actions, or to strengthen the inclination to good, and therefore cannot improve the character: they simply work on the imagination, and there-

fore influence action as do images of fancy in general; but that influence
is similarly dissipated and destroyed by all that weakens the vitality of the
imagination. If we remember, moreover, that even in the minds of the
most faithful believers these expectations are so remote, and therefore so
uncertain, that they lose much of their efficiency from the thoughts of
subsequent reformation, of future repentance, of hopes of pardon, which
are so much encouraged by certain religious ideas, it will be difficult for
us to conceive how such tenets can do more to influence conduct than the
certain belief in civil punishments, which, with good police arrangements, are near and certain in their operation, and are not to be averted by
any possibility of repentance or subsequent reformation. Provided only
that the citizen is familiarized with the retributive certainty of these punishments from his childhood, and taught to trace the consequences of
moral and immoral actions, we cannot suppose such immediate influences to be less effectual than the other, more remote ideas.

But, on the other hand, undoubtedly even comparatively unenlightened
conceptions of religion often influence a large part of the people in a
nobler fashion. The thought of being an object of loving care to an all-
wise and perfect being gives them new dignity; the trust in eternity leads
them to a higher point of view, and brings more order and purpose to
their actions; the feeling of the loving goodness of God gives their souls a
similar disposition; and, in short, religion tends to inspire men with a
sense of the beauty of virtue. But for religion to have these effects it must
permeate the mind and sensibility, which is not possible where the spirit
of free inquiry is hampered, and everything is made a matter of faith:
before such results could follow, moreover, there must have been some
latent sense of better feelings, which must be taken as an undeveloped
tendency towards morality, which positive morality subsequently merely
shaped. And, on the whole, no one will be disposed utterly to deny the
influence of religion on morality; the only question at issue is whether
that influence rests on a few religious dogmas, and, secondly, whether it
is so clear that there is an indissoluble connection between them. Both
questions, I believe, must be answered in the negative. Virtue harmonizes
so well with man's original inclinations; the feelings of love, of sociabil-
ity, of justice, have in them something so sweet, those of disinterested
effort and self-sacrifice, something so uplifting, and the relations which
grow out of these feelings in domestic and social life contribute so much

to human happiness, that it is far less necessary to look for new incentives
to virtuous action, than simply to secure for those already in the soul a
more free and unhindered operation.

Should we however wish to go further, and try to find new encouragements to morality, we should not forget, through partiality, to set their
usefulness against their possible harm. After so much has been said of the
pernicious results arising from restrictions on freedom of thought, it
hardly seems necessary to emphasize this, and I have, besides, already
dwelt sufficiently, in the former part of this chapter, on the harm done by
all positive promotion of religious feeling by the State. If the harmful
consequences were confined merely to the results of intellectual inquiries—if they occasioned nothing more than incompleteness or inexactness
in our scientific knowledge, we might reasonably assess the advantages
which might perhaps be expected to flow from such a policy. But, as it
is, the danger is far more serious. The importance of free inquiry extends
to our whole manner of thinking, and even acting. The man who is accustomed to judge of truth and error for himself, and to hear them similarly
discussed by others, without fear of the consequences, weighs the principles of action more calmly and consistently, and from a higher point of
view, than one whose inquiries are constantly influenced by a variety of
circumstances not properly part of the inquiry itself. Inquiry, and the conviction which springs from free inquiry, is spontaneity; while belief is
reliance on some outside power, some external perfection, moral or intellectual. Hence there is more self-reliance and firmness in the inquiring
thinker, more weakness and indolence in the trusting believer. It is true
that where belief has stifled every form of doubt and gained the supreme
mastery, it often creates a far more irresistible courage and extraordinary
endurance, as we see in the history of all enthusiasts; but this kind of
energy is never desirable except when some definite external result is in
question, which requires such a machine-like activity for its accomplishment; and it is wholly inapplicable in cases which imply individual decision, deliberate actions grounded on principles of reason, and, above all,
internal perfection. The strength which supports such enthusiasm is
wholly dependent on the suppression of all activity in the reason. Doubt
is torture only to the believer, and not to the man who follows the results
of his own inquiries; for, to him results are generally far less important.
During the inquiry, he is conscious of his soul's activity and strength; he

feels that his perfection, his happiness, depend upon this power; and instead of being oppressed by his doubts about the propositions he formerly took to be true, he congratulates himself that his increasing mental powers enable him to see clearly through errors that he had not till now perceived. The believer, on the contrary, is only interested in the result itself, for, the truth once perceived, there is nothing further to be sought for. The doubts which reason arouses afflict and depress him, for they are not, as in the case of one who thinks for himself, new means for arriving at truth; they deprive him of certainty without revealing any other method of recovering it. If we were to follow these suggestive considerations, we should be led to observe that it is in general wrong to attribute so much importance to any particular results, and to suppose that either so many other truths, or so many useful consequences, internal and external, are necessarily dependent on them. It is because of such a belief that the course of inquiry so often comes to a standstill, and that the most free and enlightened conclusions react against the basis of thought without which they could not have arisen. Hence it is that freedom of thought is so vital, and anything that diminishes it so fatal.

The State on the other hand has no lack of means for enforcing the authority of its laws, and preventing crime. If one closes up the sources of immoral actions to be found in the State constitution itself; if one sharpens the vigilance of the police with regard to crimes actually perpetrated; if one punishes judiciously, the desired end will be achieved. It cannot surely be forgotten that freedom of thought, and the enlightenment which only flourishes beneath its shelter, are the most efficient of all means for promoting security. While all other methods are confined to the mere suppression of actual outbreaks, free inquiry acts immediately on the dispositions and sentiments; and while everything else only produces outward conformity, it creates internal harmony between will and activity. When shall we learn, moreover, to set less value on the outward results of actions than on the inner temper and disposition from which they flow? When will the man arise to do for legislation what Rousseau did for education, and draw our attention from mere external, physical results to the internal self-education of mankind. One should not think that this freedom of thought and enlightenment would be for a few only, that to the majority, whose energies are exhausted by providing for the physical necessities of life, such opportunities would be useless or even positively harmful, and that the only way to influence the masses is to promulgate some definite beliefs, and to restrict freedom of thought. There is something degrading to human nature in the idea of refusing to any man the right to be a man. There are none so hopelessly low on the scale of culture and refinement as to be incapable of rising higher; and even though the more enlightened views of philosophy and religion could not immediately convince a large part of the community, and though it should be necessary to dress truth in different clothing before it could find a place among their ideas, so that one would have to appeal to their feelings and imagination rather than to the cold decision of reason, still, the diffusion of scientific knowledge by freedom and enlightenment spreads gradually downward even to them; and the beneficial results of complete liberty of thought on the mind and character of the entire nation extend their influence even to its humblest individuals.

In order to give a more general character to this reasoning which bears mainly on the question whether the State should try to spread particular religious doctrines, I have to reintroduce the principle that all influence of religion on morality depends especially, if not entirely, on the form in which religion exists in the individual man, rather than on the content of the propositions which it makes sacred in his eyes. Now, all State institutions, as I also tried to show earlier, act solely on this content to a greater or less degree; while the form of their acceptance by the individual is untouchable by the State. The way in which religion springs up in the human heart, and the way in which it is received, depend entirely on the whole manner of the man's existence, of his thoughts and sensations. But, if the State were in a position to remodel these according to its views (the impossibility of which is undeniable), I must have been very unfortunate in the exposition of my principles if it were necessary to repeat the reasons why the State may not make man an instrument to serve its arbitrary ends, overlooking his individual purposes. And that there is no absolute necessity, which would perhaps alone justify an exception, is apparent from the independence of morality from religion which I have already tried to establish, but which will appear in a clearer light when I show that the preservation of a State's internal security does not at all require that a prescribed direction should be given to the national morals in general. Now, if there is one thing more calculated than another to prepare a fertile soil for religion in the minds of the citizens—if there is anything to make that religion, which has been firmly grasped, and received into the prevailing system of ideas and sensibility, react beneficially on morality—it is freedom, which always suffers from the interference, however slight, of the State. For the greater the diversity and individuality of man's development, and the more sublime his feelings become, the more easily his gaze turns from the limited, temporary things around him to the notion of an infinity and totality which includes all limits and all changes—whether he hopes to find a being corresponding to this conception or not. The greater a man's freedom, the more self-reliant and well-disposed towards others he becomes. Now, nothing leads us so directly to Deity as benevolent love; and nothing renders the absence of a belief in God so harmless to morals as self-reliance—self-sufficing and self-contained energy. Finally, the higher the feeling of power in man, and the more unhindered every manifestation of it, the more willingly does he look for some internal law to lead and direct him; and thus he remains attached to morality, whether this bond is to him a feeling of reverence and love of God, or the reward of his own self-consciousness.

The difference, then, appears to me to be this: the citizen who is wholly left to himself in matters of religion will mingle religious feelings with his inner life, or not, according to his individual character; but, in either case, his system of ideas will be more consistent, and his sensations more profound; his nature will be more coherent, and he will distinguish more clearly between morality and submission to the laws. On the other hand, the man who is fettered by various regulations will, despite these, show the same variety of religious ideas, or their absence, but in any case he will have less consistency in his ideas, less depth and sincerity of feeling, less harmony of character, and so will have less regard for morality, and wish more frequently to evade the laws.

Hence, then, without adducing any further reasons, I may proceed to lay down the principle, by no means a novel one, *that all that concerns religion lies beyond the sphere of the State's activity; and that the choice of ministers, as well as all that relates to religious worship in general, should be left to the free judgement of the communities concerned, without any special supervision on the part of the State.*

CHAPTER VIII

Amelioration of morals[1]

he last means which States customarily use in order to reform morality in accordance with their design of maintaining security is the influence of special laws and enactments. But as these are indirect measures towards virtue and morality, special provisions of this nature can naturally do nothing more than prohibit particular actions of the citizens, or mark out those which, without directly infringing the rights of others, are either positively immoral or are likely to lead to immorality.

To this class of institutions all sumptuary laws in particular belong. For, it is evident, there is no such common and fertile source of immoral and even lawless actions, as an excessive propensity of the soul towards the sensual, or the general disproportion between men's desires and impulses, and the means of satisfaction which their external position affords. When continence and moderation make men satisfied with their allotted sphere, they are less inclined to try to infringe the rights of others or to do anything likely to disturb their happiness and contentment.

It would seem therefore consistent with the true end of the State to confine luxury within due bounds, since it is the source from which all clashes between man and man arise (for where spiritual feeling is predominant there can always be harmony); and since it seems the simplest and easiest method, it might be argued that the state should try, as far as possible, to suppress love of luxury altogether.

Still, to remain faithful to the principle which has guided us so far, and first of all to regard any means the State may use in the light of man's true and unmistakable interests—it becomes necessary to look into the influence of sensualism on human life, culture, activity, and happiness—

[1] This chapter first appeared in the *Berlinische Monatsschrift* (November 1792).

an inquiry which, in that it attempts to show the inner significance of human activity and enjoyment, will at the same time illustrate more graphically the harmful or beneficial consequences which flow in general from restrictions imposed on freedom. Only after doing this can we consider in all its implications the State's competence to act positively on morals, and so arrive at the solution of this part of the general question we have proposed.

The impressions, inclinations, and passions which have their immediate source in the sense are those which first and most violently show themselves in human nature. Wherever, before the refining influences of culture have given a new direction to the soul's energies, these sensuous impressions, etc., are not apparent, all energy is dead, and nothing good or great can flourish. They constitute the original source of all spontaneous activity, and all living warmth in the soul. They bring life and vigour to the soul: when not satisfied, they make it active, ingenious in the invention of schemes, and courageous in their execution; when satisfied, they promote an easy and unhindered play of ideas. In general, they animate and quicken all concepts and images with a greater and more varied activity, suggest new views, point out hitherto unnoticed aspects, and, according to the manner in which they are satisfied, they react on the physical organization, which in its turn acts upon the soul in a manner which we only observe from the results.

The influence, however, of these impressions and inclinations differs, not only in its intensity, but in the manner of its operation. This is, to a certain extent, owing to their strength or weakness; but it is also partly to be attributed to their degree of affinity with the spiritual element in human nature, or from the ease or difficulty of raising them from animal gratifications to human pleasures. Thus, for instance, the eye imparts to the substance of its impressions that outline of form which is so full of enjoyment and suggestive of ideas; while the ear lends to sound the proportionate succession of tones in the order of time. Much that is new and highly interesting could perhaps be said of the diverse nature of these impressions and their manner of operation, if this were the proper place for such a topic, but I will only pause to notice their different uses in the culture of the soul.

The eye supplies the reason, so to speak, with a more prepared substance; and our inner nature, in association with the other things with which it is always connected in our imagination, is presented to us in a definite form and in a particular situation. If we conceive of the ear merely as an organ of sense, and in so far as it does not receive and communicate words, it conveys far less distinctness of impression. And it is for this reason that Kant gives the preference to the plastic arts when compared with music. But he notices very rightly that this presupposes as a standard a culture in which the arts minister, and I would add, minister directly, to the spirit.

The question, however, presents itself whether this is the correct standard. Energy appears to me to be the first and unique virtue of mankind. Whatever raises his energies to a higher pitch is worth more than what merely puts materials into our hands for its exercise. Now, as it is characteristic of man's nature to perceive only one thing at a time, it will be most affected by what presents only one object to him at a time, and in which the relation in which the parts stand to each other being a relation of sequence, each is given a certain ranking by virtue of what has preceded it, and in turn influences what follows. Now all this is true of music. The sequence of time, moreover, is its peculiar and essential property; this is all that is specified in it. The series which it presents hardly impels us to any definite sensation. It gives us a theme to which we can supply an endless number of texts; and what the soul of the hearer contributes, in so far as he is, in general, in a receptive mood, springs up freely and naturally from his own resources, and so is more warmly embraced than what is received passively, which is more often observed than truly grasped. As it is not my province to examine the nature and properties of music, I will not consider its other striking characteristics, such as that it evokes tones from natural objects, and therein keeps closer to nature than painting, sculpture, or poetry. I only wished, in introducing it, to illustrate more clearly the varied character of sensuous impressions.

But the manner of influence just described is not peculiar to music alone. Kant[2] observes it to be possible with shifting patterns of colour, and it characterizes still more remarkably the impressions we receive from the sense of touch. Even in taste it is unmistakable. In taste, also, there are different gradations of satisfaction, which, as it were, yearn

---

[2] The references here are to Kant's *Critique of Judgement*.

towards a resolution, and when it is achieved, vanish in a series of diminishing reverberations. This influence may be least noticeable, perhaps, in the sense of smell. Now, as it is the course of sensation, its degree, its increase and decrease, its pure and perfect harmony, which attract attention more than the stuff of sensation itself, we forget that the nature of the sensations mainly determines the progression, and still more, the harmony, of the sequence; and further, as sensitive man, like the image of blossoming spring, is the most interesting of all spectacles, so also, in the fine arts, it is this visible image of his sensations which man especially looks for. Painting and sculpture make this their province. The eye of Guido Reni's Madonna[3] is not limited to a single, fleeting glance. The tense and straining muscles of the Borghese Gladiator[4] foretell the blow he is about to deal. In a still higher degree poetry makes use of the same means. And, to make my idea clearer, without wishing to give special attention to the comparative excellence of the fine arts, I would observe that they exercise their influence in two ways, and while these are shared by each, we find them combined in very different manner. They immediately convey ideas, or they excite sensations; thus they bring harmony to the soul, and, if the expression is not too affected, enrich or exalt its powers. Now the more one of these sources of influence borrows aid from the other, the more it weakens its own peculiar force. Poetry unites both in the highest degree, and it is therefore, in this respect, the most perfect of all the fine arts; but when we regard it in another light, it is also the most weak and imperfect. While it represents its objects less vividly than painting and sculpture, it does not speak so forcibly to the senses as song and music. But, not to speak of that many-sidedness which so especially characterizes poetry, we are ready to overlook this imperfection when we see that it is nearest to the true inner nature of man, since it clothes not only thought, but sensation, with the most delicate veil.

The stimulation of sensuous impressions (for I only refer to the arts by way of illustrating these) acts in different ways; partly as they are more or less harmoniously related to each other, partly as the elements of stuff of which the impressions are composed fasten more or less strongly on the

---

[3] Picture of the Assumption, then in the Düsseldorf Gallery. It has been admired by Humboldt's friend Georg Forster [L].

[4] The Borghese Warrior, a statue of the third century A.D., is now in the Louvre. (I owe this information to Mr. Andrew Martindale.)

soul. Thus, the human voice, of equal melodiousness and quality, affects us more powerfully than a lifeless instrument. For nothing is ever so near to us as the personal, physical feeling; and where this feeling is called into play, the effect produced is the greatest. But here, as always, the disproportionate power of the substance suppresses, as it were, the delicacy of the form; and there must always exist a just relation between them. Wherever there is such a disproportion, the proper equilibrium can be restored by strengthening one or weakening the other. But it is always wrong to cultivate anything by weakening, unless the energy reduced is not natural, but artificial; only when this is the case should any limitation be imposed. It is better that it should destroy itself than slowly die away. But I cannot dwell longer on this subject. I hope I have sufficiently explained my idea, although I would like to take the opportunity of acknowledging the difficulties in this inquiry; on the other hand the interest of the subject, and the impossibility of borrowing the necessary conclusions from other writers, for I know of none who proceed from precisely my present point of view, led me to enlarge on this theme; on the other, the reflection that these considerations do not strictly belong to this subject, but are only subsidiary, recalled me to my proper task. I must make the same excuse for what follows.

Although it is impossible to isolate the subject completely, I have hitherto tried to speak only of sensuous impressions as such. But the sensual and spiritual are linked together by a mysterious bond, sensed by our emotions, though hidden from our eyes. To this double nature of the visible and invisible world—to the profound longing for the latter, coupled with the feeling of the sweet necessity of the former, we owe all sound and logical systems of philosophy, truly based on the immutable principles of our nature, just as from the same source arise the most senseless enthusiasms.[5] A constant endeavour to combine these two elements, so that each may deprive the other as little as possible, has always seemed to me the true end of wisdom. The aesthetic feeling, in virtue of which the sensuous is to us a veil of the spiritual, and the spiritual the living principle of the world of sense, is everywhere unmistakable. The continual

---

[5] Humboldt habitually uses 'enthusiasm' (*Schwärmerei*) in the pejorative, eighteenth-century sense, to denote irrational fanaticism. Where we might speak of enthusiasm, Humboldt refers always to powers or energies (*Kräfte*), though Humboldt seems also to intend to connote by this the idea of cosmic, creative energy.

contemplation of this physiognomy of nature forms the true man. For nothing exercises such a widely diffused influence on the whole character as the expression of the spiritual in the sensuous—of the sublime, the simple, the beautiful in all the works of nature and products of art which surround us. Here, too, we find the difference apparent between the sense impressions which stimulate human energy and those which do not. If the ultimate object of all our mortal striving is solely to discover, nourish, and recreate what truly exists in ourselves and others, although in its original form forever invisible—if it is the intuitive anticipation of this which endears and consecrates each of its symbols in our eyes, then the nearer we approach this original essence in contemplating the image of its endlessly animating energy. We commune with it in a language which is indeed difficult, and often misinterpreted, but which often startles us with the surest premonitions of truth, whilst the form and representation, so to speak, of that energy are further from the truth.

This is the soil, moreover, on which the beautiful flourishes, and even more especially the sublime, which brings us still nearer to the divine. The need for some purer satisfaction, without any specific goal, and not to be grasped intellectually, apprises a man of his origin in the invisible and his kinship with it; and the feeling of his utter inadequateness to the transcendental object blends together, in the most human and divine way, infinite greatness with the most devoted humility. Were it not for his feeling for the beautiful, man would cease to love things for their own sake; were it not for the sublime, he would lose that sense of dutiful submission which disdains rewards and ignores unworthy fear. The study of the beautiful bestows taste; that of the sublime (if it also may be studied, and the feeling and representation of it is not the fruit of genius alone) brings a balanced greatness. But taste alone, which must always rest on greatness as its basis (since only the great needs moderation, and only the powerful, composure), blends all the tones of a perfectly adjusted being into exquisite harmony. It induces in all our impressions and impulses, even those which are purely spiritual, something measured, composed, concentrated into one focal point. Where taste is lacking, sensual desire is rude and unrestrained; and although without it, scientific inquiries may be both acute and profound, there is no refinement, no polish, nothing fruitful in their application. In general, where there is no taste, the greatest depth of thought and the treasures of wisdom are barren and lifeless, and even the sublime strength of the moral will is rough and without a warm beneficence.

To inquire and to create—these are the centres around which all human pursuits more or less directly revolve. Before inquiry can get to the root of things, or to the limits of reason, it presupposes, in addition to profundity, a rich diversity and an inner warmth of soul—the harmonious exertion of all the human faculties combined. It is the analytical philosopher alone, perhaps, who is able to arrive at his results through the calm, but cold processes of reason. But real depth of thought and a mind which has found means to cultivate all its powers to an equal degree of perfection are essential to discover the links which unite synthetic propositions.[6] Thus Kant, who, it may be truly said, has never been surpassed in profundity, will often be charged with enthusiasm when treating of morals or aesthetics, and has indeed been so accused;[7] but while I am willing to confess that there are passages (as, for example, his interpretation of the prismatic colours)[8] which, though rare, appear to indicate something of this nature, I am only led to deplore my own want of intellectual depth. To follow these ideas out would naturally lead us to the difficult but interesting inquiry into the essential difference between the metaphysician and the poet. And were it not that a thorough re-investigation of this might perhaps invalidate my previous conclusions, I would limit my definition of the difference to this, that the philosopher concerns himself with perceptions alone, and the poet, on the contrary, with sensations; while both require the same degree and cultivation of mental power. But to establish this would lead me too far astray from my immediate subject, and I trust I have shown already, by my previous arguments, that, even to form the calmest thinker, the pleasures of sense and fancy must have often played around the soul. But to pass from transcendental to psychological inquiries (where man as he appears is the object of our studies), would not the

---

[6] A synthetic proposition was Kant's term for one asserting a matter of fact, as distinct from purely logical, analytical propositions.

[7] Kant had been criticized in this fashion in the circle of Nicolai, the publisher of the *Berlinische Monatsschrift* and by others [L].

[8] Kant, *Critique of Judgement* (2nd ed. Berlin 1793), p. 172. Kant calls the modifications of light in colour a language which nature addresses to us, and which seems to have some deeper significance. 'Thus the whiteness of the lily seems to dispose the heart to ideas of innocence, and the other colours in their orders from red to violet: 1. To the idea of sublimity; 2. Of courage; 3. Of sincerity; 4. Of kindliness; 5. Of humility; 6. Of firmness; 7. Of tenderness' [L].

man to explore most deeply this most richly creative species, and represent it most truly and vividly, be the one whose own sensibility is most comprehensive in its sympathies. Hence the man whose sensibility is thus cultivated and developed displays the full beauty of his character when he enters into practical life—when, externally and internally, he creatively enriches what he receives. The analogy between the laws of plastic nature and those of intellectual creation has been already noticed by a mind* of singular power of penetration, and established by striking proofs. But perhaps his exposition would have been still more interesting, and psychology enriched with the results of a more extended knowledge, if, instead of inquiring into the inscrutable laws of biological development, the process of intellectual creation had been shown to be, as it were, a more refined offspring of the physical.

To speak first of the moral life, which seems to be the special province of cold reason; it is only the idea of the sublime which enables us to obey absolute and unconditional laws, both humanly, through the medium of feeling, and with godlike disinterestedness, through the utter absence of all ulterior reference to happiness or misfortune. The feeling of the inadequacy of human strength to the full performance of the moral law, the profound consciousness that the most virtuous man is he who feels most inwardly conscious of how unattainably high the law is exalted above him, inspires awe—a sensation which seems to be no more shrouded in a corporeal veil than is necessary not to dazzle mortal eyes by the full splendour. Now, when the moral law obliges us to regard every man as an end in himself, it becomes fused with that feeling for the beautiful which loves to animate the merest clay, so that even in it, it may rejoice in an individual existence, and which receives and embraces man all the more completely and beautifully in that it is independent of intellectual concepts, and is not therefore limited to considering the few isolated characteristics which are all that intellectual concepts can comprehend.

The union with the feeling for the beautiful seems as if it would impair the purity of the moral will, and it might, and indeed would, have this effect, if this feeling were to become the sole motive to morality. But it will only claim the duty of discovering those more varied applications of

---

* F. v. Dalberg, *Vom Bilden und Erfinden*.[9]

   [9] The correct title is *Vom Erfinden und Bilden* (1791). The book attempts to combine Kantian and organic concepts in a theory of aesthetics.

the moral law which would otherwise escape the cold, and hence in such cases, coarser processes of reason; and since we are not forbidden to receive happiness in such intimate connection with virtue, but only to barter virtue for this happiness, it will also enjoy the privilege of bestowing on human nature its sweetest feelings. In general, the more I reflect on this subject, the less does this difference to which I refer appear to be either subtle or fanciful. However eagerly man may strive to grasp at enjoyment—however he may try to represent to himself a constant union between happiness and virtue, even under the most unfavourable circumstances, his soul still remains alive to the grandeur of the moral law. He cannot screen himself from the influence and authority of this imposing grandeur over his actions, and it is only from being penetrated with a sense of it that he acts without reference to enjoyment; for he never loses the consciousness that no misfortune whatever could compel him to adopt another course of behaviour.

It is, however, true that the soul only acquires this strength in a way similar to that which I described earlier—only by a mighty internal pressure, and a complex external struggle. But all strength springs from man's sensuous nature; and however seemingly remote, still depends on it. Now the man who ceaselessly tries to heighten his powers, and to rejuvenate them by frequent enjoyment; who often calls in his strength of character to aid him in asserting his independence of sensualism, while he tries to combine this independence with the most exquisite susceptibility; whose honest and profound intelligence tirelessly searches after the truth; whose just and delicate feeling for the beautiful notices every charming form; whose impulse to assimilate his external perceptions, and to make them bear new fruit, to infuse his own individuality into all forms of beauty and to shape it creatively anew—such a man may cherish the consoling consciousness that he is on the right path to approach the ideal which the boldest flight of fancy has ventured to indicate.

I have in this brief sketch tried to show how intimately sensualism, with all its beneficial consequences, is interwoven with the whole tissue of human life and pursuits. Although such a topic is in itself somewhat foreign to a political essay, it was appropriate and even necessary in the order of ideas adopted in this inquiry; and in these remarks on sensualism, I intended to win for it greater freedom and esteem. Still, I must not forget that sensualism is also the immediate source of innumerable physical and moral evils. Even morally speaking, it is only beneficial in a proper relationship with the exercise of the mental faculties; it easily acquires a harmful preponderance. When once the equilibrium is destroyed, human pleasure becomes degraded to mere animal gratification, and taste disappears, or becomes distorted into unnatural directions. At the same time, I would make the reservation with regard to this last expression, and chiefly with reference to certain one-sided opinions, that we are not to condemn anything as unnatural which does not exactly fulfil this or that purpose of nature, but only whatever frustrates its general ultimate design with regard to man. Now this is that his nature should always be developing itself to higher degrees of perfection, and hence, especially, that his powers of thought and sensibility should always be indissolubly linked in the proper proportions. But again, lack of relation may arise between the manner in which a man develops and manifests his powers, and the means of activity and enjoyment afforded by his position; and this is a fresh source of evil. Now, according to our former principles, the State may not attempt to act upon the situation of the citizen with any positive ends in view. Therefore, the citizen's situation would not have stamped upon it such a specific and prescribed form, and this greater freedom would ensure that it would be chiefly shaped by the citizen's own ways of thinking and acting, which would diminish the disproportion between self-cultivation and the means available to it. Still, the fact that, even so, the original danger would remain—a danger which is far from being unimportant—might suggest the necessity of checking and opposing the corruption of morals by laws and State institutions.

But even if such laws and institutions were effectual, the harm they did would be proportionate to their effectiveness. A State, in which the citizens were compelled or moved by such means to obey even the best of laws, might be a tranquil, peaceable, prosperous State; but it would always seem to me a multitude of well-cared-for slaves, rather than a nation of free and independent men, with no restraint save such as was required to prevent any infringement of rights. There are, doubtless, many methods of producing given actions and sentiments; but none of these lead to true moral perfection. Sensual impulses to certain actions, or the continuing necessity of refraining from them, gradually come to create a habit; through the force of habit the satisfaction which was at first connected with these impulses alone is transferred to the action itself; the inclination, which was at first only suppressed by necessity, becomes wholly stifled; and thus man may be led to keep his actions within the limits of virtue, and to a certain extent to entertain virtuous sentiments. But his spiritual energy is not heightened by such a process, nor are his views of his vocation and his own worth made clearer, nor does his will gain greater power to conquer his rebellious desires; and hence, he does not advance a single step towards true, intrinsic perfection. Those, therefore, who look to the cultivation of man rather than to external ends will never make use of such inadequate means. For, setting aside the fact that coercion and guidance can never succeed in producing virtue, they manifestly tend to weaken energy; and what is outward morality without true moral strength and virtue? Moreover, however great an evil immorality may be, we must not forget that it is not without its beneficial consequences. It is only through extremes that men can arrive at the middle path of wisdom and virtue. Extremes, like large masses shining far off, must operate at a distance. In order that blood may be supplied to the narrowest veins in the body, there must be a considerable amount in the larger ones. To wish to disturb the order of nature in these respects is to acquiesce in a moral, in order to prevent a physical evil.

Moreover, I think we err in supposing that the danger of immorality is either so great or so urgent; and while much that I have said tends more or less to establish this, the following conclusions may serve to give it additional confirmation—

1. Man is naturally more disposed to beneficent than selfish actions. This we learn even from history of savages. The domestic virtues have something in them so inviting, and the public virtues of the citizen something so grand and inspiring, that even the man who has only just escaped being corrupted is seldom able to resist their charm.

2. Freedom heightens energy, and, as the natural consequence, promotes all kinds of liberality. Coercion stifles energy, and engenders all selfish desires, and all the mean artifices of weakness. Coercion may prevent many transgressions; but it robs even actions which are legal of a part of their beauty. Freedom may lead to many transgressions, but it lends even to vices a less ignoble form.

3. The man who is left to himself arrives with greater difficulty at just principles; but they show themselves ineffaceably in his actions. The man who is led by some preconcerted design receives such principles with

greater facility; but they still give way before his natural energies, however weakened they may be.

4. All political arrangements, in that they have to bring a variety of widely discordant interests into unity and harmony, necessarily produce various clashes. From these clashes spring a disproportion between men's desires and their powers; and from these, transgressions. The more active the State is, the greater is the number of these. If it were possible to make an accurate calculation of the evils which police regulations occasion, and of those which they prevent, the number of the former would, in all cases, exceed that of the latter.

5. How far the strictest search into crimes actually committed, the infliction of just, carefully calculated, but irrevocable punishment, and the consequent rarity of impunity, are really practicable has never yet been tried.

I have now sufficiently shown, according to my views, how questionable is every effort of the State to oppose or even to prevent any dissoluteness of morals (in so far as it does not imply injury to individual rights); how few the beneficial results to morality to be expected from such attempts; and how the exercise of such an influence on the character of a nation is not even necessary for the preservation of security.

If now, in addition to this, we bring forward the principles already developed, which disapprove of all State agency directed to positive aims, and which apply here with particular force, since it is precisely the moral man who feels every restriction most deeply; reflecting, further, that if there is one aspect of development more than any other which owes its highest beauty to freedom, it is precisely the cultivation of character and morals; then the justice of the following principle will be sufficiently obvious: *that the State must wholly refrain from every attempt to operate directly or indirectly on the morals and character of the nation, except in so far as such a policy may become inevitable as a natural consequence of its other absolutely necessary measures; and that everything calculated to promote such a design, and particularly all special supervision of education, religion, sumptuary laws, etc., lies wholly outside the limits of its legitimate activity.*

CHAPTER IX

The solicitude of the State for security more accurately and positively defined ▪ Further development of the idea of security

ow that I have completed the more important and difficult parts of the present inquiry, and approached nearer to the solution of the great problem which it involves, it becomes necessary to review its progress up to this point, and endeavour to sum up its results.

Firstly, then, the State's care was to be withheld from all objects which do not immediately relate to the external or internal security of its citizens. In the second place, this same security has been represented as the real object of political activity; and, lastly, it has been agreed that nothing is permissible for the promotion of this object which is designed to work on the morals and character of the nation itself, to bend them to or from any particular course. To a certain extent, therefore, the question as to the proper limits of State agency appears to be already fully solved, seeing that its sphere is confined to the preservation of security; and, in the means available to it, still more narrowly restricted to those which do not interfere, for State ends, with the development of national character, or, rather, do not mould and fashion it with a view to those ends. For although, it is true, this definition is so far purely negative, what remains after such a division of functions is of itself sufficiently distinct. Political activity can only extend its influence to such actions as imply a direct trespass on the rights of others; to the task of deciding in cases of disputed right; to redressing the wronged, and punishing the wrong-doers. But the idea of security—towards defining which nothing further has been observed than that it embraces security against the attacks of foreign enemies, and against the aggressive spirit of fellow-citizens—is too wide and comprehensive not to require some more special exposition. For, just as there are great and important differences between the results of persuasion by advice, and those of officious recommendation, and between these and the influence of positive coercion; and just as the degrees of unfairness and injustice may vary, from actions exercised within the limits of one's own right, but possibly harmful to another, to those which likewise do not trespass those limits, but often or always tend to disturb some other in the enjoyment of his own, and again from these to actual encroachments on another's rightful property; just in like manner does the idea of security vary in extent and application, since we may understand it as security against some particular kind or degree of coercive influence, or against some definite infringement of rights. Now the interpretation of the term security is of extreme importance; and if it is stretched too far or too narrowly circumscribed, the specification of spheres of influence is thrown into confusion by the confusion of terms, which it will be impossible to repair without a clear definition.

Again, the means the State may or may not use must be still more closely scrutinized and distinguished. For, although we have disapproved of any attempt on the part of the State directed to the reformation of morals, there still remains, in this respect, too large and indefinite a field for political enterprise. The question remains undecided, for example, how far the State's restrictive enactments are removed from those actions which immediately violate the rights of others; and how far the State may proceed in preventing actual crimes by stopping up their sources, not in the character of the citizens, but in the opportunities for their commission. Now, how far and dangerously it is possible to err in this respect is already shown by the fact that the concern for freedom itself has disposed a number of men of sound judgement to make the State responsible for the whole welfare of its citizens; believing that such a comprehensive arrangement would promote the unhindered play of human energies. I am therefore ready to confess, in view of these considerations, that I have as yet done nothing but distinguish such large areas as lie clearly outside the circle of political activity, and have not yet tried to draw its precise limit, especially where these limits were questionable and disputed.

This therefore still remains to be done; and, even though I may not be wholly successful in the attempt, I must at least try to ascertain the reasons for this failure as clearly and fully as possible. And, in any case, I hope now to be able to conclude shortly, as all the principles I require for the task have been already discussed and settled, at least as far as my abilities would allow.

I call the citizens of a State secure when, living together in the full enjoyment of their due rights of person and property, they are out of the reach of any external disturbance from the encroachments of others; and hence I would call security, if the expression does not seem too abrupt to be clear, the assurance of legal freedom. Now this security is not necessarily disturbed by all such actions as impede a man in the free exercise of his powers, and in the full enjoyment of all that belongs to him, but only by those which do this unrightfully. This sense which we assign to the word, and the definition just adopted to express it, are not arbitrarily chosen by me. Both follow immediately from our previous conclusions; and it is only with this sense of the term security that our former reasoning can be employed. For it is only actual violations of right which need to be met with any force other than that which each individual himself possesses; only what prevents such violations brings a pure gain for human self-cultivation, while every other effort of the State throws obstacles in its way; and, lastly, it alone is grounded on the infallible principle of necessity, while all others rest on the precarious basis of a deceptively plausible usefulness.

Those whose security is to be preserved are, on the one hand, all the citizens, in perfect legal equality, and, on the other, the State itself. The extent of this latter object, or the security of the State, is determined by the extent of the rights assigned to it, and, through these, by the nature and extent of its aims. As I have argued, it may not demand security for anything except the power entrusted to its hands, and the resources allotted to it. Further, it should not, with a view to this security, restrict the citizen when, without violating any actual right (and hence, with the understanding that he is not bound to the State by any personal or temporary relation, as, for instance, in time of war), he wishes to withdraw himself or his property from the political community. For the State association is merely a subordinate means to which man, the true end, is not to be sacrificed; except in the case of a conflict of interests where the individual would not be bound to sacrifice himself, and yet the community might have the right to sacrifice him. Moreover, according to our former principles, the State is not to have any positive care for the citizen's welfare; and nothing can be necessary in order to preserve security which tends to repress freedom, and with it security itself.

Disturbances of security are produced either by actions which in themselves violate the rights of others, or by those from whose consequences this is to be feared. Now, both these kinds of action (with certain qualifications which will shortly occupy our attention) are to be prohibited by the State, and, as far as possible, prevented; when once they are committed, it must try to render them, as far as possible, innocuous, by extending legal redress for the wrong sustained, and by punishment, to lessen the frequency of such actions in future. Hence, to use the usual terms, arise police, civil and criminal laws. In addition to these, however, there comes another object under the general head of concern for security; and, on account of its peculiar nature, it requires a wholly separate treatment.

There is a class of citizens to whom the principles we have unfolded (since they presuppose men to be in the enjoyment of their usual faculties) can only be applied with considerable qualifications. I allude to those who have not yet arrived at the age of maturity, or who, through idiocy or mania, have not the use of their proper human powers. It is obvious that the State must also provide for their security; and as we can easily foresee, their peculiar position must require a special policy to be adopted towards them. We must therefore, finally, consider the relation in which the State stands to all infants among its citizens, in the character of (to use the familiar expression) their chief guardian.

Having before sufficiently treated of security against foreign enemies, I believe I have now succeeded in marking out all the objects towards which the State is to direct its active concern. Far from pretending to penetrate at all profoundly into all the great and difficult subjects I have enumerated, I shall be content to develop the fundamental principles in each, as briefly as possible, and as far as comes within the scope of my present design. It is only when this has been done that we can feel that we have completed our attempt to examine the proposed question thoroughly and to consider all aspects of the activity of the State and its proper limits.

CHAPTER X

*On the solicitude of the State for security
with respect to actions which directly relate
to the agent only (Police laws)*

I n order to follow man, as we now must through all the complex and manifold relations which his life in society
presents, it will be best to begin with considering the simplest of these, the case where man, though living in association with others, remains strictly within the limits of what belongs to
himself, and engages in nothing that refers immediately to the rights of
others. It is to this aspect of civil relations that the greater number of our
so-called police, or preventive, laws are directed; since, however indefinite this expression may be, it still conveys to us the general and important idea that these laws relate to the means of averting violations of the
rights of others. Now they either restrict actions whose immediate consequences are likely to endanger the rights of others; or they impose limitations on those which usually lead ultimately to transgressions of the law;
or, lastly, they may specify what is necessary for the preservation or exercise of the power of the State itself. I must here overlook the fact that
those regulations which do not relate to security, but are directed to the
positive welfare of the citizen, are most commonly classed under this
heading; since it does not fall in with the system of classification I have
adopted. Now, according to the principles we have already determined,
the State ought not to interfere with these simple human relations, except
where there are grounds for fearing some violation of its own rights, or
those of its citizens. And as to the rights of the State, it should here be
borne in mind that such rights are granted only for the sake of protecting

security. In no case, then, should prohibitive laws be enacted when the advantage or disadvantage refers only to the State itself. Again, it is not enough to justify such restrictions that an action should imply damage to another person; it must, at the same time, encroach upon his rights. But this second position requires explanation. Right, then, is never infringed except when someone is deprived of a part of what properly belongs to him, or of his personal freedom, without his consent or against his will. But when, on the contrary, there occurs no such deprivation—when one individual does not overstep the boundary of another's right, then, whatever disadvantage may accrue to the latter, there is no diminution of rights. Neither is there when the injury itself does not follow until he who suffers becomes active on his own part, and, as it were, joins in the action, or, at least, does not oppose it as far as he can.

The application of these definitions is sufficiently evident, and I will only pause to mention two remarkable examples. According to these principles, we cannot assume the injustice of any actions which only create offence, and especially as regards religion and morals. He who utters or does anything to wound the conscience and moral sense of others may indeed act immorally; but, so long as he is not guilty of being importunate, he violates no right. The others are free to cut off all intercourse with such a person, and, should circumstances render this impossible, they must submit to the unavoidable inconvenience of associating with men of uncongenial character; not forgetting, moreover, that the obnoxious party may likewise be annoyed by the display of peculiar traits in them. Even a possible exposure to more positively harmful influences— as where witnessing some action, or listening to a particular argument, was calculated to harm the virtue, or mislead the reason and sound sense of others—would not be sufficient to justify restrictions on freedom. Whoever spoke or acted thus did not in doing so infringe directly on the right of any other; and those who were exposed to the influence of such words and actions were free to counteract the evil impression on themselves with the strength of will and the principles of reason. Hence, then, however great the evils that may follow from overt immorality and seductive errors of reasoning, there still remains this excellent consequence that in the former case strength of character, in the latter the spirit of toleration and diversity of view, are brought to the test, and reap benefits in the process. It is scarcely necessary to mention that in the instance I have just taken, I have confined my attention to its influence on the security of the citizens. For I have already tried to show the relation of such actions to national morality, and to show what may or may not be allowed to the State with regard to them, on that account.

Since, however, there are many cases where a correct judgement requires special knowledge, and since, in regard to these, security might be disturbed if anyone should unthinkingly or designedly turn the ignorance of others to his own advantage, the citizen should have the option, in such cases, of applying to the State for advice. The most striking instances of what I mean—whether we consider the frequent necessity for such special knowledge, the difficulty attending just discrimination, or, lastly, the extent of the harm to be feared—are supplied by those cases in which the professional services of physicians and advocates are required. Now, in order to meet the needs and wishes of the nation in these cases, it is not only advisable but necessary that the State should look into the qualifications of those who take up such vocations, provided they agree to submit themselves to its tests; and, giving them testimonials of fitness, when they pass these tests, acquaint the citizens that they can only confide with certainty in those thus certified. Beyond this, however, the State may not go, or prevent those who have declined, or failed in examination, from exercising their vocation, or the public from using their services. Moreover this supervision should be confined to occupations which are not intended to act on the internal, but only on the external life of man, and in which he is not himself required to cooperate, but only to remain passive and obedient, and where the truth or falsity of the results is the only thing of importance. Secondly, such regulations are only proper in those cases where correct judgement requires special knowledge, and is not attainable by the mere exercise of reason and practical discernment, and further where the rarity of their occurrence makes seeking advice itself difficult. Should the State proceed further than is prescribed by this last limitation, it falls into the danger of making the nation indolent, inactive, and too much inclined to rely on the knowledge and judgement of others; while, on the other hand, the very lack of positive assistance invites men to enrich their own knowledge and experience, and knits the citizens together in a closer and more varied association, in that they are left more dependent on each other. Should the State fail to observe the first limitation we have

pointed out, that it is not to prevent a man from the free exercise of his
chosen profession because he has not submitted himself to its tests, then,
besides the evils just alluded to, all those harmful consequences will
naturally follow which we traced in detail at the beginning of this essay.
It is evident then—to take another noteworthy example—that in the
case of religious teachers State regulations cannot be applied. For in
what should the State examine them? In the belief of some particular
dogmas? We have already fully shown that religion is in no way dependent on these. On the degree of intellectual ability in general? In the
teacher of religion, whose task it is to present things to his audience in
such a way as to relate them to their individual life, almost the sole point
of importance is the relation between his reason and theirs, and so on
this account alone such an estimate is impossible. Should it then judge
moral character and integrity? For these there is only a test to which the
position of the State is very ill-adapted: inquiry into the previous conduct and circumstances of the candidates, etc. Lastly, regulations of this
nature—even in the cases we have ourselves approved—should, in general, only be adopted when the will of the nation clearly demands them.
For, in themselves, they are not necessary among free men made cultivated by their possession of freedom; and further, they might be constantly liable to serious abuse. As, in general, it is not my intention to
pursue particular subjects, but rather to define fundamental principles, I
shall once more briefly indicate the only point of view from which I
consider such regulations. The State, then, is not to concern itself in any
way with the positive welfare of its citizens, and hence, not with their
life or health, except where these are imperilled by the actions of others;
but it is to keep a vigilant eye on their security, though only in so far as
this might suffer from the attempts of the designing to turn the ignorance
of others to their own advantage. Still, in such cases of deception, the
victim of the imposture must have been persuaded, and the complexity
and nuances of such relations make the application of any general rule
almost impossible and as the liability to fraud which freedom leaves
open tends to discipline men's prudence and foresight, I think it more in
accordance with my principles, in a theory which is necessarily remote
from practical application, to confine prohibition by law to those cases
only in which actions are done without the consent of another, or still
more, in direct opposition to his wishes. The general tenor of my argu-

ments will serve to indicate the consistent treatment of other cases, should these present themselves.*

While we have hitherto confined our attention only to the consequences of an action, which bring it under the eye of the State, we have yet to ask whether the mere possibility of such consequences is sufficient to justify restriction, or whether this is so only where the consequences necessarily follow. Freedom may suffer if we adopt the former position; if we take the latter, security may be endangered. It is therefore clear that a middle course should be pursued; but to give any general definition of this seems to me impossible. Clearly deliberation in such cases must be guided by the extent of the injury, and of the restrictions on freedom implied in the law. But estimation of these does not admit, properly speaking, of any general rule; and all calculations of probability are remarkably unreliable. Theory therefore can only point out some starting-points for deliberation. In practice, I believe that one must chiefly look at special circumstances, and not so much at cases in general, and that one should only decide on restrictions when past experience and present considerations seem to make it necessary. Natural law, when applied to the social life of men, defines the boundary lines unmistakably. It condemns all actions in which one man culpably encroaches on the province of another, and hence, includes all those cases where the injury arises from oversight, or where it is always or with some degree of probability a consequence of the action taken, so that the agent is either aware of what he is doing or becomes culpable by overlooking it. In all other cases the injury occurs by chance, and the agent is not bound to make reparation. Any wider extension than this could only be authorized by the tacit agreement of those living together; and this is again something positive. But that the State should stop here seems questionable; especially when we consider the importance of the harm to be feared, and the possibility of limiting the harm done by the restrictions on the citizens' freedom. In such a case the State's right is undeniable, since it has to provide for security, not only by enforcing reparation where a right has really been violated, but also by

---

* It might appear that the cases here mentioned do not so much belong to the present chapter as to the next, since they concern actions which relate immediately to others. But I have not here considered the case in which a physician actually treats a patient, or a lawyer really undertakes a suit; but only of the choice of a means of gaining a livelihood. I only put the question whether the State should restrict such a choice; and this choice alone does not relate directly to any other person.

preventing such wrongs. A third person, moreover, can only decide according to external characteristics. It is therefore impossible for the State to wait to see whether the citizens will fail in taking due precautions against dangerous actions, nor can it rely on the probability of their foreseeing the injury: it must rather, where circumstances make the need for supervision urgent, restrict actions harmless in themselves.

In view of these considerations, therefore, we may be justified in laying down the following principle: *in order to provide for the security of its citizens, the State must prohibit or restrict such actions, relating directly to the agents only, as imply in their consequences the infringement of others' rights, or encroach on their freedom or property without their consent or against their will; and further, it must forbid or restrict these actions when the probability of such consequences is to be feared— a probability in which it must necessarily consider the extent of the injury feared, and on the other hand the consequences of the restriction on freedom implied in the law contemplated. Beyond this, every limitation of personal freedom lies outside the limits of State action.*

Since, according to the ideas I have put forward, the protection of the rights of others is the only justification for these restrictions, the necessity for them must naturally disappear when this justification no longer exists; as when, for instance, as in most police-regulations, the danger applies only to a particular community, village or town, as soon as such a community expressly and unanimously demands that these restrictions should be abolished. The State must then draw back, and content itself with punishing only such injuries as have arisen from an intentional or culpable violation of rights. For to restrain dissension among the citizens is the only true interest of the State; and the will of individual citizens, even though they are themselves the parties injured, should never be allowed to hinder this. If we imagine a community of enlightened men—fully instructed in their truest interests, and therefore mutually well-disposed and closely bound together—we can easily imagine how voluntary contracts with a view to their security would be entered into among them; contracts, for example, that this or that dangerous occupation or manufacture should be carried on only in certain places and at certain times, or even should be wholly prohibited. Agreements of this kind are infinitely to be preferred to any State arrangements. For as it is the very persons who enter into such contracts who are most conscious of their necessity,

and feel directly the advantage or disadvantage accruing from them, it is
clear that they will not be readily formed except where there is an obvious
need for them; that they will be far more rigidly observed, being voluntarily made; that however considerable the restrictions they entail, they
will have a less harmful influence on the character, being the results of
spontaneous activity; and that, lastly, springing as they would from a
certain spirit of benevolence and enlightenment, they would still further
contribute in their turn to increase and diffuse them. The best efforts of
the State should therefore aim at bringing men into such a condition by
means of freedom that associations would arise with greater ease, and so
take the place of political regulations in these and many kinds of similar
instances.

I have not made any mention here of laws which impose positive duties
on the citizens to sacrifice or to do something either for the State or for
each other, though there are such laws everywhere among us. But, apart
from the use of his powers which every citizen, where necessary, owes to
the State (about which I shall have to speak later), I do not agree that the
State should compel any one to do anything to gratify the wish or further
the interests of another, even though he should receive the fullest compensation. For as everything and every pursuit, from the infinite diversity
of human dispositions and desires, confers on men such various and inestimable benefits, and as these benefits may likewise vary infinitely in
interest, importance, and necessity, the decision which benefits are to be
regarded as equivalent, though its difficulty should not deter us from
attempting it, has always something harsh in it, and seems like passing
sentence on the feelings and individuality of another. For this reason,
moreover, since we cannot make any exact restitution except where the
things in question are exactly of the same kind, real compensation is
often utterly impossible, and can scarcely be determined by a general
rule.

In addition to these harmful consequences of even the best laws of this
kind, there is always, moreover, the considerable possibility of abuse.

Furthermore, security, which alone prescribes the proper limits of State
action, does not render such regulations generally necessary, since every
case in which this necessity occurs must be strictly exceptional: men,
moreover, become more kindly disposed towards each other, and more
ready to render mutual assistance, the less they feel their self-love and

sense of freedom wounded by an actual right of coercion on the part of others; and even though the mere whim and wholly groundless obstinacy of a man may thwart an excellent undertaking, this is not sufficient to justify the interposition of the full power of the State. In the physical world, the State does not blow up every rock that lies in the wayfarer's path. Obstacles stimulate energy, and sharpen wits; only those which arise from human injustice are uselessly restrictive; the latter is not the case, however, with those examples of self-will which can, indeed, be humbled by laws framed to meet special circumstances, but can only really be amended by freedom. These reasons, of which a brief summary is all that can be given here, seem sufficient to make us yield to iron necessity alone; and the State should content itself with securing to men their natural right to protect themselves at the expense of the freedom and property of others.

Lastly, there are many police laws framed to meet actions which are performed, it is true, within the limits of the agent's right, but not his exclusively, it being a communal right. In such cases, restrictions on freedom are evidently far less questionable, since in property that is common, every joint proprietor has the right of gainsay. Examples of such common property are roads, rivers flowing through different properties, squares and streets of towns, and so forth.

CHAPTER XI

On the solicitude of the State for security

with respect to such of the citizens' actions

as relate directly to others (Civil laws)

T he subject to which we have now to direct our attention—
one of less difficulty, at least for the present inquiry—is the
case of actions which immediately affect others. For where
rights are infringed by such actions, it is clearly the duty of
the State to restrict them, and compel the agents to repair the injury they
have inflicted. But according to our previous definition, these actions are
unjust only when they deprive another of a part of his freedom or possessions without his consent or against his will. When any one has suffered
wrong, he has a right to redress; but when once, as a member of a community, he has transferred his private revenge to the State, to nothing
more. The man, therefore, who has committed the wrong is bound to
restore to the man who has sustained it whatever he has been deprived of;
or, if this be impossible, to make compensation to the full extent of his
means, and of what he can earn. To deprive a man of his personal liberty—as is practised, for instance, in the case of insolvent debtors—can
only be regarded as a subsidiary means, where otherwise the creditor
should run the risk of losing the debtor's future earnings. Now while the
State is not to refuse any just means of redress to the person injured, it
must take care that a spirit of revenge does not turn this fair demand into
a pretext for injustice. This seems the more necessary when we reflect,
first, that in a state of nature the person originally committing the wrong
would resist the one who sought satisfaction, if he were to overstep the
bounds of justice, whereas here, the irresistible authority of the State

comes in to check further retaliation; and secondly, that general definitions, which are always necessary when a third party is to arbitrate, invariably tend to encourage the pretext for revenge. The imprisonment of
debtors therefore might seem to require still further exceptions, as the
majority of laws relating to them allow.

Actions which are undertaken by mutual agreement are exactly similar
to those which a man performs by himself, without immediate reference
to others, and I have only to repeat of them what I have already said of
the latter. There is one class of such actions, however, which requires
wholly special regulations; I mean those which are not concluded at once,
but extend in their operation to the future. Of this kind are promises or
engagements which impose absolute duties on the parties to the engagement, whether they are mutual or not. By these, portions of property are
made over from one person to another; and if the party transferring it
retracts from his engagement by trying to recover what has been transferred, order is disturbed. It is therefore one of the most important duties
of the State to see that such engagements are binding. But the restraint
which every engagement imposes is only just and salutary, when, firstly,
the implied limitation extends only to him who enters into it; and secondly, when he has in general, and at the time of the engagement, acted
with a proper capacity for reflection, and of his own free will. Wherever
this is not the case, coercion is as unjust in principle as it is pernicious in
its effects. It must be borne in mind that judgements about the future are
always imperfect, and also that many contractual obligations are such as
to impose such fetters on liberty, as prove serious hindrances to the man's
complete development. Hence there devolves a second duty on the
State—to refuse the support of the law to such engagements as are contrary to justice, and to take all necessary precautions consistent with the
security of property to prevent a moment's want of reflection from entail-
ing such restrictions on a man as to retard or prevent his own perfect
development. It is the province of juridical theories to detail all that is
necessary for the validity of contracts or engagements. It only remains for
me to observe, with regard to their objects, that a State, which (according
to our former principles) is required only to maintain security, may not
take up any object that is not included in the general notion of justice or
justified by the concern for security. Of this class we may notice the
following cases, as being the most remarkable: 1. When the party promis-

ing cannot transfer any right of coercion without making himself a tool for the designs of others—as, for example, in every contract which ends in the slavery of the person contracting; 2. Where the party promising has no power to grant what is promised, because of its very nature—as is the case, for instance, in all matters of feeling or belief; 3. When the promise in itself, or in its implied consequences, is either incompatible with, or dangerous to, the rights of others, in which case the principles established in our last chapter are also strictly applicable here. Now the difference between these cases is this, that in the first and second the State must only refuse to provide the sanction of its laws, without preventing the formation or execution of such engagements, in so far as these are by mutual consent; while, in the last instance we have mentioned, it not only can but must forbid the act of engagement itself.

Still, even where there is nothing against the validity of a contract or engagement, the State should have the power to lessen the restrictions which men impose on one another, even with their own consent, and by facilitating release from such engagements, to prevent a moment's decision from hindering their freedom of action for too long a period of life. When, however, a mere transfer of things is implied in the contract, without any other personal relation, I do not consider such a course advisable. For, firstly, these are seldom of such a kind as to lead to a lasting relation between the contracting parties; secondly, limitations on such engagements tend to upset the stability of business arrangements, with far more harmful consequences; and lastly, for many reasons, but chiefly with respect to the cultivation of judgement and strength of character, it is good that a man's word once given should be irrevocably binding; so that such an obligation should never be removed except where this is really necessary; such a necessity does not arise in the case of a transfer of things, because however they may hinder certain manifestations of human activity, they seldom tend to weaken the force of energy itself. But with contracts which render personal performance a duty, or still more with those which produce actual personal relations, the case is wholly different. With these, coercion harms man's noblest powers; and since the success of the business which is to be conducted in accordance with the contract more or less depends on the continuing consent of the parties, such a limitation is in their case less pernicious. When therefore such a personal relation arises from the contract as not only to require certain specific actions, but, in the strictest sense, to affect the person, and influence the whole manner of his existence; where what is done or left undone is closely bound up with man's inner sensibility, repudiation should be possible at all times and without excuses.[1] This is the case with marriage.

Where the relation is indeed less intimate, while personal liberty is still narrowly restricted, the State should, I believe, fix a time, the length of which must be determined by the importance of the restriction on the one hand, and on the other by the nature of the business concerned, during which neither of the parties should be allowed to withdraw without mutual consent; but that after its expiration, the contract, unless renewed, should not remain binding, even though the parties, in concluding the engagement, had abandoned the advantage to which such a law would entitle them. For although such a provision might seem to be nothing more than a boon of the law, and not to be enforced more than any other similar privilege, the course we suggest does not debar any one from entering into a lifelong contract, but guards against the possibility of compulsory performance of an engagement, when such constraint would harm the individual's highest aims. And indeed it is the less a mere boon in this respect that the cases I have quoted, and especially matrimony (as soon as free will no longer accompanies that relation), differ only in degree from that in which one party surrenders himself as a mere tool into the hands of others, or rather is made a tool by the other to further his designs; and the competence to determine generally in these the boundary between just and unjust constraint cannot be refused to the State, that is, to the common will of society; since it would only be possible in special cases to decide accurately and truthfully where the limitation arising from a contract was such as actually to render the man who had changed his mind a mere tool of the other. Lastly, it cannot be called a compulsory boon, when we authorize its renunciation in advance.

The fundamental principles of justice themselves teach, and it has been already expressly laid down, that no one can make a valid contract, or, in general, enter into any engagement with regard to anything except what is really his property, that is, his actions, or his possessions. It is evident

---

[1] Cf. J. S. Mill: 'The principle of freedom cannot require that [a man] should be free not to be free' (*On Liberty*, Cambridge ed., p. 103; Toronto ed., p. 300). Mill thought that Humboldt had oversimplified the problem, however (pp. 103–4; 300–1).

moreover that the greatest part of the State's concern for the security of its citizens, in so far as this is affected by the operation of contracts or engagements, consists in supervising the observance of this principle. Still there are certain entire departments of business to which this fundamental rule has not been applied. Such, for example, are all dispositions of property to be observed after the death of the disposer, whether made directly or indirectly, incidentally in another contract or in a special contract or testament, or in any disposition of whatever kind. Rights of any kind can only relate immediately to the person: their relation to things is only conceivable in so far as these are connected with the person by actions. With the decease of the person, therefore, this right is also at an end. Hence, as long as he lives, man is free to dispose of his things as he pleases, to alienate them in part or altogether—their substance, use, or possession; and further, to limit his actions and the employment of his means by anticipation, as he thinks best. But he is in no way entitled to define, in any way binding on others, what shall be done with his property after his decease, or to determine how its future possessor is to act. I will not stop to examine the possible objections to these assertions. The reasons on both sides have already been exhaustively examined in the well-known dispute over the validity of testaments according to natural right; and the point of right is, on the whole, of less importance in this case, since the competence of the whole society to give to testamentary dispositions the validity which they would otherwise lack is clearly unquestionable. But in the extension afforded to testaments by our common law, which in this respect unites the subtlety of the Roman jurists with the mania for lordship of the feudal system which followed the dissolution of society—as regards this extension, it restricts that freedom which is essential to human development, and so runs counter to every principle we have put forward. For our testamentary laws provide the principal means by which one generation succeeds in prescribing laws to another—through which abuses and prejudices, not likely otherwise to survive the causes which necessarily produced them, descend by inheritance, from century to century, so that instead of man shaping things, things, on the contrary, bring man under their yoke. Further, they more than anything else divert man's attention from his true powers and their development, and direct them exclusively to external possessions; since these are clearly the only means of securing obedience to their wishes after death. Finally, the arbitrary power of disposing property by testament is often, indeed generally, made subservient to man's less worthy passions of pride, vanity, desire for dominion, etc., so that it is the less wise and good men who avail themselves of this power. It does not occur to the wise to arrange things for a future, the individual circumstances of which they are too shortsighted to foresee, while the good, far from eagerly looking for such opportunities, are glad not to find any occasion to impose limits on the will of others. Too often, even, secrecy and safety from the censure of the world may induce men to make dispositions which otherwise shame would have prohibited. These reasons may show the necessity of guarding at least against the dangers to the freedom of the individual from the practice of testamentary dispositions.

But what is to supply the place of such dispositions of property if, as principle strictly demands, the State were to abolish completely the right of making them? As the necessary preservation of peace and order precludes the possibility of just any one taking possession, there clearly remains nothing but an hereditary succession *ab intestato* to be decided by the State. But to transfer to the political power such a mighty positive influence as it would acquire by the right of settling this hereditary succession, and by utterly abolishing the personal will of the ancestor, is forbidden by the principles we have already agreed upon. The close connection which exists between laws on succession *ab intestato* with the political constitution of States has been frequently observed; and this source of influence might be employed to further other designs. On the whole, the diverse and changing wishes of individual men are to be preferred to the uniform and unchangeable will of the State. And we should remember, further, that whatever evils may flow from the practice of testamentary dispositions, it seems hard to deprive man of the innocent joy which accompanies the thought of continuing to do good with his property even after death; and although this feeling, it is true, produces an excessive concern with property, when too much encouraged, the utter absence of it might lead perhaps to the opposite evil. The liberty too, which men enjoy, of leaving their goods behind them according to their own free will, creates a new bond of union among them, which, though often the source of abuse, may also often be beneficial. And indeed the whole tenor of the ideas and arguments unfolded in this essay might fairly be reduced to this, that while they would break all fetters in human society, they would attempt to find as many new social bonds as possible. The isolated man is no more able to develop than the one who is fettered. Lastly, it differs little whether a man really gives away what belongs to him at the very hour of death, or bequeaths it by will; and to the former he has an undoubted and inalienable right.

The contradiction seemingly involved in the reasons here advanced on both sides of the question is reconciled when we remember that the dispositions of a testament can contain two kinds of settlement: 1. Who shall be the next heir to the property? 2. How is he to manage it; to whom is it to be willed in turn, and, in general, what is to be done with it for the future? We see that all the disadvantages enumerated apply only to the latter, while all the contrasting advantages spring only from the former. For if the laws have only ensured, by determining the portion due to his family, as indeed they must, that no testator can be guilty of real wrong or injustice, it seems as if the mere kindly intention to make someone a present after one's death would leave no special danger to be feared. The principles, moreover, by which men are guided in such actions will evidently be much the same at any given time; and the frequency or rarity of testaments will, in any period, show the legislator whether the order of succession *ab intestato* which he has introduced is still appropriate or not. It might perhaps, then, be advisable to make a corresponding division of the State's measures relating to testaments, according to the twofold character of the objects we have noticed as embraced by them; that is, to allow every man, on the one hand, to determine who shall inherit his possessions after his death, subject only to the limitation as regards the portion due to his family, but to forbid him, on the other, to prescribe in any way whatever how it shall be managed or employed. Now it is certain that the first of these privileges, which we assume to be allowed by the State, might be seriously abused, and made the means of doing what the State wishes to prohibit. But it should be the object of the legislator to obviate this abuse by special and precise regulations. This is not the place to enter into a full exposition of this subject, but I may propose the following as examples of such regulations: that the heir, in order that he be really the heir, should be distinguished by no express condition to be fulfilled after the death of the testator; that the testator nominate only the next heir to his possessions and never a subsequent one, since by this process the liberty of the first would be restricted; that the testator have the power of appointing several heirs, but must do this in a direct way; that he be allowed to divide a thing according to its extent, but never with respect to the rights connected with it—as, for instance, substance and usufruct, etc. From these spring manifold inconveniences and limitations of freedom, as also from the idea connected with them, that the heir is the representative of the testator—an idea which (like so many others which have since become so extremely important) is founded, I believe, on a formality of the Romans, and therefore on the necessarily imperfect arrangement of the juridical constitution of a people who were only in process of formation. But we shall be able to rid ourselves of all these false notions if we keep the principle distinctly in view that nothing further is to be granted to the testator than, at the most, to appoint his heir; and that the State, while it should assist the latter to secure possession when his appointment is valid, must not lend its aid to the enforcement of any disposition on the part of the testator extending beyond this.

In case no heir has been appointed by the dying person, the State must arrange an order of succession *ab intestato.* But it does not come within my present design to develop the principles on which such an arrangement should proceed, nor those which relate to the portion always due to the testator's family: I will content myself with observing that the State should not have scope afforded it for the furtherance of its own positive aims in these, as in the other regulations we have considered—such as maintaining the splendour and prosperity of families, or the opposite extreme, of dissipating large fortunes by increasing the number of inheritors; but that it must always act in accordance with ideas of justice, which are restricted in this case to the limits of the former co-proprietorship in the testator's lifetime, and must thus give the first claim to the family, the next to the municipality,* etc.

Very closely connected with the subject of inheritance is the question how far contracts between living persons may be transmitted to their heirs. We shall find the answer to this question in the principle we have

* I have been much indebted in the above remarks to the speech of Mirabeau on this subject; and should have availed myself still further of his reasoning, had not he proceeded from a wholly different point of view from that adopted in this inquiry. (See *Collection Complète des Travaux de M. Mirabeau l'Aîné à l'Assémblée Nationale,* V, 498–524.)[2]

[2] The speech to which Humboldt refers, published as 'Discours sur l'égalité des portages dans les successions en ligne directe' is not now attributed to Mirabeau [L].

already established: that is, that a man during lifetime may restrict his actions and alienate his property just as he pleases, but is not allowed to limit the actions of his heir after his own death, or, under such circumstances to make any other disposition except such as would secure a valid succession to his property. Hence all those obligations must pass over to the heir and must be fulfilled towards him, which really include the transfer of a portion of the property, and which therefore have either lessened or augmented the means of the testator; but, on the other hand, none of these obligations remain which have either simply consisted in actions of the testator, or related solely to his person. But, even after having made this limitation, there still remains too great a danger of entangling the descendants in relations which are binding, by means of contracts concluded in the lifetime of the testator. For rights can be alienated as well as separate lots of property, and such alienations must necessarily be binding on the heirs, who cannot come into any other position than that which has been held by the testators; and thus the several possession of divided rights in one and the same thing invariably leads to oppressive personal relations. It might therefore be advisable, if not necessary, for the State to prohibit the extension of such contracts beyond the lifetime of the persons concluding them, or, at least, to facilitate the means for effecting a real division of property, where such a relation has once arisen. To enter into fuller details to be observed in such an arrangement does not come within my present design; and this is the less necessary when I consider that it should not be based so much on general principles, as determined by particular laws having distinct reference to specific contracts.

The less a man is induced to act other than according to his wishes and his powers, the more favourable his position as a member of a civil community becomes. If, in view of this truth (around which all the ideas advanced in this essay revolve), we consider the field of civil jurisprudence, there seems to me, among other less important objects, one that especially claims attention; I mean those societies which, in contrast to actual men, we are accustomed to call moral or legal persons. As they always possess a unity, independent of the number of members who compose them, a unity which, with unimportant modifications, maintains itself through the years, they produce in the end all those harmful consequences which have been seen to arise from the practice of testamentary dispositions. For although, with us, much of their harmfulness springs from an arrangement not necessarily connected with their nature—namely, the exclusive privileges now expressly accorded them by the State, and now tacitly sanctioned by custom, as a result of which they often become true political bodies—still they lead in themselves to many inconveniences. But these only arise when the nature of their constitution either compels all the members, against their will, to accept this or that use of their corporate property, or, at least, by the necessity for unanimity, allows the will of the majority to be fettered by that of the minority. Still, unions and associations, so far from having harmful consequences of themselves, are one of the surest and most appropriate ways of promoting and accelerating human development. All that we should expect therefore from the State must be an arrangement that every corporation or association should be regarded simply as a union of the constituent members at any given time; and hence, that all obstacles should be removed which would prevent them deciding in any given case on the use of their corporate powers and property according to the will of the majority. It only remains to provide that only those members on whom the association really depends should be considered as such and not those only who are connected with it as the agents—a confusion which has often occurred, and especially in decisions on the rights of the clergy; where the rights of the clergy have sometimes been mistaken for those of the Church.

From the reasons I have brought forward I would therefore deduce the following principles—

Where man does not confine himself to the immediate province of his own powers and property, but performs actions relating directly to others, the concern for security imposes on the State the following duties—

1. *As regards those actions which are done without the consent or against the will of another, it must prohibit any injury to the latter in the enjoyment of his powers or the possession of his property; further, should he have actually sustained injury in these respects, it must compel the offender to give redress, while it prevents the sufferer from taking private revenge on this or any other pretext.*

2. *Those actions which are undertaken with the free consent of the second party must be confined within the same (and not narrower) restrictions as those which have already been prescribed in the case of actions relating to the agent only.*

3. *If of those actions already specified there are some from which future rights and obligations arise between the parties (single or mutual engagements, contracts, etc.), the State must protect the right of enforcement, where the contractor was in a proper condition to make a reasoned decision, so long as the contract refers to objects at the disposal of the transferring party, and has been transferred with full power of decision; but in no case where the latter conditions are wanting, or where a third person would be unjustly restricted without his consent or against his will.*

4. *Even in the case of valid contracts, if such personal obligations, or, still more, such a continuing personal relation follows as is calculated to restrict freedom within very narrow limits, the State must facilitate a release from the contract, even against the will of one party, and always according to the degree of the harm done by this restriction to inner self-cultivation. Hence, in cases where the discharge of the duties arising from the relation is closely connected with sensibility, it must always grant the power of unconditional release; but wherever (the limitation still being somewhat narrow) this connection is not so intimate, it must allow the power of withdrawal after the lapse of a certain time, this time to be determined according to the importance of the restriction and the nature of what is restricted.*

5. *If anyone desires to dispose of his goods in the event of his death, it might be thought advisable to allow him to appoint his immediate heir, but without any condition being appended to limit the inheritor's power of disposing of the goods according to his views and wishes.*

6. *It is necessary however to prohibit all further dispositions of this nature, to decide on some order of succession* ab intestato, *and to affix the portion due to the testator's family.*

7. *Although contracts concluded by living persons pass over to their heirs, and must be fulfilled towards them, inasmuch as they modify what is left behind, the State should not only prevent the further extension of this principle, but it would be expedient to limit certain contracts which give rise to intimate and restrictive relations between the parties (as, for instance, the division of rights in one thing among several persons) to the period of life only; or, at least, to facilitate their dissolution by the heirs of one or the other party. For although the same reasons do not apply as in the previous case of personal relations, yet the will of the heirs is less free, and the continuance of the relation indefinitely long.*

If I have succeeded in fully conveying my views by the recapitulation of these principles, they will point out the rule to be followed in all cases in which civil legislation has to provide for the maintenance of security.

It is for this reason, for instance, that I have omitted to mention, in this recapitulation, those corporate bodies to which I referred; since, according to the origin of such societies in testament or contract, they are to be judged by the principles established with respect to these. Obviously, the number and variety of the cases which come under the head of civil law forbid my priding myself on my success in this project.

CHAPTER XII

On the solicitude of the State for security

as manifested in the juridical decision

of disputes among the citizens

he security of citizens in a society depends chiefly on transferring to the State all private pursuit of redress. With this transfer the State acquires the duty of giving to the citizens what they may no longer obtain for themselves, and hence of judging disputed cases and of protecting the successful litigant in his rights.

In so doing the State merely disinterestedly takes the place of the citizens. For security is never really violated when the man who is wronged is willing, or has reasons, to waive his right of redress; but only when he who suffers, or believes himself to suffer, wrong will not patiently put up with it. Indeed, if ignorance or indolence should bring men to neglect their personal rights, the State should not interfere on its own account. It has sufficiently done its duty if it has not encouraged such errors by obscure and complicated laws, or by some which have not been properly made known. These considerations also apply to all means adopted by the State to solve the exact question of right in cases where redress is sought. That is, it must not advance a single step further in its investigation into the true nature of the case than the parties concerned require. Hence, the first principle of every judicial proceeding should be never to institute a search to discover the truth absolutely and in itself, but only to conduct the inquiry in so far as it is required by the party who is entitled to demand the full investigation. But here too there is another limitation: the State is not to comply with all wishes of the parties, but only those which bear on the question in dispute, and which employ only such means as, even outside the State, a man might justly use against his fellow-man; especially in cases where the possession of a right, only, is disputed between them, and in which there is no violation, or where this is not immediately evident. The State, the third power called in to the dispute, must use only these means. Hence arises the difference between civil and criminal proceedings: that in the former the only means of eliciting the truth is the administration of the oath, while in the latter the State enjoys far greater liberty in investigation.

Since the judge, as examiner into questions of contested right, occupies a middle place, as it were, between the two parties, it is his duty to see that neither of these is disturbed in his plans for obtaining redress or even delayed by the other; and hence we come to the second principle, equally as important as the first: to keep the conduct of the parties under special supervision during the progress of the suit, and to take care that, instead of serving its purpose, it does not actually hinder it. The most exact and consistent observance of these two principles would give us, I believe, the best system of legal proceeding. For if the importance of the latter principle is overlooked, there is too much scope for the chicanery of the interested parties and the negligence and egotism of the advocates: thus lawsuits become complicated, protracted, and costly; while the decisions are often warped and falsified, irrelevant to the object, and unsatisfactory to the persons concerned. Indeed, these disadvantages often actually increase the frequency of juridical disputes, and tend to promote the spread of a litigious spirit. If, on the other hand, the first principle is not observed, the proceedings become inquisitorial, the judge gets undue power into his hands, and is disposed to meddle in the minutest private affairs of the citizen. There are illustrations of both extremes in actual practice; while experience corroborates our conclusions, and shows that whereas the latter of these errors operates to restrict freedom too narrowly, and at variance with principles of justice, the former tends to endanger the security of property.

In order to discover, the judge needs means of proof. Hence we now notice a new principle of legislation, that is, the need for another kind of law which requires transactions to have certain characteristic features in order to be legally valid. The necessity for laws of this nature invariably decreases as the juridical constitution becomes more perfect; and this necessity is greatest when, owing to a defective constitution, the greatest number of external signs are required to establish proof. Hence we find in the most uncultivated nations the greatest number of formalities. In order to establish a claim to a field among the Romans, it was at first necessary that both the parties to the transaction should be present on the very ground; then it was enough to carry a clod from it into court; afterwards a few formal words were deemed sufficient; and, at last, even these were dispensed with. In general, and especially in the less enlightened nations, the juridical constitution has exercised an important influence on legislation—an influence often far from being limited to mere formalities. I recall here, among the possible examples, the Roman doctrine of pacts and contracts; and although it is a subject which has been little examined or explained as yet, it can hardly be regarded from any other point of view. To inquire into this influence on different systems of legislation in different times and nations would not only be useful in many important respects, but would be especially valuable in this—that it would determine what kind of enactments might be generally necessary, and what were founded only on local and peculiar circumstances.

Even though it were possible, however, it might be scarcely advisable to abolish all limitations of this nature. For, firstly, fraud, such as the substitution of false documents, etc., would become too easy; and secondly, lawsuits would be multiplied, or, if this does not perhaps appear to be itself an evil, there would be too frequent opportunities of disturbing the peace of others, by kindling useless disputes. Now it is just this spirit of contention which manifests itself in lawsuits, which (apart from the loss of time, fortune, and equanimity it occasions the citizen) has the most unfortunate effects on the character; while it has no useful consequences at all to compensate for these evils. The disadvantages, on the other hand, of too many formalities are the increased difficulty of transacting business and the restrictions imposed on freedom, which are, in any relation, of critical importance. Therefore, the law must try here also to adopt a middle course—that is, it must never require formalities for any other object than the validity of negotiations; they are not to be required, even with this object, except where particular circumstances make them necessary, where forgeries might too easily occur without them, and proof be difficult to establish; and, lastly, regulations should only be prescribed respecting them which do not raise too many difficulties, while all regulations should be abolished which would make business transactions not only more difficult, but even almost impossible.

Due consideration, therefore, of security on the one hand, and of freedom on the other, seems to imply the following principles—

1. *One of the principal duties of the State is to investigate and settle the legal disputes of its citizens. In these it takes the place of the interested parties, and the only object is to protect from unjust demands, on the one hand, and, on the other, to give to just ones that due weight and consideration which could only be won for them by the citizens themselves, in some way prejudicial to public order. During the process of inquiry, therefore, it must consult the wishes of the parties, in so far as these are founded on the strictest principles of justice, but must prevent either from using unjust means against the other.*

2. *The judge's decision in cases of contested rights can only be arrived at if particular legal requirements have been satisfied. From this arises the necessity for a new class of laws, namely, those which are designed to specify certain requirements of the validity of legal transactions. In framing such laws the legislator must be guided by two objects only: to provide for the authentication of legal transactions, and to facilitate the proof which is necessary in lawsuits; secondly, to be careful of running into the opposite extreme, of making negotiations too difficult, while he must never impose regulations where they would almost amount to rendering them impossible.*

CHAPTER XIII

On the solicitude for security as manifested in the punishment of transgressions of the State's laws (Criminal laws)

The last, and perhaps the most important, of the means adopted for preserving the security of the citizens is the punishment of transgression of the State's laws. I must therefore apply to this also the fundamental principles we have already agreed on. Now the first question which presents itself here is this: what are the actions which the State can regard and punish as crimes? The answer is, after what has been said previously, an easy one. For as the State must pursue no other end than the security of its subjects, it may impose restrictions only on actions which run counter to this ultimate object. But it also follows that such actions deserve suitable punishment. For since they impair what is most necessary both to man's pleasure and to the cultivation of his powers, the harm they do is so serious that we should use all permissible and appropriate means to oppose it. Moreover, according to the fundamental principles of justice, everyone must accept that the punishment should invade the circle of his own rights to the same extent as the offence invaded that of another. But to punish actions, on the contrary, which relate to the agent only, or which are done with the consent of the person who is affected by them, is forbidden by the same principles which do not permit their limitation; and hence none of the so-called carnal crimes (rape excepted), whether creating offence or not, attempted suicide, etc. ought to be punished, and even taking away a man's life with his own consent should not be, unless the possibility of a dangerous abuse of this exemption should make a criminal law necessary.

Besides those laws which prohibit direct violations of the rights of others, there are others of a different kind which we have already partly discussed, and must now again consider. Since, however, these laws are directed to what we have indicated as the ultimate end of the State, the State may punish breaches of them, in so far as the punishment is not implied in the transgression itself; as, for instance, in the breach of the prohibition of *fidei commissa,* the invalidity of the dispositions follows as a consequence. This is the more necessary, as there would otherwise be complete lack of sanctions for securing obedience to the laws.

From these considerations on the cases to which punishment is to be applied, I now turn to punishment itself. I believe it to be impossible in general reasoning, without reference to local circumstances, to prescribe its extent even in a very broad fashion, or to fix the point beyond which it should never go. Punishments must be evils which deter and intimidate the criminals. Now, their extent must be as infinitely varying as the differences of physical and moral feeling, which differs in different places and periods. What may be called cruelty in one case may be required by necessity in another. This much alone is certain: that, granted equal efficiency, the system of punishment becomes more perfect as it becomes more mild. For not only are mild punishments lesser evils in themselves, but they lead men away from crime in the way that is most worthy of human nature. For the less physically painful and terrible they are, the more they become so morally speaking; while great physical suffering lessens the sense of shame in the sufferer, and of condemnation in the spectator. Hence mild punishments might be much more frequently employed than at first sight would seem possible; since they gain, on the other hand, a compensating moral weight and efficiency in proportion to their mildness. The efficiency of punishments depends entirely on the impression they make on the mind of the criminal; and we might almost claim that in a graduated series of punishments it would not matter which was taken as the last and ultimate punishment, since the actual efficiency of a punishment does not so much depend on its nature in itself as on the relative place it occupies on the scale of punishments, and what the State declares to be the ultimate punishment is readily acknowledged as such. I say almost affirm, for this assertion would only hold good when the punishments inflicted by the State were the only evils to be dreaded by the citizen. But since this is not the case, it very often is real evils which actually lead him to crime; and hence the extent of the most extreme punishment, and therefore of the punishments in general, intended to counteract these evils, must be determined by reference to them as well. Now, where the citizen enjoys as great a freedom as is recommended in these pages, he will live in greater well-being, his soul will become more serene, his imagination sweeter, and punishment will be able to be relaxed in severity without losing its efficiency. So true it is that all good and beneficent things rest in a wonderful harmony that it is only necessary to introduce one of them to enjoy the blessings of all the others. The general conclusion to be derived from this is that the most extreme punishment should be the mildest possible, under existing local circumstances.

There is one kind of punishment, I think, which should be wholly excluded, and that is the loss of honour, infamy. For a man's honour and the good opinion of his fellow-citizens is something which lies wholly outside the power of the State. At most, then, such a punishment must be reduced to this: that the State may deprive the criminal of the signs of its own esteem and confidence, and leave to others the option of doing this with impunity. However unquestionable its claim to such a right may be, and however duty may seem to demand it, I nevertheless cannot consider a general declaration that it will do this by any means advisable. For, firstly, it presupposes a certain persistence in wrong-doing which is rarely found in actual experience; and, secondly, even in its mildest expression, that is if merely expressed a justified mistrust on the part of the State, it is always too indefinite not to create much abuse, and, if only for consistency's sake, would often embrace more cases than might really be necessary. For the kinds of confidence that may be extended to a man are, according to different cases, so infinitely manifold that I hardly know of any crime which would shut out the criminal from all these at once. But there is always a general expression of mistrust in such cases, and the man of whom it would be remembered only on appropriate occasions that he had transgressed any particular law carries about with him a general air of unworthiness. Now, how hard such a punishment must be we know from the feeling we all know, that without the confidence of one's fellow-men life itself ceases to be worth living. Moreover, many other difficulties present themselves when we look more closely at the way in which such a punishment shall be applied. Mistrust of honesty will always follow where the lack of it has been shown. Now, to how many cases such a punishment would have to be extended, one can see for oneself. No less difficult is the question how long the punishment shall last. Every right-thinking man would undoubtedly wish to confine it to a certain period. But will the judge be able to contrive that one who has so long borne the load of his fellow-citizens' mistrust may at once regain their confidence on the expiration of a certain day? Lastly, it is not in accordance with the principles which run through this essay that the State should give a definite direction to the opinions of the citizens in any way whatever. According to my views, therefore, it would seem advisable for the State to confine itself within the limits of its incumbent duty, to protect the citizens against suspicious persons, and hence, wherever necessary—as, for instance, in official appointments, acceptance of the testimony of witnesses, approval of guardians, etc.—to exclude, by laws expressly enacted, those who had committed certain crimes or incurred certain punishments: beyond this, the State should refrain from any general manifestation of mistrust or any deprivation of honour. In this case also it would be very easy to fix on some time beyond which such objections should cease to operate. For the rest, it is needless to show that the State always retains the right of acting on the sense of honour by degrading punishments. Neither is it necessary for me to repeat (now that I am treating of the general nature of punishments) that no punishment whatever must be inflicted which would extend beyond the person of the criminal to his children or relations. Justice and equity alike declare against such a course; and even the caution observed, in the otherwise excellent Prussian code, where such a punishment occurs, is not sufficient to lessen the severity necessarily inherent in the thing itself.[1]

Since it is impossible to fix an absolute standard of punishment, it is, on the other hand, the more necessary to fix its relative degree. That is, we should establish the standard according to which the degree of punishment attaching to different crimes should be determined. Now, it seems to follow as a consequence of the principles we have developed that this standard can be no other than what is suggested by the extent of disregard

---

[1] This paragraph of the Prussian Civil Code ran: 'Such persons guilty of high treason shall not only forfeit all goods and civil status, but their children also shall bear the guilt of their misfortune, if the State finds it necessary for the avoidance of future dangers to keep them in perpetual detention or banishment' [L].

for others' rights shown in the crime; and this (since we are not referring to the application of any penal law to an individual criminal, but to the general principles of punishment) must be decided according to the nature of the right which is violated by the crime. The most natural principle seems to be to judge according to the ease or difficulty of preventing the crime, so that the extent of the punishment should be proportionate to the strength of the motives which impelled or deterred the criminal. But when this principle is rightly understood, we find it to be identical with the one we have just laid down. For in a well-organized State, where there is nothing in the constitution itself which is calculated to incite men to crime, there cannot properly be any other cause of crime than the disregard for others' rights, which the impulses, inclinations, and passions prompting crime take advantage of. But if this principle is differently interpreted; if it is supposed that crimes should always be met with punishment to the extent that circumstances of time and locality make them more frequent, or, still more (as in the case of so many crimes against the State) to the extent that, from their very nature, moral restraints are less effective against them—then the standard would be unjust and harmful.

It would be unjust. For as it is correct to suppose the prevention of future injuries to be the end of all punishment—at least in so far as never to allow a punishment to be inflicted with any other purpose—so the necessity for the criminal to undergo the punishment arises from the fact that everyone must submit to an infringement of his own rights exactly in proportion as he has violated the rights of others. This obligation rests on these grounds not only outside political society but also within it. For to derive it from a mutual contract is not only useless, but also has this difficulty—that capital punishment, for example, which is clearly necessary at some times and in certain circumstances, could hardly be justified on these grounds, and that every criminal could escape his punishment if before undergoing it he renounced the social contract; as we see, for instance, in the voluntary exile of the ancient republics, which however, if my memory does not mislead me, was only admitted in cases of political and not private crimes. No discussion of the State's actions can therefore be allowed to the offender; and, however certain it may be that the party injured would have no new injury to fear from him, he must still acknowledge the justice of the punishment. But it follows also, on the other hand, from the same principle, that he may justly resist every punishment exceeding the extent of his crime, however certain it might be that this punishment alone, and no milder one whatever, would be effective. There is obviously an intimate connection in human ideas between the internal feeling of right and the enjoyment of external happiness, and the former seems to man to entitle him to the latter. Whether this expectation is justified by the happiness which fate grants him is a more doubtful question, but cannot be discussed here. But his right to the happiness to which he is entitled, in so far as others can arbitrarily grant or withhold it, must be acknowledged. This principle, however, seems to deny it, at least *de facto*.

But, further, this standard is harmful even to security itself. For although it may enforce obedience to this or that particular law, it disturbs and confuses precisely what is the mainstay of the security of the citizens in a State—the feeling of morality—by causing a conflict between the treatment a criminal meets with, and his own consciousness of his guilt. The only certain and infallible means of preventing crime is to secure a due regard for the rights of others; and this is never achieved unless everyone who infringes those rights is restricted to an equal extent in the exercise of his own. For it is only by such a correspondence that harmony is preserved between man's internal moral development and the success of political arrangements, without which even the most ingenious legislation will always fail in its purpose. How much the attainment of all other human purposes would suffer from the adoption of such a standard—how much it contradicts all the principles laid down in this essay, it is needless for me to show. Again, the equality between crime and punishment which is demanded by the reasons we have put forward cannot be absolutely determined; we cannot decide in a general way that this or that crime is deserving of this or that particular punishment. It is only in a series of crimes differing in degree that the means of securing this equality can be described; and in this case the respective punishments must be arranged in corresponding gradations. When, therefore, in accordance with what has been said, the absolute standard of punishment (for instance, of the most extreme punishment) is to be determined according to the amount of evil done, and to what is necessary to prevent the crime in the future, the relative extent of the others (when the highest, or indeed any, punishment has once been fixed) must be determined according to the extent to which the respective crimes are greater or less than that which the first punishment was intended to prevent. The most severe punishments, therefore, should be applied to those crimes which really infringe the rights of others, and the milder ones to transgressions of those laws which are simply designed to prevent such infringements, however important and necessary those laws may be in themselves. In this way the citizens are disabused of the idea that they are treated arbitrarily by the State, and that its conduct towards them is not grounded on proper motives—a prejudice easily awakened where severe punishments are inflicted on actions which either really have only a remote influence on security, or whose connection with it is not easy to understand. Among the crimes first mentioned, those which attack directly the rights of the State itself must be met with the severest punishment, since he who shows no regard for the rights of the State shows that he does not respect those of his fellow-citizens, whose security depends upon the former.

When crimes and punishments have been generally apportioned by the law in this way, these penal enactments must then be applied to particular crimes. Here, according to the principles of justice, the punishment must only affect the criminal to the same extent as his criminal intention or guilt in the action he has committed. But when the above principle is exactly followed, and only disregard for the rights of others punished in all cases, the application of the principle to individual cases must not be forgotten. In every crime committed, therefore, the judge must make it his business to inquire carefully into the intention of the criminal, and must have the legal power to modify the general punishment according to the particular extent to which the criminal has disregarded the right he has violated.

The proceedings against the criminal, moreover, are prescribed by the general principles of justice, in the same manner as before. That is, the judge must take all just measures to discover the truth, but must refrain from making use of any which lie beyond the legitimate limit. He must therefore draw a careful distinction between the citizen who is only suspected, and the criminal who is actually convicted, never treating the former like the latter; and, in fine, must never deprive even the convicted criminal of the enjoyment of his rights as a man and as a citizen, since he can lose the former only with his life, and the latter only by a legal, judicial exclusion from the political association. The use of means, therefore, which involve actual deceit should be as unlawful for this purpose as the employment of torture. For although it might perhaps be urged, in excuse, that the suspected person, or at least the criminal, authorized such a course by the character of his own actions, it is still wholly unworthy of the dignity of the State, which is represented by the judge; and as to the salutary effects of an open and straightforward conduct even towards the criminals, it is not only evident in itself, but also in the experience of those States (England, for example) which enjoy in this respect an honourable legislature.

Lastly, I must (now that we are treating of criminal law), examine a question that has assumed a high degree of importance by the efforts of modern legislation; the question, namely, as to how far the State is entitled or obliged to prevent crimes not yet committed. There is perhaps no project so philanthropically intended, and the sympathy which it inspires in every man of feeling is somewhat dangerous to the impartiality of the inquiry. Nevertheless, I really consider such an inquiry highly necessary, since, if we consider the infinite variety of impulses from which the intention to commit a crime may arise, it seems to me impossible to devise any method of wholly preventing such designs, and furthermore actually hazardous to freedom, to prevent their execution. As I have already attempted to define the right of the State to restrict the actions of individual men, I may seem to have already answered this question. But when I therefore established that the State should restrict those actions whose consequences might endanger the rights of others, I understood by these (as the reasons I advanced in support of this position show) only consequences which would arise solely and in themselves from the action, and might only be avoided perhaps by greater caution on the part of the agent. But when we speak of the prevention of crimes, we naturally mean the restriction of actions which give rise to other actions, namely crimes. Hence there is already this important difference, that the agent must here cooperate by a new decision; while in the former case he might either have no influence whatever, or merely a negative one, by doing nothing. This alone, I hope, will serve to show the distinction sufficiently clearly.

Now all prevention of crime must be directed to its causes. But these causes, which are so infinitely varied, might be expressed perhaps in a general formula as the feeling, not sufficiently resisted by reason, of the disparity between the inclinations of the agent and the means in his power for gratifying them. Although it might be very difficult to distinguish them in particular instances, there would be, in general, two distinct cases of this disproportion; firstly, when it arises from a real excess of desires, and, secondly, when it results from a lack of means to satisfy even ordinary inclinations. Both cases however must be accompanied by a want of strong reasoning power and of moral feeling, which fails to prevent the disparity from breaking out into illegal actions. Every effort of the State, then, to prevent crimes by suppressing their causes in the criminal must, according to the difference noticed in these cases, be directed towards changing and amending the situation of the citizens when it may oblige them to commit crimes; or to restrict the inclinations which usually lead to transgression of the laws; or, to gain greater force and efficiency for the arguments of reason and the operation of moral feeling. Lastly, too, there is another method of preventing crimes, by legally reducing the opportunities to commit them, or circumstances which even encourage the outbreak of lawless inclinations. We must not overlook any of these different methods in the present inquiry.

The first of these, which is designed only to reform the conditions leading to crime, seems to have by far the fewest disadvantages. It is in itself so beneficial and calculated to enrich men's opportunities for the exercise of their powers as well as opportunities of enjoyment; it does not directly restrict free activity; and although it is clearly undeniable that it has all those consequences which I have earlier represented as the effects of the State's concern for the physical welfare of the citizens, still they only follow here in a much smaller degree, since this protectiveness is extended only to a few persons. Nevertheless they do always really result from such a policy; the conflict between internal morality and external circumstances is done away with, and along with it its beneficial influence on the agent's strength of character, and on mutual benevolence among the citizens in general; and the very fact that such concern can only apply to particular individuals necessitates political interference in the individual circumstances of the citizens—all of which are ill effects which we could only overlook if we were convinced that the security of the State would suffer without such an arrangement. But there seems to me considerable reason to doubt such a necessity. For in a State whose own constitution does not place the citizens in such pressing circumstances, but which, on the contrary, ensures the freedom which it is the intention of this essay to recommend, it is hardly possible in general that such situations as those we describe should arise, without finding a sufficient remedy in the voluntary assistance of the citizens themselves, without any State interference; the cause in such a case must be looked for in the conduct of the man himself. But in this case it is wrong for the State to interfere in the natural consequences of men's actions. These situations, moreover, will only occur so rarely as to require no especial State interference, so that its advantages would be exceeded by those disadvantages which need no more detailed exposition here, after all that has already been said.

Exactly the reverse are the reasons for and against the second method for the prevention of crime which is designed to act on men's own passions and inclinations. For, on the one hand, the necessity seems greater for, with more unrestricted freedom, enjoyment becomes more extravagant, and desires more far-reaching; against which the regard for others' rights, although it always increases with the sense of one's own freedom, might not perhaps be sufficient. But, on the other hand, the disadvantages increase as the moral nature is more sensitive to every constraint than the physical. I have already attempted to show the reasons for holding that any political effort directed to the moral improvement of the citizens is neither necessary nor advisable. These reasons apply in this case in their full extent, and only with this difference: that the State does not here aim at reforming morality in general, but only at exercising an influence on the conduct of particular individuals which seems to endanger the authority of the law. But by this very difference the sum of the disadvantages increases. For, precisely because this effort is not general in its operation, it must fall short of its purpose, so that not even the partial good which it does is sufficient to reconcile us to the harm which it causes; and further, it presupposes not only the interference of the State in the citizen's private actions, but also the power of influencing them—a power which is still more questionable when we consider those to whom it may be entrusted. That is, there must be a superintending power entrusted either to persons specially appointed, or to the regular State functionaries who are already in office, over the conduct and the situations arising out of it, either of all the citizens, or of those who come under their immediate inspection. But in this way a new kind of domination is introduced, which is perhaps more oppressive than any other could be; and an opportunity is given for impertinent curiosity, bigoted intolerance, and even hypocrisy and dissimulation. I hope I may not be accused of having indicated only abuses here. The abuses are here inseparably connected with the thing itself; and I venture to assert that even though the laws might be the best and most philanthropic, and allow to the superintending official nothing beyond the information to be gained through lawful channels, and the use of advice and exhortation wholly free from coercion—and should the most perfect obedience be given to these laws, still such an institution would be both useless and dangerous. Every citizen must be in a position to act without hindrance and just as he pleases, so long as he does not transgress the law; every one must have the right to maintain, in reply to others, and even against all probability, so far others can tell, 'However closely I approach the danger of transgressing the law, yet will I not succumb.' If he is deprived of this liberty, then his right is violated, and the cultivation of his faculties—the development of his individuality—suffers. For the forms of morality and observance of law are infinitely different and varying; and if another person decides that such or such a course of conduct must lead to unlawful actions, he follows his own view, which, however just it may be, is still only the view of one man. But even supposing he were not mistaken in his judgement—that the result were even such as to confirm it and that the other, yielding to coercion or following advice, without internal conviction, should not this once transgress the law which otherwise he would have done—still it would be better for the transgressor to feel for once the weight of punishment, and to gain the pure instruction of experience, than to escape this particular evil, but not to gain any greater clearness of ideas, or any active exercise of moral feeling; and it would still be better that one more transgression of the law should disturb public tranquillity, and that the consequent punishment should serve as an instruction and warning, than that the very thing on which the tranquillity and security of the citizens depend—the regard for others' rights—be neither really greater in itself, nor in this case increased and promoted. Finally, moreover, such an institution cannot have the effect ascribed to it. As with all means which do not act directly on the inner sources from which actions spring, it will only give another direction to the desires which run counter to the laws, and produce a dissimulation twice as harmful. I have hitherto confined myself to the assumption that the persons to whom such supervision is entrusted do not produce inner conviction, but only work through the medium of external arguments. It may seem that I am not authorized to proceed on such an assumption. But that it is good to exercise an influence on one's fellow-citizens and their morality through the medium of a living example and convincing persuasion is too obvious to need repeating. In any case, where such an institution produces these results, our reasoning cannot apply. Only it seems to me that a legal prescription to this end is not only an inappropriate method, but even a self-defeating one. For, firstly, it is not the province of the law to recommend virtues, but only to prescribe duties which can be enforced; and it will frequently happen that virtue will lose by such an attempt, since man only enjoys a course of virtuous action when it proceeds from his own free will. And, secondly, every mere request contained in a law, and every admonition or advice which a superior gives in virtue of it, is a positive command, which theoretically, it is true, men are not forced to observe, but which in reality they always do obey. Lastly, we must take into account how many circumstances may oblige men, and how many motives may incite them to follow such advice, even wholly against their convictions. The influence which the State has over those at the head of its affairs and through whom it attempts, at the same time, to influence the other citizens is usually of this kind. Since such persons are bound to the State by special contracts, it is undeniable that it can exercise greater rights over them than over the other citizens. But if it faithfully adheres to the principles of the highest legal freedom, it will not seek to obtain more from them than the fulfilment of civic duties in general, and of those special duties which are required by their particular offices. For it obviously exercises too strong a positive influence on the citizens in general when it tries to impose on these, in virtue of their special connection with it, anything which it has no right to impose directly on the other citizens. Without the State taking any positive steps, it is quite sufficiently anticipated by men's passions; and the task of preventing the evils which arise spontaneously from these sources will fully employ its zeal and vigilance.

The State has a more direct motive for preventing crimes by the suppression of their causes in the character in the case of those who, by their actual transgressions of the law, awaken a reasonable anxiety with regard to their future conduct. Hence, the most thoughtful modern legislators have attempted to make punishments at the same time reformatory. Now it is certain not only that everything should be removed from the punishment of criminals at all calculated to do harm to their morality, but also that every means of correcting their ideas and improving their feelings must be left open to them, so long as it does not counteract the object of the punishment. But instruction is not to be thrust even on the criminal; and while, by the very fact of its being enforced, it loses its usefulness and efficiency, such enforcement is also contrary to the rights of the criminal, who never can be compelled to anything save suffering the legal punishment.

There is still, however, a completely special case, where the accused has too many things against him not to labour under a strong suspicion of guilt, but still not enough to justify his being condemned (*absolutio ab instantia*).[2] To grant to him, under such circumstances, the full freedom enjoyed by citizens of good reputation is hardly compatible with care for security; and a constant surveillance of his future conduct hence evidently becomes necessary. The same reasons, however, which make every positive effort on the part of the State so questionable, and which make it advisable to substitute the efforts of individual citizens wherever this is possible, lead us in this case also to prefer the voluntary surveillance of the citizens to the supervision of the State; and hence it might be better to allow suspected persons of this class to give security rather than to place them directly under the eye of the State, which should only be done in cases where securities could not be obtained. We find examples of such security given (not in this case, it is true, but in similar ones) in the legislation of England.

The last method of preventing crimes is that which, without attempting to act on their causes, endeavours only to prevent the actual commission of them. This is the least immediately harmful to freedom, as it least of all leads to the exercise of any positive influence. However, this method also admits of greater or less extension of its sphere and operation. For the State may content itself with exercising the most watchful vigilance on every unlawful project, and defeating it before it has been put into execution; or, advancing further, it may prohibit actions which are harmless in themselves, but which tempt to the commission or planning of crime. This latter, again, tends to encroach on the liberty of the citizens;

---

[2] 'Acquittal for the present'.

it shows a distrust on the part of the State which not only harms the character of the citizens, but helps to defeat the end in view; and is not advisable for the same reasons as the methods of preventing crime mentioned earlier. All that the State may do, without frustrating its own end, and without encroaching on the freedom of its citizens, is, therefore, restricted to the former course—that is, the strictest surveillance of every transgression of the law, either already committed or only planned; and as this cannot properly be called preventing the causes of crime, I think I may safely assert that the prevention of criminal actions is wholly outside the State's proper sphere of activity. But it must all the more assiduously take care that no crime committed shall remain undiscovered, and that no offence discovered shall escape unpunished, or even punished more leniently than the law strictly demands. For the conviction in the minds of the citizens—a conviction strengthened by unvarying experience—that it is impossible for them to infringe the rights of others without suffering an equivalent diminution of their own seems to me at once the only bulwark of internal security, and the only infallible means of creating an inviolable regard for the rights of others. This is, at the same time, the only way to act worthily on man's character, since we must not lead or compel him to certain actions, but only bring him to them by a consideration of the consequences, which, according to the nature of things, must flow inevitably from his conduct.[3] Hence, instead of all the more artificial and complicated means for averting crime, I would never propose anything but good and well-matured laws; punishments adapted, in their absolute extent, to local circumstances, and, in their relative degree, to the immorality of the crime; as minute a search as possible into all actual transgressions of law; and, lastly, the certainty of the punishment determined by the judge, without any possibility of lightening its severity. Should these methods, so simple in their operation, be somewhat slow in their effects, as I will not deny they may be, they are, on the other hand, sure and infallible; they do not harmfully affect the freedom of the citizen, and they exercise a salutary influence upon his character. I need not dwell longer on this subject to point out the consequences of these principles such as, for example, the truth so often observed, that the right of the

---

[3] This, it will be remembered, was the central doctrine of Rousseau's *Emile*, which is here applied to criminal law.

sovereign to grant reprieve or mitigation of the punishment must cease completely. Such consequences are easily derived from the principles themselves. The detail of arrangements to be adopted by the State for the discovery of crimes actually committed, or for the prevention of those which are only planned, depends almost entirely on the individual circumstances of particular situations. We may only generally observe that here also the State must not go beyond its rights, and hence that it must not do anything contrary to the freedom and domestic security of the citizens. But it may appoint proper officers to be on the watch in public places where misdemeanours are most commonly committed; establish public prosecutors, who may, in virtue of their office, proceed against suspected persons; and, lastly, make it legally binding on all the citizens to lend their assistance to the task, by denouncing not only crimes which are contemplated but not yet committed, but those which are already perpetrated, and the criminals concerned in them. Only, in order not to harm the character of the citizens, it must demand this only as a duty, and must not incite them by rewards and benefits; and it must absolve them from even this duty where it could not be fulfilled without breaking the closest family ties.

Lastly, before concluding this subject, I ought to observe that all criminal laws, both those which fix the punishments and which prescribe the forms of procedure, must be fully and clearly made known to all the citizens without distinction. I am well aware that a contrary practice has been repeatedly recommended, and the reason given is that the citizen should not be given the choice of purchasing the advantages of his unlawful action by being prepared to accept the punishment for it. But, even granted the possibility of concealment, however immoral such a balancing of advantages would be in the man who adopted it, still the State must not forbid it, nor indeed can any man forbid it to another. It has, I hope, been sufficiently shown above that no man is justified in injuring another, under the name of punishment, any further than he has himself suffered by the crime. If there were no legal determination of punishment, the criminal ought to expect about the same extent of injury as he would think equal to his crime; and as this estimate would vary too much according to the variety of men's characters, it is very natural that a fixed standard should be determined by law, and hence that there should be a contract, not indeed to confirm the obligation to suffer punishment, but to prevent the arbitrary transgression of all limits in inflicting it. Still more unjust does such concealment of the law become as regards the process of investigating and searching out crimes. In this case it could evidently serve no other purpose than that of exciting fear of such means as the State does not think fit to employ; and the State should never seek to act through fears, which can depend on nothing else than the ignorance of the citizens of their rights, or distrust of the State's respect for them.

I now deduce from the previous arguments the following ultimate principles of every general system of criminal legislation—

1. *One of the chief means for preserving security is the punishment of transgressions of the laws. The State must inflict punishment on every action which infringes on the rights of the citizens, and (in so far as its legislation is guided by this principle alone) every action in which the transgression of one of its laws is implied.*

2. *The most severe punishment must be only that which is the mildest possible, according to particular circumstances of time and place. From this all other punishments must be determined, in proportion to the disregard for the rights of others in the crimes committed. Hence, the severest punishment must be reserved for the man who has violated the most important right of the State itself; one less severe must be inflicted on the one who has violated an equally important right of an individual citizen; and, lastly, one still milder must be applied to one who has only transgressed a law designed to prevent such injuries.*

3. *Criminal laws are to be applied only to one who has transgressed them intentionally or culpably, and only to the extent to which the criminal thereby showed a disregard for the rights of others.*

4. *In the inquiry into crimes committed, the State may indeed employ every means consistent with the end, but none which would treat the citizen who is only suspected as already a criminal, nor any which would violate the rights of man and citizen (which the State must respect even in the criminal), or which would render the State guilty of an immoral action.*

5. *The State must only adopt special arrangements for preventing crimes not yet committed, in so far as they avert their immediate perpetration. And all others, whether they are designed to counteract the causes of crime, or to prevent actions, harmless in themselves, but often leading to criminal offences, are wholly beyond the State's sphere of action. If there seems to be a contradiction between this principle and that laid down with regard to the actions of individual men, it must not be forgotten that the previous question applied to actions which in their immediate consequences were likely to*

infringe the rights of others, and that here we are considering those from which, in order to produce this effect, a further action must proceed. The concealment of pregnancy[4]*—to illustrate what I mean by an example—ought not to be forbidden in order to prevent infanticide (unless we were to regard it as already an indication of the mother's intention), but as an action which, in itself, and without any such intention, might be dangerous to the life of the infant.*

[4] Humboldt had been interested in this question for some time. See R. Leroux, *Guillaume de Humboldt. La formation de sa pensée jusqu'en 1794* (Paris, 1932), p. 57.

CHAPTER XIV

On the solicitude of the State for the welfare of minors, lunatics, and idiots

ll the principles I have hitherto attempted to establish presuppose men to have the full use of their mature powers of understanding. For they are all grounded on the conviction that the man who thinks and acts for himself should never be robbed of the power of voluntarily deciding on all that concerns himself, according to the results of his deliberations. Hence, then, they cannot be applied to persons such as lunatics and idiots, who are almost wholly deprived of reason, or to those in whom it has not reached that maturity which depends on the maturity of the body. For, however indefinite and, strictly speaking, incorrect, the latter standard may be, still there can be no other generally valid test to enable us to judge. Now, all these need, in the strictest sense, a positive care for their physical and moral well-being, and the merely negative preservation of their security is not enough in their case. But, to begin with children, who constitute the largest and most important class of such persons, it is evident that the care for their welfare, in virtue of the principles of justice, belongs to certain persons, that is, their parents. It is their duty to bring up their offspring to full maturity; and from this duty, and as a necessary condition of fulfilling it, arise all their rights with regard to them. The children, therefore, retain all their original rights as regards their life, their health, their goods, if they already possess any, and should not be limited even in their freedom, except in so far as the parents may think necessary, partly for their own development, and partly to preserve the newly created family relations, while such limitations should not extend beyond the time required for their training. Children must never be compelled to actions which

extend in their immediate consequences beyond this period of development, or even over their whole life. Hence, for example, they cannot be
bound in the matter of marriage, or be obliged to follow any particular
career. With the age of maturity the power of the parents must necessarily
cease altogether. The duty of the parents, then, may be thus generally
defined—to put their children in a condition, partly by personal care for
their physical and moral well-being, and partly by providing them with
the necessary means, to choose a plan of life for themselves, while they
are only restricted in that choice by the circumstances of their individual
position; the duty of the children, on the other hand, consists in doing all
that is necessary for the sufficient performance of that duty on the part of
the parents. I shall not consider in detail all that these respective duties
may and must include. Such an examination belongs rather to a theory of
legislation, and even these could hardly be fully presented, seeing that it
depends to a great extent on the individual circumstances of particular
situations.

Now, it is clearly incumbent on the State to provide for the security of
the rights of children against their parents; and hence to determine, first, a
legal age of maturity. Now, this must naturally differ not only according
to the difference of the climate and the time in which they live, but also
according to individual circumstances, and the greater or less degree of
intellectual maturity required in them. In addition to this, it must see that
the paternal power does not exceed its limits, and must always watch
closely over it. Still this supervision must never seek to prescribe any
positive rules for the definite training and instruction of the children by
their parents, but must confine itself to the negative precautions necessary
to preserve in both the due observance of the mutual limits and relations
assigned them by the law. It seems, therefore neither just nor advisable to
require parents to be continually rendering account of their conduct
towards their children; they must be trusted not to neglect the discharge
of a duty which lies so near to their hearts; and only in cases where actual
neglect of this responsibility has occurred, or is immediately about to do
so, has the State any right to interfere with these family relations.

To whom the care of the children's upbringing must fall, after the
death of the parents, is not so clearly determined by the principles of
natural law. Hence, it becomes the duty of the State to decide on which of
the kinsmen the guardianship is to devolve; or, if none of them should be

in a condition to undertake the duty, to declare how one of the other citizens may be chosen for the trust. It must likewise determine what are the necessary qualifications for guardianship. Since the guardians appointed undertake all the duties which belonged to the parents, they also enter on all their accompanying rights; but as, in any case they do not stand in so close a relationship to their wards, they cannot claim an equal degree of confidence, and the State must therefore double its vigilance over them. With guardians, therefore, it might be necessary to require a regular account of their trusteeship. According to our principles, the State should exercise as little positive influence as possible, even indirectly. Hence, then, as far as its care for the children allows, it must try to make possible the choice of a guardian by the dying parents themselves, or by the surviving relatives or by the municipality to which the children belong. It is in general advisable to transfer the supervision of all special precautions to be taken in such cases to the respective municipalities; their measures will not only always be more suitable to the individual circumstances of the wards, but will be more diverse and less uniform; and so long as an overall supervision remains in the hands of the State itself, the security of the wards is sufficiently provided for.

In addition to these arrangements, the State should not content itself with protecting minors like other citizens from the attacks of others, but must go further in this respect. It has been laid down above that every man may dispose of his goods or decide on his actions, as the case may be, of his own free will. Such freedom might be dangerous, in more respects than one, to those whose judgement was not fully matured. It is, indeed, the duty of the parents, or of the guardians, to avert such dangers, and they have the right to guide the minor's actions. But the State must aid them both in this, and declare their actions void when the consequences of them would be harmful. It must therefore prevent others with self-interested motives from deceiving them or persuading them against their better judgement. Where this happens, the State must not only enforce reparation, but must also punish the guilty ones; and thus actions may become punishable which would otherwise be beyond the competence of the law. I may here mention illicit sexual intercourse as an example; according to these principles, the State must punish the perpetrator, when the offence has been committed with a minor. But as human actions require many different degrees of judgement, and judgement only matures gradually, it is desirable, in deciding the guilt of various actions, to relate them to different periods or stages in the minor's maturity.

What we have here said of minors applies also to the treatment of idiots and madmen. The difference chiefly consists in this, that these do not require education and training, unless we apply this name to the efforts made to restore them to the use of their reason, but only care and supervision; that in their case, moreover, it is principally the injury they might do to others which is to be prevented, and that they are generally in a condition which forbids the enjoyment either of their personal liberty or goods, though it must not be forgotten that as their return to reason is still possible, the temporary exercise of their rights is all that should be taken from them, and not those rights themselves. As my present design does not permit me to take the matter further, I shall conclude the subject with a statement of the following general principles—

1. *Those persons who have not the use of their powers of understanding, or have not yet reached the age necessary for the possession of them, require special care for their physical, intellectual, and moral welfare. Persons of this kind are minors and those deprived of reason. First, of the former class; and, secondly, of the latter.*

2. *In the case of minors, the State must determine the duration of their minority. It must provide in this that the period be neither too long nor too short to be essentially harmful, deciding according to the individual circumstances of the condition of the nation, and guided by considerations of the period required for the full development of the body, as an approximate guide. It is advisable that different times should be appointed for the expiration of minority in respect of the validity of different actions, and that the freedom of minors should be gradually enlarged while the supervision of their affairs is correspondingly diminished.*

3. *The State must see that the parents strictly fulfil their duty towards their children, that is, to fit them, as far as their situation allows, to choose a plan of life of their own; and that the children, on their part, discharge the duty they owe to their parents, that is, to do all they can to enable the latter to fulfil their duty with regard to them; while neither should be allowed to overstep the rights which the discharge of their mutual duty gives them. The State's object must be restricted to this; and every attempt to bring about positive ends in this connection—such as, for example, to encourage a particular development of the children's faculties—lies outside the limits of its activity.*

4. *In the event of the death of the parents, guardians have to be appointed. The State, therefore, should determine the way in which they are to be chosen, and the qualifications needed in them. But it will do well to provide that they be appointed by the parents before their death, or by the surviving relatives, or by the municipality to which the minors belong. The conduct of the guardian in the discharge of his duty requires special supervision on the part of the State.*

5. *In order to provide for the security of minors, so that their inexperience and rashness shall not be exploited by others to prejudice their interests, the State must declare all such self-interested actions void whose consequences are likely to be harmful and must punish those who have taken advantage of the minors in this way.*

6. *All that is said here of minors applies equally to those who are deprived of reason, with the difference which is suggested by the nature of the case itself. No one moreover should be regarded as such until he has been formally declared to be so, after an inquiry into the circumstances by medical men, and under the supervision of the magistrate; and the evil itself must always be considered as temporary, and the return of reason possible.*

I have now considered all the objects to which the State's actions should be directed, and have attempted to lay down the ultimate principle by which it should be guided in each case. Should this essay appear imperfect, and should I seem to have omitted much that is important in legislation, it must not be forgotten that it was not my intention to construct a theory of legislation, a task beyond my knowledge and abilities, but only to make it clear how far legislation in its different branches might extend or restrict the State's activities. For, as legislation may be divided according to its objects, it can also be arranged according to its sources; and perhaps the latter system of division, particularly for the legislator himself, is more fruitful. There seems to me to be only three such sources, or, to speak more correctly, three main points of view from which the necessity of laws is apparent. Legislation in general must deal with the actions of the citizen and their necessary consequences. The first point of view, therefore, arises from the nature of those actions, and of their consequences, which alone spring from the principles of justice. The second point of view is the special purpose of the State, the limits to which it resolves to restrict or to extend its activities. Lastly, the third point of view is suggested by the means which it needs to maintain the State edifice itself, and to make the attainment of its ends at all possible.

Every conceivable law must properly fall under one of these three points of view; but none should be made and enacted without regard to all three, and the one-sided outlook in which they have originated is an essential defect in too many laws. Now from this threefold aspect we have three preliminary essentials for every system of legislation. 1. A complete general theory of justice. 2. A complete exposition of the end which the State should set itself, or what is, in fact, the same thing, an accurate definition of the limits within which it is to restrict its activity, or a depiction of the special ends which are actually pursued by this or that State association. 3. A theory of the means necessary to the existence of a State; and as these means are necessary partly for the sake of preserving internal cohesion, and partly in order to make its activities possible, a theory of political and of financial science, or, again, a depiction of actual systems of politics and economic science. In this general classification, which allows various subdivisions, I would only observe that the first category alone is eternal and immutable as human nature itself, while the others allow of various modifications. If, however, these modifications do not proceed from general considerations, derived from all these different aspects of legislations, but from accidental circumstances; if, for example, there exists in some State a fixed political system, and financial arrangements which are unchangeable, then the second category we have mentioned falls into great difficulties and the first suffers as a result. The reasons for very many political imperfections might certainly be traced to these and other similar conflicts.

Thus I hope I have sufficiently defined the point of view I took up in this attempted exposition of the principles of legislation. But, even with these limitations, I am very far from flattering myself with any great success in my design. The correctness of the principles laid down may in general be unquestionable, but there is doubtless much incompleteness in the attempt to support and accurately define them. Even to establish the most fundamental principle, and especially with such a purpose, it is necessary to enter into the most minute details. But it was not in accordance with my plan to enter into these; and while I did my best to conceive them in my own mind as the model for the little I wrote down, I constantly fell short of doing so. I must, therefore, rest satisfied with having pointed out what remains to be done, rather than with having fully developed the whole subject. Still I hope I have said enough to make my own position in this essay clearer, or to show that the chief point to be kept in view by the State is the development of the powers of its citizens in their full individuality; that it must, therefore, pursue only that object which they cannot procure for themselves, namely security; and that this is the only true and infallible way to connect, by a strong and enduring bond, two apparently incompatible things: the general end of the State and the ends of all the individual citizens.

CHAPTER XV

Measures for the maintenance of the
State ▪ Completion of the theory

ccording to the plan I proposed to myself in a former chapter,* I have now completed the remainder of my task, and have, therefore, given as full and accurate a solution of the question before us as my ability would allow. I could conclude, then, at this point, if I were not obliged to refer, before doing so, to one final consideration, which is of the greatest importance for the whole subject; I allude to the means which are necessary, not only to make the activity of the State possible, but even to secure its existence.

In order to accomplish even the most limited objects, the State must have sufficient sources of revenue. My ignorance of everything concerned with finance prevents my entering here on an elaborate disquisition. So, according to the plan I have chosen, this is not necessary. For, as I observed at the outset, we are not supposing the case of a State whose ends are determined by the extent and efficiency of the means it may happen to possess, but rather that of one in which the latter are subordinate to and determined by the former.[1] I have only to observe, for the sake of consistency, that it is no less our duty to regard, in financial arrangements also, the true end of man as member of the body politic, and the limitations arising from this. Even a moment's reflection on the close interdependence between police and financial regulations is sufficient to convince us of this. There are then, it seems to me, only three sources of State revenue—1. The property which has been reserved for

---

* Chapter IX.
[1] At this point there is a reference in the manuscript to the section which is now missing.

the State, or subsequently acquired; 2. Direct taxation; 3. Indirect taxation. All State property has pernicious consequences. I have already shown that the State must, by its very nature, obtain a predominant influence compared with private individuals; and in becoming a proprietor, it must necessarily become involved in many private relations, while it preserves all its peculiar attributes. That is, the power of the State, which it is allowed only to serve the needs of security, takes up a role in cases where security is not an issue. Indirect taxation likewise has harmful consequences. Experience teaches us what a multiplicity of institutions is required to arrange and levy them; and of all these, according to our previous reasoning, we must unquestionably disapprove. Direct taxation, then, is all that remains. Now, of all the possible systems of direct taxation, the physiocratical[2] is unquestionably the simplest. But, as it has been frequently objected, one of the most natural products of all is overlooked in such a system; I mean human power, whose labour and works, under our institutions, is also a disposable commodity, and must therefore be subject likewise to direct taxation. If, however, the system of direct taxation to which we are reduced is not unjustly condemned as the worst and clumsiest of all financial systems, we must not forget that the government, whose activity we have so narrowly circumscribed, needs no great income, and that a State which has no special interest of its own, apart from those of its citizens, will be more assured of support from a free and therefore, according to the experience of all the ages, a prosperous nation.

As the administration of financial affairs may create obstacles to the practical application of the principles we have laid down, this is equally or still more the case with the internal arrangements of the political constitution. That is, some means must be provided to connect the governing and governed classes of the nation together, to secure the former in the possession of the power confided to them, and the latter in the enjoyment of what freedom remains. Different methods have been adopted in different States for this purpose: in some, it is by attempting to strengthen the physical power of the government—clearly dangerous to freedom; in others, by the equilibrium of a number of contending powers; and in

---

[2] The physiocrats regarded land alone as productive, and hence advocated a land tax.

others, by diffusing throughout the nation a spirit favourable to the constitution. This last method, although it has produced splendid results, as we notice more especially in antiquity, is too harmful to the individual development of the citizen, too easily induces one-sidedness in the national character, and is therefore least advisable in the system we have proposed. According to this, we should look for a constitution which should have the least possible positive or special influence on the character of the citizens, and would fill their hearts with nothing but the deepest regard for the rights of others, combined with the most enthusiastic love for their own liberty. I shall not here attempt to discover which conceivable constitution this may be. Such an investigation clearly belongs only in a theory of politics proper; and I shall content myself with a few brief considerations, which may show more clearly at least the possibility of such a constitution. The system I have put forward tends to strengthen and multiply the private interests of the citizens, and it may therefore seem calculated in this way to weaken the public interest. But it interweaves the two so closely together that the latter seems rather to be based on the former; and especially appears so to the citizen, who wishes to be at once secure and free. Thus then, with such a system, that love for the constitution which it is so often vainly sought to cultivate in the hearts of the citizens by artificial means will be best maintained. A State, moreover, whose sphere of action is so narrow needs less power, and this needs correspondingly less defence. Lastly, it is understood of course that, as power and enjoyment have often to be sacrificed for results, in order to protect both sides from a greater loss, the same will be the case here.

I have now succeeded, then, in answering the question I put, as far as my present powers would allow, and have traced out the sphere of political activity, and confined it within such limits as seemed to me most conducive and necessary to man's highest interests. In this I have taken the point of view of what was best; that of justice might also seem, in conjunction with this, not uninteresting. But when a State has taken a certain end and has voluntarily set certain limits to its activity, those ends and limits are naturally in accordance with justice, so long as those who defined them were adequate to their task. Where such an express definition of ends and limits has not been made, the State must naturally attempt to limit its activity to what pure theory prescribes, but must also be guided by the consideration of obstacles which, if overlooked, would lead to more harmful consequences. The nation can always demand the adoption of such a theory, in so far as these obstacles make it practicable, but no further. I have not hitherto taken these obstacles into consideration, but have contented myself with developing the pure theory. I have in general aimed at discovering the most favourable position which man can occupy as member of a political community. And it has appeared to me to be that in which the most diverse individuality and the most original independence coexisted equally with the most diverse and profound associations of human beings with each other—a problem which nothing but the most absolute liberty can ever hope to solve. To point out the possibility of a political organization which should limit the achievement of this end as little as possible has been my only purpose in these pages, and has for some time been the subject of all my thoughts and researches. I shall be satisfied if I have shown that this principle should at least hover before the legislator as an ideal in all political constitutions.

These ideas might have been forcibly illustrated by history and statistics. On the whole there has often seemed to me to be much need of reform in statistical science. Instead of giving us the mere data of area, population, wealth, and industry in a State, from which its real condition can never be fully and accurately determined, it should proceed from a consideration of the real state of the country and its inhabitants,[3] and attempt to convey the extent and nature of their powers of activity, endurance and enjoyment, and to show by degrees the modification of these, partly by the national community, partly by the institution of the State. For the State constitution and the national community, however closely they may be interwoven, should not be confused. While the State constitution, by the force of law, or custom, or its own power, sets the citizens in a specific relationship to each other, there is another which is wholly distinct from this—chosen by their own free will, infinitely various, and in its nature ever-changing. And it is strictly speaking the latter—the free cooperation of the members of the nation—which secures all those benefits for which men longed when they formed themselves into a society. The State constitution itself is strictly subordinate to this end, as only a

---

[3] Humboldt later amplified these suggestions in his *Plan einer vergleichenden Anthropologie* (1795).

necessary means; and, since it is always attended with restrictions of freedom, as a necessary evil.

It has, therefore, been my secondary design in these pages to point out the fatal consequences for human enjoyment, energy, and character, from confounding the free activity of the nation with the enforced working of the political constitution.

CHAPTER XVI

Practical application of the theory proposed

Every development of truths which apply to human nature, and more especially to human activity, leads to a wish to see worked out in practice what theory has shown us to be right. To man, who is seldom satisfied with the calmly beneficent influence of abstract ideas, this desire is perfectly natural, and it is quickened by benevolent sympathy with the well-being of society. But, however natural in itself, and however noble in its origin, this desire has not infrequently led to harmful consequences, indeed, often to greater evils than the colder indifference, or—for the same effects can follow from opposite causes—the burning enthusiasm, which comparatively heedless of reality, delights only in the pure beauty of ideas. For as soon as truth strikes deep roots in human nature, if only in a single man, it slowly and silently spreads its beneficial influence into practical life, while on the other hand, if it is put directly into practice, it often changes character as a result and does not react on men's ideas. Hence there are some ideas which the wise man would never attempt to put into practice. Indeed, reality, in any period, is never ripe for the ripest and finest fruit of the spirit; the ideal must always float before the soul of the artist, whatever the art he practises, only as an unattainable standard. These considerations, therefore, show the need for more than ordinary prudence in applying even the most consistent and generally accepted theory; and they impel me all the more to examine, before concluding my task, as fully and at the same time as briefly as possible, how far the principles developed here can be transferred into actual practice. This examination will, at the same time, serve to defend me from the charge that I wished directly to prescribe rules to actual life in what I have said, or even to disapprove of anything in it contrary to what I have advocated. I would wish to repudiate such a presumption even if I were sure that everything I have said is perfectly correct and unquestionable.

In every remodelling of the present, the existing condition of things must be replaced by a new one. Now every situation in which men find themselves, every circumstance communicates a definite shape to their internal nature. This form is not such that it can change and adapt itself to any other a man may choose to receive; and man's end is frustrated and his energies suppressed when we impose something incompatible upon it. If we glance at the most important revolutions in history, we see at once that the greatest number of these originated in the periodical revolutions of the human mind. And we are still more convinced of this when, considering the powers that have done most to change the world, we find the human the most important. For physical nature, on account of its measured, uniform, eternally recurring cycles, is less important in this respect; as is the brute creation, considered by itself. Human power[1] can only manifest itself in any one period, in one way, but it can infinitely modify this manifestation; at any given epoch, therefore, it exhibits a one-sided aspect, but in a series of different periods these combine to give the image of a wonderful multiformity. Every preceding condition of things is either the complete and sufficient cause of what succeeds it, or, at least, exercises such modifying influences that the external pressure of circumstances can produce no other. This prior condition, then, and the modifications it receives, act also to determine in what way the new order of circumstances shall exercise an influence on human nature; and the force of this determination is so great that these very circumstances are often wholly altered by it. Hence it comes that we might be justified in regarding everything which is done on earth as both good and beneficial; since it is man's internal power which masters and subdues everything to itself, whatever its nature, and because this internal power, in any of its manifestations, can never act other than beneficially, since each of these operates in different degrees to strengthen and develop it. In view of this consideration, we understand how the whole history of the human race

---

[1] The passage which follows takes up the arguments already put forward by Humboldt in his earlier essays, *Ideen über Staatsverfassung* and *Über die Gesetze der Entwicklung der Menschlichen Kräfte* (1791) and foreshadows those developed later in his *Plan einer vergleichenden Anthropologie* (1795) and *Betrachtungen über die Weltgeschichte* (1814). None of these essays were published during his lifetime. See Editor's Introduction, pp. xxix, xxxii.

could perhaps be represented merely as a natural result of the revolutions of human energy; and while the study of history in this light would be perhaps more pregnant than any other in interest and instruction, it would at the same time point out to the man who wishes to influence his fellow-men the way in which he should attempt to sway and guide human energies, and what he should never expect of them. While, therefore, this inner human force deserves our special attention, commanding our respect and admiration as it does, by its intrinsic worth, it has double claims on our consideration when we recognize the mighty influence with which it subjects all other things to its sway.

Whoever, then, would attempt the difficult task of ingeniously introducing a new state of affairs and grafting it to what already exists should never lose sight of this all-important fact. He must wait, therefore, in the first place, for the full working out of the present in men's minds; if he should attempt to cut through the difficulty, he might succeed, perhaps, in transforming the external aspects of things, but never the inner disposition of human nature, which would carry over into everything new that had been forcibly imposed on it. One should not imagine, moreover, that the more one allows the present tendencies to work themselves out, men become more averse to any subsequent change. In human history, it is extremes which lie most closely together; and the external state of affairs, if we leave it to run its course undisturbed, so far from strengthening and perpetuating itself, works towards its ruin. This is not only proved by the experience of all ages, but is in strict accordance with human nature; for the active man never remains longer with one object than his energy finds in it material for exercise, and hence he abandons it most quickly when he has been most uninterruptedly engaged on it; and as for the passive man, although it is true that a continuing pressure blunts his powers, it also causes him to feel the influence more keenly. Now, without directly altering the existing state of things, it is possible to work upon the human mind and character, and give them a direction imcompatible with it; and this is precisely what the wise man will attempt to do. Only in this way is it possible to reproduce the new system in reality, just as it has been conceived in idea; in every other method, apart from the evils which arise from disturbing the natural order of human development, it is changed, modified, disfigured by the remaining influence of preceding systems, in the actual state of affairs or in the minds of men. But if this obstacle is removed—if the new state of things which is decided upon can work itself out fully, unimpeded by what has gone before, and by the present state of things in which the influence of the past is still alive—then nothing further must be allowed to stand in the way of the contemplated reform. The most general principles of the theory of all reform may therefore be reduced to these—

1. *We should never attempt to transfer purely theoretical principles into reality, before the latter offers no further obstacles to achieving results to which the principles would always lead in the absence of outside interference.*

2. *In order to bring about the transition from present circumstances to those which have been planned, every reform should be allowed to proceed as much as possible from men's minds and thoughts.*

In my exposition of abstract theoretical principles in this essay, I have always proceeded strictly from considerations of human nature; I have not presupposed in this, moreover, any but the usual degree of energy and capacity; still, I have assumed man to be only what his humanity makes him, not moulded by any particular social relations. But we never find man thus: the circumstances amidst which he lives have in all cases already given him some determinate form or other. Whenever a State, therefore, contemplates extending or restricting its sphere of action, according to correct theoretical principles, it must pay special attention to this. Now the difference between theory and reality, on this point of political administration, will in all cases consist, as may easily be foreseen, in too little freedom; and hence it might appear that the removal of existing bounds would be at all times possible and at all times beneficial. But however true in itself this may be, it should not be forgotten that the very thing which cripples men's power on the one hand, on the other provides the material for its activity. I have already observed, in the beginning of this essay, that man is more disposed to domination than freedom; and a structure of dominion not only gladdens the eye of the master who rears and protects it, but even its servants are uplifted by the thought that they are members of a whole, which rises high above the life and strength of single generations. Wherever, then, there is still such a commanding spectacle to sway men's admiration, and we attempt to constrain man to act only in and for himself, only within the narrow circle of his own individual powers, only for his own lifetime, his energy will vanish, and lethargy and inaction ensue. It is true that this is really the only way in which man can act on illimitable space and time, but he does so indirectly; he sows seeds which grow spontaneously rather than erects structures which show directly the traces of his hand; and it requires a higher degree of culture to rejoice in an activity which only creates energies and leaves them to work out their own results, rather than in one which establishes them at once. It is this degree of culture which shows the time is ripe for freedom. But the capacity for freedom which arises from such a degree of culture is nowhere perfect; and this perfection, I believe, is destined to remain beyond the reach of man's sensuous nature, which always disposes him to cling to external objects.

What, then, would be the task of the statesman who should undertake such a reform?[2] First, in every new step which is outside the course of things as they exist, he must be guided strictly by pure theory, except where there are circumstances in the present which, if one attempted to graft changes on to them, would partially or wholly destroy the proper consequences of theory. Secondly, he must allow all restrictions on freedom to remain untouched which are rooted in the present state of things, so long as men do not show by unmistakable signs that they regard them as fetters, that they feel their oppressive influence, that they are ripe for an increase of freedom in these respects; when this is shown, he must immediately remove them. Finally, he must make men thus ripe for increased freedom by every possible means. This last duty is unquestionably the most important, and at the same time, the simplest. For nothing promotes this ripeness for freedom so much as freedom itself. This truth, perhaps, may not be acknowledged by those who have so often used this unripeness as an excuse for continuing repression. But it seems to me to follow unquestionably from the very nature of man. The incapacity for freedom can only arise from a want of moral and intellectual power; to heighten this power is the only way to supply this want; but to do this presupposes the exercise of the power, and this exercise presupposes the freedom which awakens spontaneous activity. Only it is clear we cannot call it giving freedom, when bonds are relaxed which are not felt as such by him who wears them. But of no man on earth—however neglected by nature, and however degraded by circumstances—is this true of all the

---

[2] In the manuscript 'reform' (*Umänderung*) is substituted for '*Revolution*' [L].

bonds which oppress him. Let us undo them one by one, as the feeling of freedom awakens in men's hearts, and we shall hasten progress at every step. There may still be great difficulties in being able to recognize the symptoms of this awakening. But these do not lie in the theory so much as in its execution, which clearly allows no special rules, but in this case, as in every other, is the work of genius alone. Theoretically, I should attempt to solve this admittedly intricate problem as follows:

The legislator should keep two things constantly before his eyes—1. The pure theory developed to its minutest details; 2. The particular condition of things which he intends to reform. He must command a view of the theory, not only in all its parts, and in its most careful and complete development, but must, further, never lose sight of the necessary consequences of each of its several principles, in their fullest extent, in their manifold inter-connection, and, where they cannot all be realized at once, in their mutual dependence on each other. It is not less his duty, although it is doubtless infinitely difficult, to acquaint himself with the actual condition of things, with the nature of all restrictions which the State imposes on the citizens, and which these, under the protection of the State, impose on each other, contrary to the abstract principles of the theory, and with all the consequences of these restrictions. He should now compare these two pictures with each other; and the time to translate a theoretical principle into reality would be recognized, when it was shown by the comparison that the principle could be realized, unaltered, in its full purity. It would be sufficient, even if this were not completely the case, if it could be foreseen that the discrepancies would be removed as reality approached the theory. For the gaze of the legislator must be constantly bent towards this aim, this complete coincidence.

There may seem to be something strange in the idea of these imaginative representations, and it might be thought impossible to preserve the truth of such pictures, and still more to institute an exact comparison between them. These objections are not without foundation; but they lose much of their force when we remember that the theory demands only freedom, while reality, in so far as it differs from theory, is characterized by coercion; that the only reason we do not exchange coercion for freedom is because it is impossible, and that the reason for this impossibility can only be found in one of these two considerations—either that man or the situation is not yet adapted to receive that freedom, so that freedom would destroy the very conditions without which not only freedom but even existence itself would be inconceivable; alternatively—and this could result only from the incapacity of men for it—freedom would not produce the beneficial results which otherwise invariably accompany it. Now we cannot judge either case unless we imagine both the actual and the altered circumstances in their fullest extent and carefully compare their structure and consequences. The difficulty still further decreases when we reflect that the State itself is never in a position to introduce any important change until it observes in the citizens themselves indications which show it is necessary to remove their fetters before they become oppressive; so that the State only occupies the place of a spectator, and the removal of restrictions on freedom implying nothing more than a calculation of possibility is only to be guided by the dictates of sheer necessity. Lastly, it is scarcely necessary to observe that we are alluding here to cases in which reform seems to the State not only physically but morally possible, and which therefore do not contradict the principles of justice. Only we must remember, with regard to this last condition, that natural and universal justice is the only true basis of all positive law; that therefore we should always refer back to this; and hence that, to adduce a principle of law which is, as it were, the source of all the others, no one can at any time, or in any way, obtain a right to dispose of the powers or goods of another without his consent or against his will.

Under this heading I would venture to lay down the following principle—

With regard to the limits of its activity, the State should endeavor to bring the actual condition of things as close to those prescribed by the true and just theory as is possible, and in so far as it is not opposed to reasons of real necessity. Now, the possibility consists in this that men are ready to receive the freedom which theory always approves, and that this freedom can succeed in producing those salutary consequences which always accompany its unhindered operation. The reasons of necessity which may oppose this are: that freedom, once granted, is not calculated to destroy those conditions, without which not only all further progress, but even existence itself, is endangered. In both of these cases the statesman's judgement must be formed from a careful comparison between the present state of things, and the contemplated change, and between their respective consequences.

This principle follows from the application, in this particular case, of the principle laid down earlier with regard to all methods of reform. For, when there is an incapacity for greater freedom, or when the essential conditions referred to would suffer from increasing it, the real state of things prevents the theory from producing its normal consequences. I shall not develop this principle any further. I might, perhaps, go on to classify the possible variety of real situations, and demonstrate the application of the theory to them. But in attempting this, I should only contradict my own principles; for I have observed that every such application requires a commanding view of the whole situation and its inter-relations, and this can never be done in a mere hypothesis.

If we add to this rule, which we have laid down for the practical guidance of the State, those laws which are imposed on it by the theory we previously developed, we shall conclude that its activity should always be left to be determined by necessity. For the theory we have advanced allows to it only the care for security, since security alone is unattainable by the individual man, and hence this protection alone is necessary; and this practical rule binds that State strictly to the observance of the theory, in so far as the present conditions do not necessitate a departure from it. Thus, then, it is the principle of necessity towards which all the ideas advanced in this essay converge. In pure theory the limits of this necessity are determined solely by consideration of man's proper nature as a human being; but in its application we have to look, in addition, at the individuality of man as he actually exists. This principle of necessity should, I think, prescribe the great fundamental rules to which every effort to act on human beings and their manifold relations should invariably conform. For it is the only thing which leads to certain and unquestionable results. The consideration of the useful, which might be opposed to it, cannot be clearly and definitely determined. It presupposes calculations of probability, which, even setting aside the fact that, from their very nature, they cannot be infallible, always run the risk of being falsified by the minutest unforeseen circumstances; while, on the other hand, necessity impresses itself powerfully on men's feelings, and whatever necessity demands is not only useful, but absolutely indispensable. The useful, moreover, since its degrees are as it were infinite, presupposes a constant succession of new arrangements and expedients; while the limitations, on the contrary, which necessity enjoins, tend actually to lessen its demands, since they leave ampler scope to individual energies. Lastly, the concern for the useful encourages for the most part the adoption of positive arrangements; the necessary chiefly requires negative measures; since, owing to the strength of man's spontaneous energies, necessity does not often require anything but the removal of oppressive restrictions. From all these reasons, to which a more detailed analysis of the subject might add many more, it will be seen that there is no other principle so in accordance with the reverence we owe to the individuality of spontaneous beings, and with the concern for freedom which that reverence inspires. Finally, the only infallible means of securing power and authority to laws is to see that they originate in this principle alone. Many plans have been proposed to secure this great object; to most it has appeared the surest method to persuade the citizens that the laws are both good and useful. But even although we admit that they possess these qualities in given cases, it is always difficult to convince men of the usefulness of an arrangement; different points of view give different opinions; and men's own inclinations resist persuasion, since however ready they may be to accept necessities they have recognized for themselves, they always resist what is thrust upon them. But to the yoke of necessity everyone willingly bows the head. Still, when a complicated situation actually arises, it is more difficult to discover exactly what is necessary; but by the mere acknowledgment of the principle, the problem invariably becomes simpler and the solution easier.

I have now gone over the ground I marked out in the beginning of this essay. I have felt myself animated throughout with a sense of the deepest respect for the inherent dignity of human nature, and for freedom, which alone befits that dignity. May the ideas I have advanced, and the expression I have lent to them, be not unworthy of such a feeling!

Index

Individualism
circumstances where development suffers, 120
of Rousseau, xxv–xxvi
Individuality
in *Bildung* concept, xxx
of energy and self-development, 11–12,
15, 67–68
joy in peak of, 31
state interference hinders, 27–28
Indolence (of trusting believer), 66
Ingenuity of man, 19
Inheritance, 100–22
Inner life, 21–22
Inquiry
actions and effect of free, 66–67
consciousness during, 66–67
in judicial proceeding, 106
spontaneity of, 66
of State for crimes committed, 123–24
See also Philosopher, analytical; Psychological inquiries
Institutions
origin of, 7–8
promoting public security, 46–48
See also National institution; Political
institutions
Intellect, 21
Intellectual perfection, 56–57
Intent (criminal), 116

Jacobi, Friedrich, xxiii
Judge
decisions of, 39–40
duty of, 110
role in criminal proceedings, 116–17
Judicial proceedings, 106–7
See also Civil proceedings; Criminal
proceedings
Justi, J. H. G., xxvii
Justice
as basis for law, 145
in criminal proceedings, 116–17
fundamental principles of, 97–99
State must act within ideas of, 101

Kant, Emmanuel
enthusiasm of, 76
humanism of, xxviii

Humboldt's efforts to complete ideas
of, xliii, xlvii–xlviii
ideas similar to Humboldt's, xliv
on influence on man of arts, 72
moral law of, xxi, xlvi

Laboulaye, Eduard, xviii
Lasalle, A. C. L. C., xlix
Laws
circumstances for formalities in, 108–9
crimes and punishments apportioned
by, 115–16
effect of sumptuary, 70
imposing duties on citizens, 92
justice as basis for, 145
limit sphere of morality, 20–21
necessity for, 131–32
prescribe duties to be enforced, 121
punishment for transgressions of, 124
requiring certain characteristics of transactions, 107–9
in uncultivated nations, 108
used to reform morality, 70
See also Criminal law; Legislation; Natural law; Police, or preventive laws;
Regulation; Roman law; Testamentary laws
Legal disputes, 109
Legal freedom, 84
Legislation
essentials for system of, 132–33
points of view necessitating, 131–32
principle related to validity of transactions, 110–12
principles of criminal, 124–26
Legislative system, 132
Leibniz, Gottfried W., xxi, xxv, xli
Lessing, Gotthold E., xxi, xxix
Liberalism
Humboldt anticipates nineteenth cen-
tury, liv, lvi–lvii
Humboldt's, xxiii, liv–lv, lvi–lviii
Liberty
of citizen "to act without hindrance,"
120
of thought, 68
See also Freedom
Licensing, 88–89
Litigious spirit, 107
Locke, John, xlviii

COMPARATIVE TABLE OF SUBJECTS

IN WILHELM VON HUMBOLDT'S

THE LIMITS OF STATE ACTION

AND JOHN STUART MILL'S

ON LIBERTY

In *On Liberty* and his *Autobiography,* John Stuart Mill points to the influence on his work of Wilhelm von Humboldt's *The Limits of State Action.* The following table lists passages from each work where discussions occur of various subjects relevant to this relationship. We hope that this table will allow the reader to explore more easily areas of possible influence and, thus, form a clearer understanding of the similarities and the differences between Mill and Humboldt. Such a comparison may also help to reassess Humboldt's place in the history of nineteenth-century political thought and the history of liberty.

Because an examination of liberty is ubiquitous throughout *On Liberty* and *The Limits of State Action,* we did not think it necessary to have a separate entry either for "liberty" or for any "liberties." Because Mill's work is far better known than Humboldt's, we have tended to choose his idiom for the names of the subjects rather than Humboldt's somewhat different idiom. The page references to *On Liberty* cite two different editions: *On Liberty: With The Subjection of Women and Chapters on Socialism,* ed. Stefan Collini, Cambridge Texts in the History of Political Thought (Cambridge: Cambridge University Press, 1989); and *Collected Works of John Stuart Mill,* ed. J. M. Robson, 33 vols. (Toronto: University of Toronto Press, 1963–91), vol. 18, *Essays on Politics and Society.*

Subject	The Limits of State Action, Liberty Fund Edition	On Liberty, Cambridge Edition	On Liberty, Toronto Edition
Ancients and moderns	pp. 6–9, 14, 32, 38–45, 47–48	pp. 17, 48	pp. 227, 253
Character	18, 41, 50–51, 75	15, 23, 28–29, 41–43, 52, 53–63	226, 232, 236, 247–48, 256, 258–66
Citizenship	49, 50–51, 54	105, 109	301, 305
Coercion (individual harm to others)	94–105, 110–11, 121–22	13, 15, 56–57, 75–78, 80, 83, 98, 102–5, 108	223, 225, 260, 276–78, 280, 283, 299–301, 304
Constitutions	3, 32–33, 48, 52, 54, 111, 139–41	87, 109–12	286, 305–8
Contracts	26–27, 94–97, 101–2	97, 103	295, 300
Culture	5, 12–14, 56, 64, 68, 70–71	40, 58, 60, 72	246, 261, 264, 274
Diversity (variety)	4, 5, 7–8, 10, 12, 14, 18, 32–33, 76, 99	3, 45, 47, 49, 52, 57–58, 68, 72, 74, 106, 110	215, 250, 252, 254, 257, 260–61, 270, 274, 275, 302, 306
Education	19–20, 48–52, 67, 81	46, 51, 57, 72–73, 76, 102, 105–8	251, 255, 261, 273–74, 277, 299, 301–4
Equality		48, 89	254, 288
Family	21, 100–101, 127–31	61, 81, 105, 108	264, 281, 301, 304–5

Subject	The Limits of State Action, Liberty Fund Edition	On Liberty, Cambridge Edition	On Liberty, Toronto Edition
Freedom of the will	23	5	217
Human nature	8–9, 18, 27, 35, 64–65, 142, 147	17, 60–63, 69, 69n, 77	227, 263–66, 271n, 272, 278
Individuality	7, 10–12, 15, 27–28	8, 49, 57–61, 63–67, 69, 71, 73–77, 81, 106, 110	220, 254, 261–64, 266–69, 271, 273, 275–78, 281, 302, 306
Justice	94–105, 110, 127–28, 132	14, 28, 63, 70, 83	224, 236, 266, 272, 282
Marriage (contract)	26–27, 96–97	91–92, 103, 108	290, 300, 304
Natural law	90, 128		
Order	56, 61	48, 112	253, 307
Progress	37, 44	5–6, 9, 13, 41, 43, 47–48, 57, 70, 92–93	217–18, 220, 224, 247, 249, 252–53, 261, 272, 291
Property	33, 35, 84, 91, 94–105	48, 56, 68	254, 260, 271
Punishment	38–39, 64–65, 110–26	19–20n, 29, 34, 56, 78–81, 94, 98, 100, 108	228n, 237, 241, 260, 278–81, 292, 295, 297, 304

Subject	The Limits of State Action, Liberty Fund Edition	On Liberty, Cambridge Edition	On Liberty, Toronto Edition
Religion	53–69, 81, 87	11–12, 17, 28–29, 33–34, 33n, 37–40, 43–44, 49–53, 62, 69n, 83–87, 85n, 90–92, 107	222, 227, 236–37, 240–41, 240n, 244–46, 249–50, 254–58, 265, 271n, 283–86, 285n, 289–90, 303
Rights	46, 82, 84–87, 91, 93, 94, 99, 114, 116, 123–26	6, 11, 59, 63, 73, 75, 78, 89, 102, 105	218, 222, 262, 266, 274, 276, 279, 288, 299, 301
Self-development	3–5, 12–13, 15, 22, 32–33, 41, 128, 133	3, 8, 35, 57, 63–64, 66–68, 72, 79, 89, 109, 115	215, 220, 242, 261, 266–67, 269–70, 274, 279, 288, 305, 310
Self-perfection	56–57, 62–63	77, 89–90	278, 288
Self-regarding conduct	3–4, 5, 90–91, 127	10, 13–16, 75–84, 98–99	221, 223–26, 276–84, 295–96
State: proper and improper ends	9, 16–38, 40–45, 62–69, 82–126, 132–33	5–9, 13–16, 19–20, 56–58, 75–93, 94–115	217–20, 223–26, 228–29, 260–61, 276–91, 292–310
Utilitarianism		14, 27	224, 235
Virtue	7, 44, 51, 63, 87	20n, 27–28, 32–33, 60	228n, 235–36, 239–40, 264

The text of this book was set in a type called Times Roman, designed by Stanley Morison for the *London Times*, and first introduced by that newspaper in 1932. The *Times* was seeking a typeface that would be condensed enough to accommodate a substantial number of words per column without sacrificing readability and still have an attractive, contemporary appearance. It is one of the most popular typefaces in use for book work throughout the world and quite justifies the claim made for it of being the most important type design of the twentieth century. Stanley Morison has been a strong forming influence, as typographical advisor to the English Monotype Corporation, as director of two distinguished English publishing houses, and as a writer of sensibility, erudition, and keen practical sense.

Editorial services by Custom Editorial Productions, Inc., Cincinnati, Ohio
Design by Hermann Strohbach, New York, New York
Typesetting by Alexander Typesetting, Inc., Indianapolis, Indiana
Index by Shirley Kessel, Primary Sources Research, Chevy Chase, Maryland
Printed and bound by Worzalla Publishing Company, Stevens Point, Wisconsin